CRANBORNE CHASE

This enchanted and strangely remote region spreads over three counties (Dorset, Hampshire, Wiltshire) and yet is a remarkably coherent entity. It owes its character to its history, as for so many centuries it was preserved by stern laws for the hunting of deer: a royal hunting ground from the Conquest until the Stuarts, and still a hunting ground until comparatively recent times. So it is no accident that there are no towns within the Chase: Shaftesbury, Blandford, Ringwood, Wimborne and Salisbury lie like harbours round the edge of some great lake—a lake of some 150,000 acres.

Desmond Hawkins has been associated with several BBC programmes about Cranborne Chase, on radio and television, and has known the region for over thirty years. He takes us through its fascinating history: its ancient laws and rights; how it was administered; the great families; the more recent eccentrics; the battles between keepers, poachers and smugglers.

Mr Hawkins's account of the countryside; its wild life (past and present); its roads, old (Roman and even pre-Roman) and new; the rivers, and the places along their banks; the railways, and their influence; the old way of life—the sheep, the watercress beds, the local potteries—all this and much more is delightfully interwoven with personal recollections. Here is a re-creation of a unique region: an ideal companion for both an active and an armchair traveller.

Desmond Hawkins was on the staff of the BBC from 1945 to 1970, finally becoming Regional Controller for the South and West of England. During his BBC career he developed wild-life programmes and founded the BBC Natural History Unit. More recently he has dramatised some of Hardy's novels. Before joining the BBC and since leaving it he has worked as a freelance broadcaster and author and has written a number of books on literary and natural history subjects, as well as two novels. He has also received several awards for his work in these two fields.

A Chase keeper, portrait by Romney

CRANBORNE CHASE

by

DESMOND HAWKINS

LONDON
VICTOR GOLLANCZ LTD
1983

© Desmond Hawkins 1980

First published March 1980
This edition 1983

ISBN 0 575 03392 4

'I am well aware that there are many young persons who are very indifferent and care little about what was practised by their ancestors, or how they amused themselves; they are looking forward, and do not choose to look back; but there may be some not so indifferent.'

Anecdotes and History of Cranbourn Chase
William Chafin 1818

Printed in Great Britain at
The Camelot Press Ltd, Southampton

CONTENTS

ILLUSTRATIONS

General Pitt-Rivers (*photo Dorset Evening Echo*)
Traditional Chase use of brick and flint in building
Larmer Tree Gardens, Tollard Royal, *c.* 1895 (*photo Dorset Evening Echo*)
The Cross Roads Pottery, Verwood, in the 1920s
Whitemill Bridge over the River Stour

Following page 144

Horace Pitt, the sixth and last Baron Rivers
Ferne Tennis Club, 1879: Ladies' Committee
A stone curlew (*photo Norman Orr*)
Veiny Cheese Pond, Long Crichel
Typical downland coombe near Win Green
Martin Village (*photo Norman Orr*)
Ackling Dyke, the Roman road from Badbury to Old Sarum

All unacknowledged photographs were taken by the author

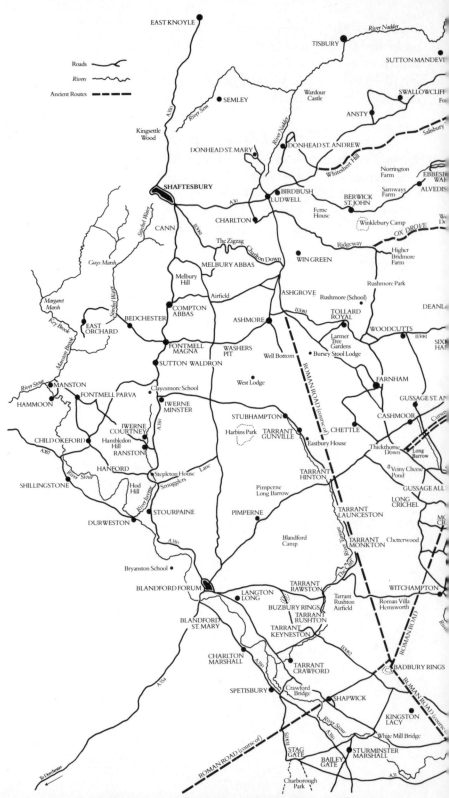

CRANBORNE CHASE

TEFFONT EVIAS

Roads

Rivers

Ancient Routes

EAST KNOYLE

River Nadder

TISBURY

SUTTON MANDEVI

SWALLOWCLIFF
For

Wardour
Castle

ANSTY

SEMLEY

Kingsettle
Wood

River Sem

DONHEAD ST. MARY

DONHEAD ST. ANDREW

River Nadder

Whitesheet Hill

Norrington
Farm

EBBESB
WAR

ALVEDIS

SHAFTESBURY

BIRDBUSH
LUDWELL

BERWICK
ST. JOHN

Samways
Farm

Ferne
House

Winklebury Camp

OX DROVE

W
De

Salisbury

CANN

CHARLTON

The Zigzag

Charlton Down

Ridgeway

Higher
Bridmore
Farm

Guys Marsh

MELBURY ABBAS

WIN GREEN

Rushmore Park

Margaret
Marsh

Melbury
Hill

Airfield

ASHGROVE

Rushmore (School)

Key Brook

Stour West

COMPTON
ABBAS

BEDCHESTER

ASHMORE

TOLLARD
ROYAL

DEANL

EAST
ORCHARD

WOODCUTTS

SIX
HA

Manston Brook

FONTMELL
MAGNA

WASHERS
PIT

Larmer
Tree
Gardens

Bursey Stool Lodge

River Stour

SUTTON WALDRON

Well Bottom

MANSTON

Claysmore School

West Lodge

FARNHAM

HAMMOON

FONTMELL PARVA

IWERNE
MINSTER

STUBHAMPTON

GUSSAGE ST. AN

CASHMOOR

IWERNE
COURTNEY

Harbins Park

TARRANT
GUNVILLE

CHETTLE

CHILD OKEFORD

Hambledon
Hill

RANSTON

Eastbury House

Thickthorne
Down

Long
Barrow

River Stour

HANFORD

Stepleton House Lane

TARRANT
HINTON

Veiny Cheese
Pond

GUSSAGE ALL

SHILLINGSTONE

Hod
Hill

Smugglers

Pimperne
Long Barrow

LONG
CRICHEL

STOURPAINE

PIMPERNE

TARRANT
LAUNCESTON

M
CR

DURWESTON

Blandford
Camp

TARRANT
MONKTON

Chetterwood

Bryanston School

BLANDFORD FORUM

LANGTON
LONG

TARRANT
RAWSTON

Tarrant
Rushton
Airfield

Roman Villa
Hemsworth

WITCHAMPTON

BUZBURY RINGS

BLANDFORD
ST. MARY

TARRANT
KEYNESTON

TARRANT
RUSHTON

BADBURY RINGS

CHARLTON
MARSHALL

TARRANT
CRAWFORD

SPETISBURY

Crawford
Bridge

SHAPWICK

KINGSTON
LACY

White Mill Bridge

To Dorchester

ROMAN ROAD (course of)

STAG
GATE

BAILEY
GATE

STURMINSTER
MARSHALL

River Stour

Charborough
Park

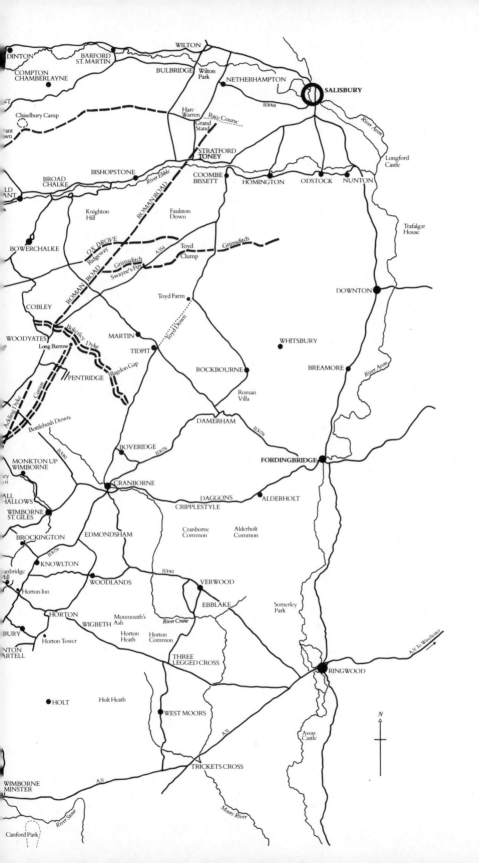

FOREWORD

CRANBORNE CHASE spreads untidily over three counties—Dorset, Wiltshire and Hampshire—and has been neglected perhaps for that reason. No book has been written about it since 1841, so I can at least claim to be repairing an omission. My interest in the Chase is deeply rooted, dating back to the 1940s when I was much involved with the BBC's *Country Magazine*. I devoted a special edition of this programme to Cranborne Chase and became so interested in the area that I made several more broadcasts about it over a period of years. Two are worth recalling. In 1953 I prepared a radio documentary with Sir Mortimer Wheeler on the great archaeologist of the Chase, General Pitt-Rivers. In 1974 I wrote the script for a television documentary on the Chase for the BBC2 series *The World About Us*. My research for that film became the basis of this book, which I began to prepare in 1975. It therefore embodies my notes and impressions extending over thirty years and the intensive research of the past three or four years.

A work of this kind would be impossible without the assistance of those many who have some item of knowledge or experience to contribute to the whole design. I have ransacked the available literature, as my bibliography will show; and I have knocked on many doors in the Chase, to be received with a friendly interest and a ready co-operation that I acknowledge with warm feelings of gratitude. To name individuals is always invidious but I must nevertheless record my personal indebtedness to the present owner of the Rushmore Estate, Michael Pitt-Rivers of Tollard Royal, and to Anthony Pitt-Rivers of Hinton St Mary, for access to family papers and a magnanimous endurance of my enquiries; to Richard Prior, whose professional studies of deer—particularly *The Roe Deer of Cranborne Chase*—gave me invaluable guidance, and who generously found time in a very busy life to read my draft with an expertly critical eye; to Douglas Judd of Sixpenny Handley, hurdle-maker, bandmaster, man of many parts, in whose company I feel at one with the spirit of the Chase; Eric Ashby, who filmed the wildlife sequences for my television script and, as always, taught me many things about the nature of the Chase; Norman Orr, who invited me to watch stone curlew from his hide and gave me a photograph of the bird to reproduce in these pages; Penny Trehane, whose enthusiasm for Verwood pottery spills over into other Chase topics; Professor Barry Cunliffe, who prescribed my archaeological reading; and Ronald Farquharson of Eastbury whose conversations of earlier days I treasure.

I am indebted to the Marquess of Salisbury for the opportunity to spend several days at Hatfield House where his archivist, Richard Harcourt-Williams, was extremely helpful. I recall gratefully other archivists and librarians whose knowledge and willing interest have made my task much easier: the archivists in the County Record Offices of Wiltshire and Dorset and at Stratfieldsaye, the librarians in the public libraries of Salisbury, Blandford and Christchurch, the library of Southampton University, and most particularly the county library at Dorchester. Their patience and encouragement go far beyond the call of duty and I thank them unreservedly.

A word about four earlier authors will be appropriate here, since I am more than commonly obliged to them. They are William Chafin, whose *Anecdotes and History of Cranbourn Chase* was published in 1818; William West, who published in 1816 his *History of the Forest or Chace Known by the Name of Cranborne Chace*; Charles Bowles whose *Hundred of Chalke* appeared separately in 1830 and was also incorporated in Richard Colt Hoare's *History of Modern Wiltshire*; and T. Wake Smart, whose *Chronicle of Cranborne and the Chase of Cranborne* appeared anonymously in 1841. After the first instance I shall refer to them in abbreviated form as Chafin, West, Bowles and Wake Smart. Chafin was a sporting parson and a celebrated character whose exploits appealed to Sir Walter Scott. A passionate hunter, he was the last of the Chafins of Chettle, a family which had provided members of Parliament and rangers of the Chase in earlier generations. In the great controversy over the disfranchisement of the Chase he was in favour of the preservation of deer and therefore supported Lord Rivers. His book, like West's, was evidently inspired by the legal actions of the time.

West was in the opposite camp. He was a journalist who in 1813 began to prepare a book on the Chase 'with a view only to agricultural purposes', but he tells us he was 'indulged with the inspection of a number of authenticated papers' which encouraged him to tackle 'the still contested question of the bounds of the chace'. Reading between the lines it becomes obvious that he was being briefed by the farmers and landowners who argued that Lord Rivers's rights as lord of the Chase did not extend into Wiltshire. By 1816 his book needed further revision, in his opinion, but 'several circumstances forbid a further delay'. It is not difficult to guess what forbade further delay: the Lent Assize at Salisbury in 1816 included what was to become the decisive case of Rivers *v* King. West's allegiance was to Thomas King.

Charles Bowles was Recorder of Shaftesbury and a brother of the poet, William Lisle Bowles. Bowles published his book in 1830, the year of disfranchisement. He had therefore no continuing motive for partisanship, since the issue was now settled, but his loyalty to Lord Arundell is unmistakable and shows itself in a guarded coolness towards Lord Rivers. By 1841, when Wake Smart completed the quartet, passions had cooled and the disfranchisement issue had passed into history. Smart's *Chronicle* is objective in tone and, saving an occasional inaccuracy, is as good a piece of local history as one could wish for. I have drawn on it freely.

The late Mrs Pleydell-Railston of Whatcombe kindly allowed me to select photographs from her family albums. Those of 'Colonel Augustus Lane Fox as a young man', 'Horace Pitt, 6th and last Baron Rivers' and 'Ferne Tennis Club 1879' have been reproduced. Small quotations have been made from the following copyright material: Sir Mortimer Wheeler's radio documentary 'The Old General' (pp. 22 and 145), by kind permission of Sir Mortimer Wheeler; *General Pitt-Rivers* by M. W. Thompson (p. 139), by courtesy of the publisher, Moonraker Press; *The Ladies of Alderley* and *The Stanleys of Alderley*, both ed. Nancy Mitford (chapter 11 *passim*), Hamish Hamilton, reprinted by permission of A. D. Peters & Co., Ltd; *Autobiography* by Bertrand Russell (p. 142), Allen & Unwin; 'The Wiltshire Downs' from *The Complete Poems of Andrew Young* (p. 123), Secker & Warburg; *The Royal Forests of England* by J. C. Cox (p. 52), Methuen; *The Englishman's Food* by J. C. Drummond and Anne Wilbraham (p. 80), Jonathan Cape; *English Downland* by H. J. Massingham (pp. 91 and 168), Batsford; *The Wessex Heathland* by Ralph Wightman (p. 149), Robert Hale; *The Story of the Rev. Peter Ince* by T. H. L. Jones (p. 157), Independent Press.

Some sections of my book derive from articles I have contributed to *Country Life* and the *Dorset Evening Echo*. To their editors I offer the customary acknowledgments, and my thanks to Ann Bellchambers who has battled with my calligraphy to produce something that the printers could read.

D. H.

PART ONE

MAP ONE: showing Outer Bounds and Ancient Features—Roman road known as Ackling Dyke. Badbury Rings. Bokerley Dyke. The Ox Drove. Pons Petrae—the stone bridge over the Allen near Horton (an important landmark on the Outer Bounds). Via regalis (the upper road from Blandford to Shaftesbury) referred to in the King John perambulation.

The principal 'noble seats'—Cranborne, Wimborne St Giles, Eastbury, Wardour Castle, Wilton.

The Lodges and Walks—West, Bursey Stool, Rushmore, Staplefoot, Cobley, Verndicth, Alderholt and Chettered.

The Great Western Turnpike connecting Blandford and Salisbury; and the Ringwood to Shaftesbury Turnpike which is now the B3081.

The principal monastic centres—Shaftesbury, Wilton, Damerham, Tarrant Crawford, Cranborne, Horton, Wimborne and Iwerne Minster.

CHAPTER ONE

A First Impression

THE SOUTHERN COUNTIES of England have not been able to preserve many surprises to offer to their visitors, but there are still a few quiet corners that can arouse our sense of wonder and refresh the spirit. One such comes to the traveller who passes southwards through Shaftesbury towards Ringwood and Christchurch. Here the chalk scarp rears up steeply: a winding zigzag road twists round hairpin bends to reveal suddenly a broad plateau that undulates into the blue distance. To come upon it in this dramatic way is like stumbling on to a lost world. By day, in clear weather, one can see the Needles, thirty miles away. And as night gathers, in this upper twilight, the eye ranges in an eagle's vision across the dark sandy heathlands of Hardy's Egdon to the twinkling lights of the coastal towns. It is a bold landscape, an unexpectedly big landscape, with the satisfying amplitude that makes line more important than colour.

This is Cranborne Chase. There are other and tamer ways of approaching it, but the best way to recognize its essential character is to climb the Zigzag on to Charlton Down and look across to Win Green—the highest point in the Chase, only ninety feet short of the magical thousand that so often eludes the peaks of southern England. Now happily the property of the National Trust, Win Green concedes nothing in grandeur to loftier mountains. So steep are its tumbling declivities into deep combes that I have looked downwards from its summit on to the back of a soaring buzzard as it rode a thermal air-current.

Physically the Chase is a chalk plateau, bordered by the valleys of the Stour and the Avon, rising steeply along its northern escarpment and sloping gently southward to lose itself in the wastes of heather, gorse and pine that run westward from Christchurch to Wareham—where they have not been engulfed in the urban developments of Bournemouth and Poole. The chalk is not unrelieved, however: other soils, notably greensand and clay, appear in places to give a variety to the general style of the landscape. The open simplicities of rolling downland are bordered and diversified by the many woods and copses that still survive from the days when no tree or shrub could be destroyed without the consent of the lord of the Chase.

In *Tess of the d'Urbervilles* Thomas Hardy described Cranborne Chase as 'a truly venerable tract of forest land, one of the few remaining woodlands in England of undoubted primeval date, wherein Druidical mistletoe was still found on aged oaks, and where enormous yew-trees, not planted by the hand of man, grew as they had grown when they were pollarded for bows'. That Victorian picture has been altered of course in the many years since Hardy wrote it: even so it is still easier here than in most places to make contact with an older England and to trace the patterns of history and prehistory. Though time has not stood still in the Chase, its hours have chimed with a slow deliberation that lags behind the sharper pace of modernity.

This slower evolution, and the special character that goes with it, can be reckoned as the outcome of the restrictions that hunting imposed. Like the New Forest, which marched with it along the Avon Valley above Ringwood, the Chase was for centuries preserved for kings and their noble relatives. William the Conqueror gave it to his queen. Their son, William Rufus, gave it to a cousin. An illegitimate son of Henry I acquired it by marriage. So did King John later: he is known to have made at least fourteen visits in order to hunt in the Chase. The lordship of the Chase was never far from the Crown until James I gave it to his 'little beagle', Robert Cecil—Lord Burghley's second son, who served James well as his chief minister and was created Viscount Cranborne and subsequently Earl of Salisbury.

This gift did not diminish royal interest in the Chase. Lord Salisbury promptly enlarged the manor house at Cranborne and equipped it to entertain the king when he chose to visit for a hunting trip. In 1609 James spent a couple of nights in August at Cranborne and killed five bucks in two days' hunting. Charles I similarly, in legislation reinforcing the preservation of deer in one of the Chase walks, let it be known that he 'did chiefly delight to hunt in the said walk or chase as the late King James had done'. In effect, therefore, by direct ownership or active patronage, Cranborne Chase enjoyed the privileges and suffered the restrictions that stemmed from the royal preservation of hunting grounds, from the Norman Conquest to the Civil War.

What happened subsequently is a remarkable story that, in all the detail of its various aspects, will appear later. In brief, ownership of the Chase rights and its lodges was sold after the Restoration and passed through several hands before it came to George Pitt in 1714. Pitt's grandson was created Baron Rivers, and it will be convenient therefore to speak of the Pitt-Rivers family as being, for over a hundred years, the last lords of the Chase. The peculiarity of their position was that they could legally impose restrictions of an obnoxiously 'mediaeval' character on other landowners whose properties lay within the established boundaries of the Chase. And no less extraordinary was the fact that those boundaries had survived almost intact in spite of the centuries of pressure which had diminished, disafforested or disfranchised so much of England's traditional hunting grounds.

To gain a tolerably accurate impression of the size of Cranborne Chase it is sufficient to sketch a rough quadrangle with Shaftesbury, Salisbury, Ringwood and Wimborne at the four corners. It has been estimated as a circuit of eighty miles. In 1816 William West calculated that the land subject to damage by deer comprised 7,000 acres of woodlands, 10,000 of sheep walks and commons and 15,000 arable. But it was not merely a question of the right to kill deer in this large area, which covered parts of three counties—Dorset, Wiltshire and Hampshire. Without the consent of the lord of the Chase nobody was permitted to interfere with the vegetation on which the deer browsed and in which they found shelter. The fact that you might own this tree or that bush did not release you from the legal obligations of Chase law. Furthermore you could be required to pay a toll called 'cheminage' for any form of transport over the Chase roads if this might be harmful to the deer, notably when they were breeding. As late as the early 1800s a pair of antlers was set up on Harnham Bridge in the outskirts of Salisbury during the 'fence' month—fifteen days before Midsummer Day and fifteen days after—to indicate that Lord Rivers was exercising his right to levy fourpence for every waggon and one penny for each packhorse using the bridge, as recompense for the disturbance to deer within the Chase at the time when they were dropping their fawns.

The tensions and frustrations inherent in such a system grew in intensity as the eighteenth century pursued elsewhere its special preoccupations of land clearance and enclosure, improved agricultural methods and the sharper definition of territorial rights and autonomies among the landed gentry. An overlordship that stultified any impulse to change the landscape or depart from the *status quo* was bound to generate friction. Gentry and peasantry, in their different ways, defied or disregarded the laws of the Chase. Some took to litigation, arguing for instance that the Chase did not extend into Wiltshire—in which they were wrong. Others erected fences, only to have them thrown down. Others again took to poaching deer, and the affrays between keepers and parties of illicit hunters became increasingly savage and bloody, to the point where lives were lost. As the Chase gained a reputation for the violence of lawless and sometimes desperate men it attracted the smugglers from the coast between Christchurch and Poole. In 1779, to quote a single example, there was a pitched battle in Hook Wood, in which a party of dragoons were defeated after they had ambushed a band of fifty smugglers, travelling through the Chase with twenty packhorses. The dragoons lost their horses and their weapons, and had to find what comfort they could in the fact that one of the smugglers died of his wounds.

All in all, it was a high price to pay for the preservation of deer. However important venison may have been in the twelfth century it was an expendable luxury by the end of the eighteenth. The need to disfranchise the Chase was seen to be urgent, and informal conversations with Lord Rivers were started to establish the terms on which he would allow his rights to be extinguished. When negotiations over the scale of compensation broke down a committee of local landowners published an open letter to Lord Rivers in 1791, in which they urged not only the injury to their own property by the exercise of Chase rights but the evil effects on the community at large. Because of its special character the Chase had become 'a nursery for and a temptation of all kinds of vice, profligacy and immorality'. Whole parishes were said to have become 'nests of deer-stealers, bred to it by their parents'. What was more, the Chase served as 'a great harbour for smugglers, the woods being very commodious for secreting their goods, and the deer-stealers always at hand to give them assistance'.

The committee's case, in a nutshell, was that 'no private property ought to exist so prejudicial to the community at large'—an interesting sentiment in its context of time and place. Nevertheless, it took forty years of hard bargaining to reach the agreement which was finally embodied in an Act of Parliament. Lord Rivers received an annual payment in compensation for the annulment of all the rights and privileges that had been associated with the lordship of the Chase. The preservation of 'vert and venison' ceased. Henceforward each landowner did as he pleased with his woodlands and his fences.

So ended a long and in some ways unique tradition which had indelibly marked the way of life in this part of England. Increasingly the hunting fraternity concentrated on the preservation of the fox as a substitute for the deer: it was certainly a more suitable quarry to be at large in the nineteenth-century countryside, since it did no damage to woods or arable crops and it offered no temptation to the poacher. The ending of the fallow deer's reign as the sovereign beast of the Chase has not however meant there are no deer to be found there. Fallow deer are still present and a deer of another kind—the more retiring and secretive roe deer—has taken possession of the Chase woodlands in sufficient force to require a planned and systematic study and regulation of numbers by those engaged in forestry.

The social structure of the Chase villages seems to reflect the character of a hunting ground. The towns are all just outside the bounds of the Chase. Shaftesbury, Blandford, Ringwood, Wimborne and Salisbury are situated like harbours round the edge of some great lake, in which the villages appear as little islands. There is no town inside the Chase. Cranborne itself came nearest to developing as a centre of small-scale trade and industry, with an incipient middle class, but the new lines of communicaation in the eighteenth and nineteenth centuries—first the turnpike roads and then the railways—bypassed Cranborne and left it to languish and decline.

The real centres of activity in the Chase over the centuries were the big manor houses, to which the villages are appendages. At first it was the religious houses that dominated the scene—the various establishments of monks and nuns at Wilton, Shaftesbury, Horton, Breamore, Tarrant Crawford, Wimborne, Gussage St Andrew, Cranborne and Iwerne. When the monastic estates were dissolved, the new men of Tudor England emerged—the Ashleys, the Cecils, the Arundells, the Groves, the Napiers. With the growth of the Empire came the new wealth of the Pitts, the Beckfords and the Dodingtons. The City of London in the eighteenth century provided its own invasion of the Chase—the Sturts, the Glyns, the Farquharsons. Their memorials are the magnificent buildings that they erected as their private palaces. Some, like Rushmore Lodge and Wardour Castle, have become schools. Some, like Ferne House of the Groves or Bubb Dodington's Eastbury, have been wholly or partially demolished. Others are converted into flats. Others again remain in the ownership of the family. Enough survive to give the Chase a sense of style and opulent dignity that few areas of England can rival. By contrast the churches, in many cases largely composed of rough flint walls, have a homely austerity.

In such ways the centuries write their history on a landscape. But in Cranborne Chase the page on which they wrote—these Plantagenets and Tudors, Georgians and Victorians—was already covered with the mysterious writings of prehistory. Behind and beyond the civilization we understand, and to which indeed we belong, are other cultures—dimly, remotely ancestral, still exerting some measure of influence on us perhaps, but now cryptic and silent, at best ambiguous and at worst undecipherable. On these chalk uplands of Wiltshire and Dorset one is more aware of the distant dead than anywhere else in England. A collective spirit of the past, a congress of ghosts, broods over the visible relics—the barrows, the henge monuments, the raised mounds and ditches that speak in a kind of dumb-show of the work of men's hands.

However little one may know of archaeology it is impossible to pass through Cranborne Chase without a sense of wonder at the relics of antiquity that catch one's attention. Quickly to mind come the complex of barrows on Oakley Down; the two massive long barrows near the Thickthorn crossroads; the strange line of the Neolithic cursus intersected by one of the finest stretches of Roman road; the firm boundary of Bokerley Dyke stretching across Martin Down; the concentration of fortresses along the flanks of the Stour valley, with Hod Hill and Hambledon looking across to Badbury Rings; and if any one of these memorable sights can epitomize the long continuity of human habitation here it is the little ruined church at Knowlton, Norman in origin or perhaps even Saxon, and standing with a sort of hopeful defiance in the midst of a Neolithic circle, sanctifying an old forgotten ritual with a later one, testifying to something shared that bridges millennia.

How appropriate then that the heir to the Rivers estates, when the direct line became extinct on the death of the sixth baron in 1880, should be General Augustus Lane-Fox, who thereupon assumed the more appropriate name of Pitt-Rivers—a name which he was to make famous by his work as a pioneer archaeologist. Suddenly in command of ample resources, and taking up his new residence in an area so rich in promise for a skilled excavator, the general set in motion what has come to be regarded as the first responsibly scientific and systematic examination of the prehistoric settlements that had come into his possession. Of him Sir Mortimer Wheeler has said: 'Pitt-Rivers is the bridge between the old world of science and the new. . . . It is not altogether unfair to say that the assured place occupied by Darwin in the history of natural science is held by Pitt-Rivers in the humanistic science which we call by the clumsy name of archaeology.'

This remarkable man also shared to the full the passion for constructing new buildings and amenities which, in the nineteenth century, animated other Chase grandees like the Sturts and the Farquharsons. While they were busy with stables and kennels, churches, mansions and lakes, Pitt-Rivers created an anthropological museum embodying his own original ideas at Farnham, a folly temple of Vesta at Rushmore to mark the birth of his first grandson, and the Larmer Tree Gardens which brought visitors in their thousands to Tollard Royal in the 1890s and early 1900s. In September 1895 Thomas Hardy and his wife spent two or three days as the general's guests at Rushmore in order to attend the annual sports and entertainments at the Larmer Tree. An open-air theatre had just been erected that year in the gardens, to be added to the other ornamental buildings which included some brought to Tollard Royal from the Indian Exhibition at Earls Court in 1890.

The Larmer Tree itself was an ancient wych-elm. The meaning of the word 'larmer' is obscure, but the tree was presumably important as a boundary mark and there is a traditional belief that King John's huntsmen assembled here. What is more certain is that 44,817 people gathered about the Larmer Tree as visitors to the gardens in 1899—the peak figure in a steadily rising sequence of annual attendances, which in 1887 had been 15,351. In the gardens a piano and an American organ were available for picnic parties to make their own music at times when the general's own band was absent and when there were no professional entertainers hired by him in the open-air theatre. Understandably the holidaymakers at the growing resort of Bournemouth rode out in carriages and wagonettes for a day at the Larmer Tree, and cyclists came from all directions.

For the local inhabitants the occasion of the sports in September was one of the highspots of the year, with races on foot and on horseback. In the evening the gardens were illuminated with thousands of Vauxhall lamps, and there was dancing in the open air—'the prettiest sight I ever saw in my life' was how one old man described it to me. Thomas Hardy led the house party into the dance in 1895 with one of the general's daughters and carefully preserved a report in the *Dorset County Chronicle*, which claimed that 'probably at no other spot in England could such a spectacle have been witnessed at any time. One could hardly believe that one was not in a suburb of Paris, instead of a corner in old-fashioned Wiltshire, nearly ten miles away from a railway-station in any direction.'

Another big event in the Chase year was the nut harvest. In the seventeenth century John Aubrey noted that 'the nutts of the Chase are of great note, and are sold yearly beyond Sea. The price of them is the price of a buschell of wheate.' Whole families used to travel to the Chase from distant places and lived for weeks at a time in the woods during the eighteenth century, joining the local inhabitants after corn harvest in gathering the hazel nuts. William Chafin, writing his *Anecdotes and History of Cranbourn Chase* in the early years of the nineteenth century, stated that the crop sold particularly well in the sea ports of the region. At the turn of the present century the nut harvest was 'a real godsend for the villagers' in the words of Frank Fry of Ashmore, who said 'the women and children used to go up in the woods and stay there all day, picking. I've known a two-horse load at night. Sixpence a peck was about the price, and that used to pay for our clothes for the year.'

Nowadays few of the human inhabitants of the Chase set much value on hazel nuts and the bulk of the crop is left for other creatures that have a liking for them—particularly the abundant grey squirrels and the occasional dormice. The acreage of hazel coppice is declining anyway.

There is no longer the demand for sheep hurdles, for which so much of the hazel used to be cut. The number of sheep grazing on the Chase downland is beginning to rise again, after falling to a very low level, but it will not recapture the scene that Defoe recorded as he travelled the fourteen miles from Shaftesbury to Salisbury and marvelled at the ever-present shepherds 'keeping their vast flocks of sheep, which are everywhere. . . . The Arcadian plains of which we read so much pastoral trumpery in the poets, could be nothing to them.' This was the classic association between the open short-grassed plains and the close-shadowed woodlands—the association of shepherd and hurdle-maker, of sheep and hazel. Its true memorial perhaps is the headstone in Martin churchyard which commemorates the shepherd Lawes who is better known by the fictitious name of Isaac Balcombe that W. H. Hudson gave him in *A Shepherd's Life*.

Hudson's classic belongs to the time when sheep were penned in hurdled enclosures by night and released to roam by day over the sheep-walks and commons. This is not the way of modern farming methods, which are designed for enclosed land; but an area of common grazing has survived by a happy coincidence on Martin Down, and it is here—on the unbroken turf that Hudson knew so well—that the music of sheep bells still signals the release of a flock from their hurdles to start their day's grazing. For a nature-lover, and more particularly a botanist, to follow the sheep up the slope of this noble downland is a memorable experience, with the recently added pleasure that the area is now designated a Nature Reserve. The sward has the increasingly rare distinction of surviving undisturbed in its pristine state, with all the variety of plants that over the centuries have found a place in the complex community of the turf. Standing here on a fresh clear morning it is easy to recognize what impelled Hudson to write: 'Just as the air is purer and fresher on these chalk heights than on the earth below, and as the water is of a more crystal purity, and the sky perhaps bluer, so do all colours and all sounds have a purity and vividness and intensity beyond that of other places.'

CHAPTER TWO

Early Days of the Chase

THE DAY MAY come when the entire English landscape is standardized in four categories—urban centres, lines of communication, areas of food production, and leisure parks—with each part looking the same as every other in the same category. Indeed we are well down that road already, as a glance at your nearest shopping centre, dairy herd and motorway will show. If then any justification be needed for a book about Cranborne Chase it will rest primarily on the fact that the Chase is still very different from other parts of southern England and is in some ways unique. The differences and the uniqueness are being gradually blurred but they are real enough to be treasured and enjoyed; and since their nature is essentially historical we must find our starting point in the history of the Chase.

The concept of a large area being preserved by stern laws for the hunting of deer is so remote from our present-day world that it requires an effort of the imagination to envisage it. What did our ancestors really mean by words like 'chase' and 'forest' and 'warren'? More specifically, how did Cranborne Chase get its name and what did it signify? The pat answer is that a forest was a royal hunting ground, while a chase was a hunting ground belonging to one of the monarch's subjects. Like many another pat answer it is not quite good enough. William West, writing in 1816 his *History of the Forest or Chace known by the Name of Cranborn Chace*, came to the conclusion that Cranborne Chase 'partakes most of the nature of a forest'.

As good a definition of a forest as any was that made by an earlier writer, James Lee, which Thomas Hearne included in his *Curious Discourses on English Antiquities*:

The word *forest* . . . doth signify . . . all things that are abroad, and neither domestical nor demean [demesne]: wherefore *foresta* in old time did extend into woods, wastes and waters, and did contain not only *vert* and venison, but also minerals and maritimal revenues.

But when *forests* were first used in England I find no certain time of the beginning thereof; and, although that ever since the Conquest it hath been lawful for the King to make any man's land (whom it pleased

him) to be *forest*, yet there are certain rules and circumstances appointed
for the doing thereof.

For, first, there must issue out of Chancery a writ of *perambulation*,
directed unto certain discreet men, commanding them to call before
them XXiiij Knights and principal freeholders, and to cause them, in the
presence of the officers of the forests, to walk or perambulate so much
ground as they shall think to be fit or convenient for the breeding,
feeding, and succouring of the King's deer, and to put the same in
writing, and to certify the same under the seals of the same Commissioners and Jurors unto the Chancery.

From this it is clear that forest territory was originally the wilderness
that lay beyond those areas that men had enclosed and cleared and put to
agricultural or pastoral use. These wild undomesticated territories would
belong to the king or paramount lord since—by definition—they had not
been granted to any subject to clear and enclose for his own use and were
therefore literally 'no man's land'. Where it became necessary to define a
hunting ground there was a recognized procedure which involved a
formal perambulation, followed by a registration of the boundaries.
Where people wanted to enter a hunting ground for purposes unconnected
with hunting, and indeed to reside in it, it was not difficult to regulate
their activities so that they did not conflict with the conditions required for
hunting. The system of regulation was what is known as forest law. It was
a system that could and did become oppressive, but it probably worked
well enough in the conditions which gave rise to it.

What forest law upheld was the primacy of the beasts that were hunted.
The 'breeding, feeding and succouring of the king's deer', to borrow Lee's
words, had precedence over every other consideration. Not only were the
beasts themselves preserved: equally so was their habitat. In the traditional
words—'vert' was no less sacred than 'venison', and 'vert' meant the
vegetation, every growing thing that could be serviceable to the deer.
Provided this general intention was honoured, however, the 'vert' could
be put to other uses by those who acquired the right to do so. These
rights—of pannage, turbary, haybote and the like—still survive in some
parts of the country though the ancient words are unfamiliar to most of us.
What they define are the ways in which a forest could be useful without
detriment to the deer. The supply of timber for such purposes as house-
building and fencing was one way; the grazing of domestic animals was
another; a third was the cutting of peat and furze for fuel. These things
were permissible up to the point where they began to compete with the
deer; and at that point they were cut off. Consequently each 'right' was

defined with great precision and could be a matter for detailed and pro-
tracted bargaining. Even the unforeseen was foreseen, if one may put it
that way: an unusually hard winter which jeopardized the feed the deer
required would be met with the declaration of a period of 'heyning'
during which the normal 'agistment' of domestic animals was suspended.

This protection of vert emphasizes the importance of deer; there was
even an extra penalty for harming the species of trees that bore fruit for
the deer. Resistance to the growing oppressiveness of forest law came to a
climax in Magna Carta and more specifically in the Charter of the Forest
which followed two years later, in 1217. The causes of friction, and eventually of organized resistance, were three. One was the arbitrary extension
of forest limits beyond what was lawfully established. The second was the
day-to-day disputes over individual rights. The third was the special
nature of the courts which administered forest law and which were outside the common law.

This is not the place to probe in detail the complexities of mediaeval law
but it is perhaps not a dangerous oversimplification to say that the difference between a forest and a chase resides in the way the law was administered. Put crudely—the calendar of offences might be the same but the
system of punishment was different. The chase courts operated within the
general framework of common law: the forest courts had an independence
which could be despotic since the king or his representative was ultimately
both prosecutor and judge. Arraigned under forest law one faced anything
from a fine to a sentence of death. The chase courts, by contrast, could
impose relatively minor punishments only, on the spot; more serious
prosecutions had to be remitted to the civil courts.

The rules that governed the Chase, therefore, were just as rigorously
addressed to the preservation of vert and venison as in the New Forest or
any other forest, but the application of legal sanctions was in the milder
forms appropriate to a chase; and this was just as true when the owner of
the Chase was the monarch himself as when it belonged to one of his close
relatives or to a mere subject. The status of the Chase was not altered by the
rank of its owner. Neither was it influenced by the kind of animals that
were hunted therein—although this is a popular notion and will be
examined later. If we are to account for the co-existence of the two legal
systems we should perhaps look to specific acts by individual monarchs in
declaring to be 'royal forest' those hunting grounds with which they
particularly wished to be associated—the most obvious example being
William I's association with the New Forest.

It is worth recalling that at the time of the Norman Conquest the
population of Britain was probably no more than about a million and a

quarter—not much greater than present-day Birmingham. In such circumstances the wilderness areas were reservoirs of food and materials. To
appreciate their value in terms of meat on the hoof we must look to
modern Africa as a contemporary equivalent, where it can still be argued
that wild animals systematically protected and culled can yield more
protein per acre than the domestic animals that might replace them at a
similar standard of husbandry. The fact that our ancestors took a delight
in the pleasures of the chase should not blind us to the severely practical
importance of hunting in their time. The pursuit of deer and wild boar
was not just something the Plantagenets did at weekends because they
had no golf courses.

The domestication of farm animals demands an ability to enclose, feed
and water them throughout the year. For the mediaeval British farmer it
was the shortage of winter feed that was the limiting factor and led to the
autumn slaughter and salting down of surplus beasts. Wild animals that
could survive on nothing more than the natural vert must have been an
important element in mediaeval economy. What underlines that importance is the size of royal and noble households—the armies of retainers who
had to be fed. For them the contribution from organized hunting grounds
must have been of considerable value, and the ability to dispense a buck to
a foreign ambassador or an influential courtier was not the least of the
monarch's advantages.

The origins of the Chase of Cranborne are more obscure than one might
expect or hope—at any rate until we come to evidence of the kind of
perambulation that James Lee described in the passage already quoted.
Before that it seems to have been the case that north-west of the New Forest
large areas of Dorset and Wiltshire were regarded indiscriminately as
forest. Cranborne Chase itself adjoined the New Forest along the Avon
valley. South of the Chase, on the sandy waste east of Wimborne
Minster, was Holt Forest. To the north, in Wiltshire, was Groveley
Forest. Along the borders of Wiltshire, Dorset and Somerset were the
Forests of Gillingham and Selwood; and to the west of the Chase, in what
is now Blackmoor Vale, was the Forest of the White Hart. It must have
been possible to hunt almost from Southampton to Bath without straying
for long outside forest territory. In the contemplation of this larger picture
it is easy to comprehend the elaborate infrastructure of individual rights
that must have been necessary to combine the preservation of vert and
venison with human settlement: easy too to realize that the niceties of
legal distinction between forest and chase were often blurred.

The definition of the Chase first takes substance in a document of 1280—
quoted here in the English of a seventeenth-century translation—which

records a dispute between the king, Edward I, represented by William de Giselham, and Gilbert de Clare, the Earl of Gloucester, who was accused of extending the 'metes and bounds' of his chase illegally to the west of 'the royal way which leads between Shaston (Shaftesbury) and Blandford' and making 'the water of Stour' his western boundary. This was not an isolated case but part of a general examination of such alleged transgressions. Henry III during his long reign had frequently seemed ready to yield to pressures to reduce the afforested areas, as he was expected to do in consequence of the Charter of the Forest, but the results showed little zeal on his part. Accordingly when Edward I succeeded him in 1272 it was prudent to show a willingness to give some genuine effect to the declared policy of disafforestation. Even absolute monarchs cannot stall indefinitely when undertakings have been solemnly given.

Sensing their opportunity several districts tried to clip the wings of Gilbert de Clare, and their juries 'presented' against him. There was pressure also from some of the religious houses at this time, notably from Glastonbury which was a substantial landowner at the eastern end of the Chase. In 1281 de Clare made a special agreement with Abbot John of Glastonbury which eased the normal restrictions on abbey property in Damerham. Meantime the action by the king brought to a head the general feeling that ownership of the manor of Cranborne by the de Clares entitled them to claim a lordship over only the Inner Bounds of the Chase, as they came to be called, and not over the much larger area which they were thought to have usurped by illicit extensions of their 'metes and bounds'.

The details of these two boundaries, the Inner and the Outer, must perhaps be reckoned a matter for specialists and enthusiasts. Without a close knowledge of the district they can mean little, and a full discussion of them is therefore placed in a separate appendix. What matters immediately is the defence de Clare offered. As Earl of Gloucester he claimed that there had been a perambulation of the boundaries of the Chase at the time when the earldom of Gloucester was held by King John; and further, that the details of that perambulation had later been confirmed unanimously on oath by the jurors at an inquisition held at Salisbury in the twenty-ninth year of the reign of Henry III—'the father of the King who now is'.

The ability to cite a formal inquisition defining and approving King John's bounds was decisive. In due course a warrant containing the words 'Dominus Rex concessit' instructed the Sheriff of Dorset to recognize the Earl of Gloucester's right to retain within the Chase the disputed land west of the royal road and as far as the banks of the Stour. It was a considerable territory, involving the villages of Compton Abbas, Fontmell Magna,

Iwerne Minster and Iwerne Courtney, Child Okeford and Stourpaine and
the town of Blandford.

It is worth dwelling briefly on the detail of Edward I's *Quo Warranto* for
what it reveals of the nature of this part of the Chase and, more generally,
of the way boundaries were defined. The significance of the royal road
from Shaftesbury to Blandford is that it keeps to the high ground of the
western scarp of the chalk downs. Its course is therefore as far west as was
practicable for a north-south route, if it can be assumed that the low-lying
land beyond the scarp—through which the present A350 links Blandford
and Shaftesbury—was in those days unsuitable for an essential through-
road. North of the great fortress complex of Hod Hill and Hambledon lies
what must have been a marshy landscape in which, even to this day, the
extent of human settlement is unusually light. The villages seem to cling to
the skirts of the chalk scarp and their earliest lines of communication
tended to run east-west. The royal road would therefore be a reasonably
well-defined boundary down the western side of the Chase and the best
one available in the absence of a watercourse.

The ideal boundary in all circumstances was undoubtedly water in the
form of river, lake or sea—normally immutable, easy to recognize and
define, difficult to pass, easy to defend. On the western flank of the Chase
the natural water-line was the River Stour, and accordingly the King John
perambulation had extended beyond the royal road to 'the water of
Stour'. As the whole pattern of the authorized 'metes and bounds' unfolds
in the warrant it becomes clear that rivers and streams have been used to
define the perimeter wherever possible: on the west the Stour, on the
north the Sem and the Nadder, on the east the Avon, on the south the
Crane and the Allen. The sectors where there is uncertainty in the interpretation of landmarks are in the linking zones between one stream and
the next.

The verdict of 1280 has at first the appearance of a victory by a member
of the nobility over the monarchy, since it was the king who tried to
reduce the size of the Chase and failed to do so. A closer look at the
relationship between the earls of Gloucester and the regal line will suggest
that this is too simplistic an interpretation; it will also throw some light on
the origins of the Chase and its connection with the village of Cranborne.
In Saxon times Cranborne was one of the manors that were grouped
together in what was known as 'the Honour of Gloucester'. In this sense
of the word 'honour' means—according to the Oxford dictionary—'a
seigniory of several manors held under one baron or lord paramount'. The
Honour of Gloucester was a substantial seigniory which included Bristol
among its manors. Its last Saxon owner was Brictric who served as English

Roe-deer fawn

Roe-deer in rut. The buck can be seen licking the back of the doe

Horton Tower

Knowlton Circles: Norman
church within neolithic henge

ambassador to Baldwin, Count of Flanders; and it was in the course of this embassy that Brictric made a fatal mistake which changed the course of the history of Cranborne manor and its chase.

The Count of Flanders had a daughter, Matilda, who took a fancy to the English ambassador. Possibly Brictric was not looking for a wife at the time, or maybe he simply failed to reciprocate Matilda's amorous feelings: whatever the reason Matilda considered herself to have been slighted by Brictric, and hers was not a forgiving nature. She married instead the man who later invaded and conquered England, with consequences for Brictric that are not difficult to predict. The discourteous ex-ambassador was imprisoned. The new Queen of England, Matilda, replaced him as owner of the Honour of Gloucester. From her it passed to her son, William Rufus. Cranborne Chase was therefore firmly in royal hands during the reigns of the first two Norman kings, when forest law in England was intensified and made more severe. Of William I it was said that he loved the deer as if he were their father, with disagreeable consequences for any who did not share that love; while it was William II who introduced the death penalty for killing a deer and imposed the 'lawing' or maiming of dogs which might otherwise hunt illicitly.

The transfer from direct royal ownership to the earls of Gloucester began when William Rufus gave the honour to his cousin Robert Fitz-Haymon. Fitz-Haymon's daughter, Mabel, was thought to be a suitable bride for Henry I's illegitimate son, Robert, but a wise precondition of the marriage was that Robert should first be given a suitable rank and title. The man Mabel met at the altar, therefore, was the newly created Earl of Gloucester. It was their grand-daughter, Hadwisa, who married Prince John, later to become King John (and then to divorce her). By his marriage John acquired the title of Earl of Gloucester and the rights that accompanied the title. The perambulation of the Chase bounds that John caused to be made was therefore concerned with land that, for more than a century, had been held by the royal family or by relatives as close as cousinhood or bastardy provided.

Cranborne was acquired by the de Clares when King John's first wife, Hadwisa, died childless. Her estate—including of course the Chase—passed to her sister, Amicia, who married Richard de Clare, Earl of Hertford. Their son, Gilbert, took his title from both parents, becoming Earl of Gloucester and Hertford, but it is as earls of Gloucester that the subsequent de Clares are known; and it is with their possession of the Honour of Gloucester, in which Cranborne Chase was included, that we are concerned.

By the thirteenth century, if not earlier, Cranborne was the administrative centre of Chase law. Here were held the courts in which those who transgressed Chase law were prosecuted. The claim of manorial rights and liberties made by Gilbert de Clare during the Edward I inquisition included 'free court of his chase aforesaid, and to plead in the same concerning vert and venison, with attachment of men taken in the fact or on open suspicion, and to take from such as are convicted emendals in the same court'. In other words he claimed the right to set up his own law court to enforce his authority as lord of the Chase by arresting men caught in the act of breaking the laws of vert and venison, or reasonably suspected of doing so, and to punish them by fines or temporary incarceration or—for more serious offences—by prosecuting them under common law before the king's justices.

The kind of offence that was dealt with in this way is well illustrated by two examples of the period. In the first, which concerned the right of certain religious houses to take timber from specified areas, the three abbesses of Shaftesbury, Wilton and Tarrant joined forces in a legal action which obliged the earl to make concessions to them; and the following year he released the powerful Abbess of Shaftesbury from the obligation to send her woodwards to attend the court at Cranborne, provided they came once—when they were first appointed—to swear to honour the laws of vert and venison and to report offenders. In the other example there were complaints that Gilbert de Clare's father had afforested all the country towards the north of the Chase, from Shaftesbury to Salisbury's Harnham Bridge along the River Nadder, 'placing seven foresters, amercing such as enclosed their own woods, laying hands unjustly at their will on men dwelling in Wilts, under pretence of taking venison, obliging them to go to Cranborne, and there amercing them without proof'.

As one examines such cases it becomes clear that a major cause of the resentment was the requirement to make the journey to Cranborne, with the near certainty of being fined in an arbitrary fashion. Anyone who has paid for a questionable parking offence rather than give up a day and make a journey to defend it will find it easy to sympathize with the thirteenth-century parson of Bishopstone, halted peremptorily with his cartload of thorns, who made a vigorous protest but paid on the spot the half-mark 'amercement' demanded of him. He was certainly neither the first nor the last who paid up 'for the sake of peace'.

When Edward I came to the throne one of his most valued supporters was Gilbert de Clare. The king's complaint about the metes and bounds of the Chase was in no sense a personal issue: rather the reverse. It was part of a general policy to honour earlier pledges to disafforest territories which could be shown to have been illegally annexed to existing forests. An instance of success in this intention, in an area adjacent to Cranborne Chase, affected Blackmoor Forest (otherwise known as the Forest of the White Hart) which lay on the western side of the water of Stour and was partly disafforested as a result of Edward I's general enquiry at this time. The ability of the Earl of Gloucester to support his claims by a valid and well-attested perambulation did nothing to impair his good relations with the king. If there were any doubt of that when the *Quo Warranto* was issued, such a doubt was dissipated ten years later when Gilbert de Clare married Joan Plantagenet, the king's daughter.

Once again the Chase was back in the hands of the king, for in April 1290 the Earl of Gloucester—as a prospective son-in-law—made a token surrender to Edward I of some or all of his possessions including *Maneria de Cranborn cum chacea ejusdem*—the manor of Cranborn with the chace of the same. The king thereupon regranted them to the earl and his newly-wedded wife, to be held by them and their heirs—a manœuvre which West has suggested was specifically intended to bear on the Chase boundaries, either by adding the king's authority to the earl's or conversely by making possible a withdrawal from the more extreme features of the boundary claim.

Neither interpretation has much to commend it. The *Quo Warranto* had already set out the king's approval in fine and legal terms, and there is nothing subsequently to suggest that the earl chose to yield any part of the lordship he had established. A much simpler explanation seems to fit the facts. De Clare's possessions, located in several counties, were on a scale that made the hunting lordship of Cranborne Chase a very minor and incidental item. The point of the ritual of surrender and regrant was surely to recognize the importance of a royal princess, and accordingly to endow and fortify her position as the earl's wife. In essence she was not to be beholden to her husband but to her kingly father. Put crudely the earl's rôle in the wedding ceremony was to say 'With all my worldly goods your father thee endows'. Nor was the gesture an empty one: if the earl's issue failed his estate reverted to the Crown.

In the event de Clare's issue did not fail though his immediate heir suffered a melancholy fate, dying at the hands of the Scots in the battle of Bannockburn in 1314. By his death Cranborne and its Chase passed to one of his three sisters, Elizabeth de Burgh. Her importance in the present context is that it was she who, in 1352, made a successful application to have the *Quo Warranto* of Edward I 'exemplified in Chancery under the Great Seal'. This was presumably a definitive act of official registration of the original document. The metes and bounds of the Chase were thus put on record in a final and irrevocable way—or as nearly irrevocable as the law could guarantee. What Edward I had conceded was to endure for over five centuries, and at the last to be overturned only with the consent of the owner and by a special Act of Parliament.

CHAPTER THREE

Royal Lords of the Chase

THE PRECISE ACREAGE of the Chase is a matter for argument but there can be no doubt that the figure usually cited is wrong. William West put it at between seven and eight hundred thousand acres in 1816, and subsequent authors have accepted and repeated his estimate uncritically. Converted to square miles this acreage would exceed 1,000 square miles—equivalent to eight New Forests. A more realistic figure for the area confined within the ancient metes and bounds of Cranborne Chase would be about 250,000 acres, which still compares impressively with the 92,365 acres which in 1860 comprised the whole area within the bounds of the New Forest.

The administration of this large tract of land altered as century followed century and successive lords of the Chase adapted their practices to the changing conditions in which they lived; but the main themes and customs and traditions persisted over long periods of time. While the fundamental legal and social rules held good there was little impulse for a new generation to depart substantially from the ways of its predecessors. The life of a keeper or a woodward in one of the Chase villages was probably not greatly different whether he served a Plantagenet noble, a Tudor monarch or a Georgian aristocrat.

Of the whole area of the Chase a large part would consist, even in its earliest period of recorded history, of open downland and of the arable fields attached to each human settlement. Some idea of the woodlands comes from a survey of Gilbert de Clare's property made in 1296 which indicates 1,433 acres of woodland where the pasture was worth 100 shillings a year but could not be sold because of the wild animals, i.e. the deer. Similarly a survey of 1362 speaks of 'a certain chase worth nothing by the year beyond the sustenance of the deer'. There was however a revenue that accrued from this land, in the form of fines and distraints levied in the Chase court. The 1296 survey valued 'the pleas and perquisites of the Chase, at 60 shillings annually'.

The Chase court was held twice a year and its proceedings contain much information about Chase life. The senior officials in Tudor times and earlier were the lord warden and the head ranger. The warden was a nobleman whose rôle was to be the monarch's representative and he might have a local lieutenant as his deputy: as for instance Sir John Ashley was Lord Pembroke's lieutenant during Queen Elizabeth's reign. The ranger was more of a bailiff or steward in charge of daily operations. It is quite possible however that at some times one man filled both posts, perhaps subcontracting a part of the duties to a subordinate of his own selection. A good example is Sir Giles Strangways or Strongwich, appointed by Henry VIII as 'steward of our lordship or manor of Cranborne' and also as 'warden and master ranger and keeper of our chase of Cranborne, in our county of Dorset, and in our county of Wilts, and of all wild beasts in the said chase being and to be'. It was a life appointment and the annual fees were to him as steward of the manor 66s 8d, as warden of the Chase 100s, and as ranger £6 1s 8d.

The Earl of Wiltshire's appointment in the reign of Henry VI was presumably as lord warden. In the following reign the appointment in 1461 by Edward IV of Walter Harding as 'Ranger of the Chace of Cranborn' points to the other rôle; and when Harding died King Edward replaced him with the royal *valet de chambre*, Thomas Dakham or Daccomb, who also became the keeper of Rushmore Lodge. At this period the Daccombs were a family of substance in the Chase. During the previous reign William Daccomb had by marriage acquired the manors of Iwerne Stepleton and Fontmell Parva. A descendant, John Daccomb, became Chancellor of the Duchy of Lancaster and was knighted in 1616. We may assume therefore that Rushmore Lodge was already something more than a keeper's cottage. It had the advantage of being centrally situated in the Chase woodlands, where the deer were concentrated; and it was located strategically within Wiltshire in a commanding position above the Ebble valley. It emerged gradually as a sort of operational head-quarters, separated from the legal and titular functions of Cranborne from which it was distanced, moreover, by a not inconsiderable journey of about ten miles.

In its earliest history Rushmore was the dwelling of the Abbess of Wilton's woodward. In 1341 an old charter was cited to show that at some period before 1341 Robert de Ryshmere had occupied the place with about fifteen acres of land, some pasture for his cattle and the right to cut wood for certain purposes. The annual rent he paid was made up of two shillings, two dozen hens and 400 eggs. For the seventy or eighty years following 1341 Rushmore was occupied by three generations of the Saleman or Solyman family at the same rent, which they seemingly had difficulty in paying. In 1413 Robert Saleman was distrained for arrears.

The enhanced status of Rushmore Lodge seems to coincide with the return of the Chase to the Crown later in the fifteenth century. The Abbess of Wilton must have parted with it at or before the time of Daccomb's appointment. From Edward IV onwards Rushmore Lodge was administered by the Crown. In Henry VIII's reign, for example, when the Chase was allocated to Queen Katherine Parr, her counsellors approved the expenditure of 33s 4d 'for repairs made upon the Lodge of Rushmore within the Chase of Cranborne by the Ranger there this year'.

In the troubled years that ended the Wars of the Roses the Chase warden was Sir Francis Chaine—a name that one is tempted to transcribe in the more familiar form of Cheny. He was apparently exiled by Richard III and returned with the accession of Henry VII to hold his post for so long as he and the king lived. A similar life appointment was that of Thomas Benbow as ranger of Rushmore. Of these two officials, warden and ranger, we have a clear account in a deposition made in 1594 by a keeper who lived at Sixpenny Handley. This man, Thomas West, had heard from his father, William, who was also a keeper, that Chaine had been warden 'when King Richard was King' but that the king 'gave Chaine out of the land' so that he remained 'beyonde sea' for two years and 'came in againe with Kinge Harry the VIIth'. Among Henry VII's supporters at the battle of Bosworth in 1485 was John Cheyne, Cheyney or Cheney who was knighted in that year and later became Lord Cheyne, dying in 1499 and being buried in Salisbury Cathedral: presumably a kinsman of the Chase warden or possibly the same man.

During the reigns of Henry VII and Henry VIII the wardens who followed Sir Francis Chaine were Sir William Compton, Sir John Rogers, the Marquess of Exeter and lastly Sir Giles Strangways; but during much of that period the 'Ranger of Rushmore' was Thomas Benbow whom Henry VII appointed for life: 'whosoever was Warden yet hee was Ranger ther as longe as he lived'. His career as ranger cannot have been brief because Thomas West recalled that Benbow occupied Rushmore Lodge until he had twenty children 'borne within the lodge by one woman'.

Elizabeth I's choice of a lord warden was the Earl of Pembroke, to whom she entrusted Cranborne Chase and the royal park at Blagdon. When the Chase passed finally out of royal hands the concept of an honorific lord warden died out and the ranger became the senior post effectively. In 1681 Captain Thomas Chafin was ranger of the Chase, and the Chafin family enjoyed a long association with the management of the Chase. George Chafin, MP for Dorset, was head ranger until his death in 1766 when the post was abolished, although the family connection persisted. The subsequent practice was to allocate the individual 'walks' of the Chase to local landowners, thereby sharing the costs, the responsibilities and the privileges and incidentally forming a formidable alliance. For example, in the early 1800s Lord Rivers retained Rushmore and Staplefoot Walks for himself, while the other rangers were Sir Arthur Paget in West Walk, Charles Sturt in Chettered, Rev. William Chafin in Bursey Stool, and the Prince of Wales in Cobley during his residence at Crichel. Cobley passed later into the hands of Lord Shaftesbury and J. J. Farquharson, the celebrated hunting 'Squire', and West Walk similarly had other rangers in Lord Dorchester and Peter Beckford.

When history begins to identify individually named 'walks' and parks like the one mentioned at Blagdon the Chase comes into sharper focus as something more than a monotonously undifferentiated hunting ground. We begin to discern an infrastructure that we can relate to the landscape of modern times. It will therefore be helpful to itemize the various sectors of the Chase and define their characteristics.

There were eight named walks in all. Five were grouped together in the area of the Inner or Lesser Bounds. These were, from west to east, West Walk, Bursey Stool, Rushmore, Staplefoot and Cobley. Until the final act of disfranchisement these five walks remained under the direct control of the lord of the Chase and within them the wellbeing of the deer was always paramount. In each the woodland area was divided into copses. Thomas Aldwell's map of 1618 shows Cobley Walk, for example, as an unbroken block of over fifty copses, each individually named and in many cases corresponding with names still in use today. Taken together these five walks of the Inner Bounds were and are the heartland of the Chase. In terms of today's maps they lie north of the A354 up to about the line of what is known as the Ox Drove.

The three other walks were Vernditch, Alderholt and Chettered: each quite separate and distinct. Vernditch, Fernditch or Fernbushes as it was variously known is best described as an eastern addition to the group of five, lying more or less alongside Cobley Walk. The evidence of early Chase court proceedings suggests that it was not then considered as a separate entity but as one of the walks of the central group, like Cobley or Staplefoot. It acquired a separate history when the Earl of Pembroke bought it from the second Earl of Salisbury and by so doing detached it from the rest of the Chase. Alderholt and Chettered were more obviously independent of the rest. Under Henry VII the Chase court considered matters affecting the central group of walks in two anonymous sections— the east part and the west part. When these were disposed of, the court addressed its attention to 'Alreholte' and 'Chyttrede'. Of all the walks Alderholt was reputed to be the largest; and it was the one closest to Cranborne. It was indeed a part of the parish of Cranborne until 1894, by which time Cranborne had become the largest parish in Dorset and was therefore split into three—releasing Alderholt and Verwood as new parishes. The other distinctive feature of Alderholt was the fact that it was mainly an area of acid heathland, whereas the other walks were on the chalk downs. The survey that Norden made for Robert Cecil shows large tracts of waste and common land to the east of Cranborne in what would have been Alderholt Walk. Much of it was barren and sometimes boggy land attracting only the occasional squatter who found here a chance to put up a hovel without fear of reprisal.

Chettered Walk is something of an anomaly. It lay apart from the other walks, circumscribed on three sides by the valleys of the Allen, the Tarrant and the Crichel stream. Its axis followed a diagonal from Tarrant Rushton to Long Crichel, and it still retains this form in its diminished modern guise as Chetterwood. Lying outside the Lesser Bounds and away from Cranborne it was sometimes treated as a separate chase. In the time of Charles I, when Lord Salisbury took action to restrain John Cole of Witchampton from hunting and killing deer in Chettered, it was stated that this was the particular area in which the king, like his father before him, 'did chiefly delight' to hunt; and it was referred to as 'the said walk or chase', which raises the tricky question of whether a chase can exist within a larger chase. For Salisbury it was argued that 'Chitred Walk' was sometimes known as Chitred Chase but was linked together with Cranborne Chase. This apparent separation of the two was evidently an administrative convenience only: so far as the preservation of deer was concerned Chettered remained an integral part of the lordship.

It is in the changing status of Verndicth and Alderholt that the tidemarks of history can be discerned. They reflect the shifts in the balance of power within the Chase, once it had passed finally out of royal hands. The transfer of ownership of the territories within the Outer Bounds began with Henry VIII and was concluded by James I. The various stages, with all their legal niceties, are too complicated to be worth unravelling in detail but the main theme is clear enough. It starts with the dissolution of the monasteries and it concerns the rise of five families—the Arundells of Wardour, the Herberts of Wilton, the Cecils of Cranborne, the Ashleys of Wimborne St Giles and the Frekes of Iwerne Courtney. In the course of events the Herberts will become the earls of Pembroke; Robert Cecil will first become Viscount Cranborne and shortly afterwards Earl of Salisbury; the Ashleys will become Ashley Coopers, earls of Shaftesbury; and the Frekes, failing in the male line, will pass by marriage into the Pitt-Rivers.

The acquisition of monastic lands, buildings, rents, tithes, advowsons and so on gave successive monarchs a great miscellany of assets that could readily be turned into cash or given in return for services rendered. The new dynasts were men with cash to invest, services to offer and positions of influence which gave them a good view of the state of play. The Arundells seem to have held land in the Chase as early as 1422 but their big moment came under Henry VIII when, in 1530, Sir Thomas Arundell married Margaret Howard, who was not only a grand-daughter of the Duke of Norfolk but also a sister of the future queen, Katherine Howard. In the three years 1535–38 he acquired a large slice of the possessions of Shaftesbury Abbey, including the Hundred of Sixpenny Handley and a string of Chase villages—Tollard Royal among them. He added others, including Tisbury, in 1544; and three years later he bought from Sir Fulke Greville the castle at Wardour, the future seat of the family from which his grandson in 1605 took the title Baron Arundell of Wardour. Also in 1544 Sir Thomas Arundell bought Shaftesbury Abbey itself or what remained of it.

While Arundell was securing the north-west of the Chase, in the wake of the Shaftesbury convent, William Herbert was busy in the north-east where the monastic owner had been the Abbess of Wilton. 'Black Will', as he was known, was a remarkable character who started life as—in John Aubrey's words—'a mad fighting young fellow', made a reputation as a soldier and married Ann Parr before her sister, Katherine, married the king. From Henry VIII he acquired Wilton Abbey and a knighthood. In connection with Wilton, which was to become the family seat, Aubrey tells an amusing story of Black Will's changing fortunes when Queen Mary restored the Catholic religion and the nuns returned to Wilton Abbey:

> this William Earl of Pembroke came to the gate which lookes toward the court by the street, but now is walled up, and fell upon his knee to the lady abbesse and nunnes, crying *peccavi*. Upon Queen Mary's death, the Earl came to Wilton (like a tigre) and turned them out, crying 'Out ye whores, to worke, to worke—ye whores, goe spinne.'

It is a diverting anecdote, in Aubrey's raciest style, but it demands a good deal of storyteller's licence—even though it does contain the essential truth that Pembroke had an exceptional talent for survival. When Sir Giles Strangways, the warden of the Chase, died in the same year as Henry VIII, the new King Edward VI appointed Will Herbert as warden. On at least one occasion during his brief reign the young king spent a week in August between Woodlands and Wilton, hunting in the Chase when, over Faulston Down, his courtiers lost contact with him and found him again in Faulston Lane.

The six years of this ailing boy on the throne of England brought very different fortunes to Arundell and Herbert. Arundell was one of the casualties involved in the overthrow of 'Protector' Somerset. Herbert acquired a second Wiltshire abbey, Ramsbury, and became Earl of Pembroke in 1551. He also acquired Wardour from Arundell, whose son recovered it later in a deal combining purchase and exchange. The nearly fatal mistake made by Pembroke was to support the plot to make Lady Jane Grey queen but he changed course quickly enough to be accepted by Queen Mary, who came to rely on him—although with some suspicion. He was indeed a great power in the land, reputed to have a thousand men in his livery. At Mary's wedding he was one of the three noblemen who, on behalf of England, gave her as a bride to the King of Spain. And when Mary died Pembroke went with William Cecil, Matthew Arundell and one other to Elizabeth at Hatfield where they were sworn as her Privy Council.

It is not with his part in national events that we are concerned, however, but with his impact on the smaller world of Cranborne Chase. Here, from 1530 until his death in 1570, he was the dominant figure as a major landowner who was also for the last two decades the lord warden of the Chase. This appointment, made by Edward VI for a term of twenty-one years, had still two or three years to run when Lord Pembroke died. Queen Elizabeth promptly appointed his son, Henry, the second earl, as seneschal of her manor of Cranborne and warden of the Chase. From their family seat at Wilton the Pembrokes therefore wielded enormous power in the Chase throughout the second half of the sixteenth century.

Serving under the Pembrokes four deputies or lieutenants are mentioned. The earliest was Sir John Rogers, followed by Sir Matthew Arundell. According to the testimony of a keeper there was a 'difference' between Arundell and Pembroke; and Arundell was replaced by Sir Henry Ashley. Sir John Ashley held the post during part of Elizabeth's reign, and in general the Ashleys begin to emerge at this period as the family most likely to snap up any opportunities that might arise in their part of the Chase. Towards the end of Elizabeth's reign Anthony Ashley was taking a keen interest in Cranborne itself. Seated at Wimborne St Giles he was eager to buy the adjacent manor of Cranborne Priory.

The priory had of course passed to Henry VIII when it was dissolved. Subsequently the Crown contractors had put it out on lease. In Queen Mary's reign Robert Freke took it for twenty years and his lease was renewed for a further twenty-one years in 1573. Freke was a teller in the

Exchequer and father of Sir Thomas Freke. He had bought the manor of Shroton, otherwise known as Iwerne Courtney, from Pembroke in 1560, and Hinton St Mary also belonged to the Frekes. Sir Thomas Freke was twice knight of the shire and for thirty years deputy lieutenant: he was also a great patron of the church, rebuilding at his own cost and having it said of him that 'hee always presented orthodox men to his tenn churches freely'. In short they were a substantial family, accumulating wealth and making alliances by marriage in the manner of the time. In 1600 Sir Thomas was renting the woods of Cranborne manor, so one may presume that he, like Anthony Ashley, would be interested in any decision by the Crown to put Cranborne on the market.

But there was someone else. This was the Secretary of State, Robert Cecil, second son of Elizabeth's elder statesman, Lord Burghley. In the late 1590s Robert began to see interesting possibilities in Cranborne. In 1599 he bought a large mixed bag of Crown properties in the west of England, including a substantial stake in Cranborne. He lost no time in consolidating his position, buying the priory and rectory in 1601 and enraging Ashley in the process. Ashley reckoned he had already bought the priory from Sir Ralph Horsey, who seems to have sold it to both parties and mortgaged it to a third man as well.

At this point Elizabeth died and Robert Cecil helped James I to secure the throne. No man was more firmly entrenched in the esteem of the new king and he set about the improvement of the manor house at Cranborne to make it fit for James to visit. The nuisance of Ashley's opposition becomes clear when we read that the king 'every second year lyeth a fortnight in his Progress' at Cranborne: and 'without the use of this parsonage house the Earl cannot lie at his great house, it serving for the out-offices and stables to the great house'. Eventually Ashley had to surrender in return for a promise that Cecil would help him to regain favour at Court.

In the summer of 1605 John Norden spent a month in the district, making his great survey with its maps and drawings and detailed descriptions. Cecil's grip on the Chase was evidently tightening. In the previous year he had become Viscount Cranborne. 1605 brought him the earldom of Salisbury, while his elder brother became Earl of Exeter. In 1608 Salisbury was made lord treasurer and held that office until his death in 1612. In his latter years he transformed and largely rebuilt the manor house. Before he died he had secured the lordship of the Chase, which had been held by the Crown without interruption ever since the distant days of Edward IV.

CHAPTER FOUR

Noble Lords of the Chase

IN LOCAL TERMS the sudden supremacy of Cecil in a rôle that had for so long been the monarch's was a dazzling manœuvre, the significance of which was not lost on men like Pembroke, Arundell, Freke and Ashley. The reign of the Pembrokes as lord warden was ended, and the post itself became obsolete. The new chief ranger was Thomas Hooper of Boveridge, very much a member of the Cecil entourage: in 1616 he became tenant of the demesne lands at Cranborne. Pembroke sold Berwick St John and Damerham to Salisbury as useful additions to the Cranborne territory—particularly Berwick St John where a new lodge for Staplefoot Walk was built. It was part of Salisbury's policy to restore existing lodges and build new ones where necessary in the Chase walks as part of a general enforcement of his rights.

The first sign of trouble came in about 1609 when a dispute arose between Salisbury and Pembroke in connection with the bounds of the Chase. The deputy ranger was ordered by Salisbury to accompany Norden, who was charged to prepare a map of the inner bounds. It was not until after Salisbury's death, however, that what might be termed the counter-offensive was launched. The second Earl of Salisbury was not the powerful political figure that his father had been. His attempts to enforce the full extent of his Chase rights met with stiffening resistance and he was openly defied by one of Lord Arundell's tenants who argued that Tollard Royal, being in Wiltshire, was outside the Chase. A jury found against Salisbury, with the implication that the form of the royal grant was inadequate. Salisbury therefore surrendered the grant of the Chase to the king who promptly regranted it in a modified form involving an annual payment of twenty shillings to the Exchequer. The effect of this was to transfer any question affecting the bounds of the Chase from the courts of common law to the Exchequer court, where Salisbury reckoned to have favourable verdicts.

Strengthened in this way Salisbury decided to reverse the Tollard Royal decision and to clear up some other disagreements by starting a comprehensive action in the Exchequer against Arundell, Pembroke and others. He was undoubtedly sheltering behind the king, who continued to make his hunting visits to Cranborne. The people of Tisbury petitioned the king in plain terms to 'signify to the Court of the Exchequer his Royal pleasure that his name should not be used to the hindrance and prejudice of justice'. The next development in the Exchequer actions was the issuing of a commission to have maps prepared by both sides, showing clearly the larger bounds claimed by Salisbury and the lesser bounds as defined by the defendants. It is to this commission of 1618 that we owe the maps of Aldwell and Harding. There is an amusing sidelight in a letter from Salisbury's steward, Christopher Keighley, to Norden about the map made previously by the surveyor. It had been mislaid and Norden was asked to prepare a new one urgently but he replied that a new perambulation would be too 'tedious' for him to do in the time required. After what must have been a frantic search the original map was retrieved; Keighley wrote again to Norden, entreating him to 'be at Westminster tomorrow' to testify that he made the map and, Keighley added, 'leaste it might be objected that you came voluntarilie I have sente yowe his majesty's writ of suppenas by this bearer'.

For more than three years, while these legal battles threatened to undermine Salisbury's authority in the Chase, the keepers' normal tasks became increasingly difficult. The king wrote to the Lord Chief Justice of the Pleas requiring the inhabitants of the Chase to forbear to spoil the game or to offer violence to the keepers. Letters were sent to the principal landowners having coppices in Wiltshire, urging them to permit the keepers to walk as they had been accustomed. The response was disappointing. The lord chamberlain put in a keeper of his own in his Wiltshire coppices; and this keeper, with others, was hunting the deer with crossbows. Sir Edmund Ludlow similarly had appointed his own keeper. As for Tollard Royal, the Chase keepers were staying out of there. It was also difficult to get favourable testimony from men who, in so many cases, owed their livelihood to Arundell or Pembroke.

At the end of it all, however, the chancellor and Barons of the Exchequer found in favour of Salisbury. A petition was presented to the House of Commons urging a reversal of the Exchequer decree and emphasizing the grievances of 20,000 inhabitants within the seventy parishes affected, but without success. The matter was closed, and remained so for the next 200 years. Or so it appears—until one looks behind the scenes. Almost in the hour of his triumph Salisbury sold Vernditch Walk to Pembroke.

It was Vernditch that had been the bone of contention between the two men. During the trial Pembroke had called witnesses to urge that Vernditch was never accounted part of the Chase and that in earlier years he had employed his own ranger there 'to walk the ground and look to the deer in its own right and not as part of Cranborne Chase'. There is no knowing whether Salisbury made this concession as the price of victory over his other opponents or as a conciliatory gesture to his most powerful neighbour. Whatever his motive, Vernditch was detached from the Chase in 1620—the first of the walks to be treated in this way.

It must be emphasized that Pembroke acquired the franchise of Vernditch, the liberty of feeding and preserving deer there. In 1672, for example, in the course of a minor negotiation with Lord Shaftesbury who in the previous year had bought the Chase from Lord Salisbury, the sixth Earl of Pembroke had included—for Shaftesbury's signature—a clause in which he disclaimed any right to Vernditch and acknowledged that Pembroke owned the territory and also the franchise there. In the latter stages of Chase history, when the disfranchisement negotiations began with Lord Rivers, the then Lord Pembroke took his own individual line over Vernditch: he elected to disfranchise it thirty years before the rest of the Chase.

The waning of the Salisbury interest in Cranborne during and after the Civil War is hardly surprising. It was Hatfield and not Cranborne that was the family seat, and political support for the Parliamentary cause did not spare the manor house at Cranborne from the looting and vandalism of the soldiery. In such troubled times the administration of the Chase must have been a burden hardly justified by the occasional requisitioning of venison for the Hatfield kitchens. The lands and properties in the Chase were retained, the manor house was put to other uses—one of John Ogilby's maps shows Lord Sussex living there in the 1670s—and the lordship of the Chase was for sale.

In June 1671 George Stillingfleet, whose family had served the Cecils long and well in Cranborne, wrote to inform Lord Salisbury that Lord Ashley—soon to become Earl of Shaftesbury—was interested in the purchase of the Chase. However, three months later Salisbury's steward, Sam Eyre, complained that there was little interest in the Chase and he had therefore sold it, except Chettered Walk, to the Earl of Pembroke for £3,000, with the manor of Berwick St John for a further £2,171 10s 6d. And yet only eight days later Lord Ashley bought 'the whole Chase of Cranborne with all its privileges' on virtually the same terms—£3,000 for the Chase and a slightly reduced figure, £2,097, for Berwick St John.

It is a strange episode which leaves one wondering what Lord Pembroke thought of it all, and particularly of Sam Eyre who moved to Wimborne St Giles and presided over Lord Ashley's first Chase court as the steward of this new lord of the Chase. It was to prove only a short régime: twenty-four years later the second Earl of Shaftesbury was ready to sell.

In the mind of William Chafin this short period of Shaftesbury ownership prompted an interesting speculation, that the principal aim was to suppress Alderholt Walk and rid it of the deer which were damaging the young timber trees in the extensive plantations that the Shaftesburys were making at this period. Just as Pembroke had got control of the deer population in his north-eastern sector of the Chase by buying Vernditch, so the Shaftesburys would control the south-east by acquiring and retaining Alderholt.

Chafin offers no proof, but the circumstantial evidence supports him. The whole of the eastern end of the Chase was singularly free from the eighteenth-century disputes and affrays that occurred in the remaining walks. Moreover the list of villages on which Lord Rivers's compensation was ultimately levied omits these eastern territories. It is at least probable that the Chase bought by Thomas Freke in 1695 did not include Alderholt Walk, just as it certainly did not include Vernditch. By degrees Cranborne Chase was shrinking. What George Pitt inherited in 1714 by his marriage connection with the Frekes could have been better described in practical terms as Rushmore Chase rather than Cranborne Chase. It was Rushmore Lodge which now became the occasional residence of the owner of the Chase as well as its administrative centre, while Cranborne retained only a vestigial significance in the light of its history.

In addition to its various walks the Chase included a number of separate enclaves in the form of parks. Hutchins lists nine parks approved by special grant and all lying beyond the inner bounds but within the perimeter of the Chase. Three were in Wiltshire—Wardour, Wilton and Faulston; three in Hampshire—Breamore, Burgate and Rockbourne; and three in Dorset—Alderholt, Blagdon and Gunville. Such parks were useful for herding or catching deer, and the owner might be granted the right to 'impark' any stray deer that entered—though not to attract deer deliberately from the Chase. A park would not normally be allowed in close proximity to a chase or forest area frequented by deer. For example, when John Bisset sought to enclose Rockbourne Park in 1236 he was closely questioned about its likely effect on the deer of Cranborne Chase.

It was Henry VIII's policy to dispark these enclosures as opportunity offered. Alderholt Park, which was reputed to comprise 154 acres 'within the ditch', was one that he disparked. The deer in it were destroyed. The parks at Breamore, Burgate and Faulston also disappeared at about this period, and so did the most important one of all—Blagdon. Situated a couple of miles north of Cranborne the park of Blagdon or Blakedon dates from 1321 when Roger Damory was permitted to enclose 500 acres of his woodlands; but for many years it was a royal park in the care of a parker, who made his own individual presentment at the Chase court. It was the only park to be treated in this way in the court's procedure. The duties of the parker extended to the rabbit warren associated with the park. In the reign of Edward IV Henry Langshaw was granted for life the office of parker; and with it 'the ferme of the cunnyes'.

Blagdon was disparked about 1570. In his survey of 1605 Norden provided an interesting account of the place. The great ornamental park, formerly full of large timber trees and wood for burning, was now bare of both. There were only some scanty coppices and thinly growing underwoods. It used to be rich in fallow deer but was now turned into six holdings of arable and pasture. There was a keeper's lodge and the rabbit warren was still maintained.

Quite different was the park at Wardour, which was not disturbed by Tudor policy. Its owners, the Arundells, were politically powerful; and the park was very near the northern limit of the Chase. It was in fact not one park but two. Harding's map of 1618 shows one park designated 'Fallow Deer' and a second contiguous park for 'Red Deare'. The different styles of spelling raise the question of whether 'Fallow Deer' is a later addition to the map; or alternatively 'Red Deare' may have been copied by Harding from an earlier map. Aldwell's map shows Wardour within a single enclosed area and does not use the word 'park' in this context although it appears elsewhere.

While some parks suffered the fate of being disparked, other new ones came into existence. Wilton was one such—a symbol of the prestige of the Pembrokes in Tudor times. In his testimony of 1618 Walter Snelgar referred to the new grounds enclosed with a wall 'and intended for a park, called Wilton park'. Another example from the same period was the park that Robert Cecil formed at Rushmore. Having bought the manor of Berwick St John from Pembroke he built there a new Rushmore Lodge and enclosed the adjoining waste to form a park. In so doing he deprived the Berwick tenants of their grazing rights, for which he promised compensation in the form of a buck in the summer and a doe in the winter 'with their skins entire'—a promise which gave rise to sixty years of acrimonious dispute before it was fulfilled. A more recent case was the 1672 permission by Lord Shaftesbury to 'Sir Gerard Napier of More Critchell' to enclose his park of about thirty acres for the preservation of a stock of deer for his own sole use. This was a lifehold lease on three lives and required an annual rent of sixpence.

The proliferation of such special privileges and obligations, of which the origins were all too easily forgotten or disputed, was the cause of much of the friction that appears in Chase history. And of all the parks the one which remains to be mentioned was the most contentious—the park at Gunville. This lay wholly in West Walk—or it bordered it on two sides, as opinions differed. Either way it was remarkably close to the deer preserves of the inner bounds. That its location there should be obnoxious to the lord of the Chase is hardly surprising, on the assumption that the park fence would normally be of such a height as to allow a deer to leap into the park, where a steeply sloping ditch would prevent it from jumping out again. There is little doubt that Gunville park was so fenced and ditched as to accumulate numbers of deer from the Chase, entering not only by leaping over a low-enough section of the fence but, in the case of fawns, creeping through holes in the fencing; and once inside, and across the ditch, none could escape.

The conflicts inherent in this situation provoked several incidents which illuminate the ways such matters were dealt with at various times, starting with the case of John Swayne in the fifth year of Queen Elizabeth's reign. According to Swayne the park at Gunville had been recognized as such 'time out of mind', but this was disputed by the queen's warden, Lord Pembroke, and an action was started by Pembroke's deputy, Sir John Ashley. An account of the action was preserved in a manuscript at Iwerne House from which Hutchins quotes, in modernized spelling.

The judgment of the court seems almost to reflect an agreed compromise. The legality of Swayne's park was affirmed but with the proviso that 'the Queen's Majesty's deer of the said chase [Cranborne] may not come into the same: provided always that the said John Swayne or any others for him shall not make nor have any Deer creep out of the said chase into his said park of Gunville'. In addition to his park Swayne was also granted the freedom to cut down and enclose his woods and coppices, but again with a proviso—to observe 'the laws of the forest and the customs of the said chase'. In particular this obliged him, not merely to leave any deer unmolested, but to permit the Chase keepers to come on to his land in order to 'hunt and rechase her Majesty's game out of his purlieu', which was described as 'next adjoining to the said chase of Cranborne'.

In the course of the judgment the words 'forest' and 'chase' are applied indiscriminately to Cranborne Chase, which supports the view that the distinction between the two was never so clear cut as the lovers of tidy definitions like to suggest. The reference to Swayne's 'purlieu' adds a further modification which is of great importance. When land once subject to forest law was disafforested it acquired a 'twilight' status which those who know Dartmoor will recognize as *venville* land and which elsewhere was known as forest purlieu or *percursus*. A good modern example of the word surviving in a place-name is Dibden Purlieu, on Southampton Water along the border of the New Forest.

In such areas the preservation and hunting of deer continued to be a major preoccupation though now with due regard for other consider-ations. Keepers could not enter purlieus or outgrounds to chase a deer back into the forest without the permission of the landowner or a legal undertaking such as Swayne was required to give. On the other hand the owner of the purlieu was not allowed to harm the deer in any way and it was therefore an unwelcome visitor, likely to damage his woodlands or his crops; there was a strong incentive accordingly to admit the keepers and enable them to 'hunt and rechase'. If they then failed to do so with reasonable expedition they were at fault. In an interesting case in 1685 the commoners of Martin made a formal complaint against Lord Pembroke's keeper for allowing deer to graze on Martin Down where they competed with the sheep by eating 'upon our land and grasses'. This, the commoners emphasized, was 'to our great damage and detriment'. It was the keeper's duty to hunt the deer back into Lord Pembroke's Vernditch woodlands—a reminder incidentally that the right to preserve deer in Vernditch had passed decisively from Salisbury to Pembroke when Salisbury sold him the woodlands of Vernditch Chase in 1620.

For most of the time, however, when there was a neighbourly atmos-phere of give-and-take, the relationship between the landowner and the lord of the Chase in these purlieu areas was a satisfactory and co-operative one. It would indeed be no great exaggeration to say that areas outside the Lesser Bounds were often the subject of mutual forbearance appropriate to purlieus without either party caring to determine the precise status in a legal definition. The signal for a renewed conflict was usually the emer-gence of a more aggressive and self-assertive personality, in the form of a new owner of the land or a fresh lord of the Chase, or both. It so happens that the continuing history of Gunville provides two striking examples.

The Gunville of John Swayne in the 1560s was very different from the Gunville of Bubb Dodington in the middle of the eighteenth century. In place of an autocratic monarch, deputing her lordship of the Chase to an earl as her warden, there was now a commoner, George Pitt, entrusting the conduct of the Chase and the protection of his rights in it to a head ranger, George Chafin. Among the new hazards that the ranger had to cope with at Gunville was the temperament of the owner of the gigantic palace that Sir John Vanbrugh had designed at Eastbury. Dodington, born George Bubb—son of a Weymouth pharmacist—took his uncle's name when Mr Dodington died childless and left his fortune, including the newly begun Eastbury House, to his nephew.

A trial of strength was not unexpected when Dodington introduced the new-fangled concept of a gamekeeper on his estate, at a time when no such person was employed throughout the Chase. Pitt's view was that his rights extended beyond the preservation of the deer to the ownership of 'all under-game of every denomination also', which could not therefore be shot or hunted without his consent. Dodington on the other hand sent his gamekeeper off with gun and dogs to beat for game in Bursey Stool Walk. While doing so the gamekeeper was confronted by the head ranger who ordered him 'to go home, and tell the person who sent him, that if he ever came there again, or into any part of the Chase, with guns and dogs, the dogs should be shot, and he himself prosecuted'. This plain speech could hardly be misconstrued, but it was ignored. A few days later the gamekeeper and the ranger met in the same circumstances. Three of the gamekeeper's dogs were drinking from a puddle with their heads close together: with one shot the ranger killed all three.

The immediate consequence was a challenge from Dodington to Chafin, to give him satisfaction for the affront. The ranger bought himself a sword and sent his second to wait on Dodington in the customary manner. These hostile preliminaries, however, were followed by an invitation to dine with Dodington who acknowledged that he was in the wrong. The reconciliation between the two men was described as 'very jovial' and they remained on friendly terms thereafter, according to George Chafin's son, William, in whose *Anecdotes* this episode is fully recorded. Dodington's diaries confirm the later friendship. In 1752 George Chafin was one of the members of the hunt invited to dine at Eastbury. In 1753, when the body of John Carver was conveyed to Ashmore church for burial, after a fatal fall from his horse, two of the bearers of the coffin were Chafin and Dodington. The four other bearers, incidentally, are worth naming as they represent great landowning families of the Chase at this period—Lord Arundell of Wardour and Messrs Beckford, Grove and Okeden. The event is commemorated on a tablet in Ashmore church.

How long George Chafin served as head ranger is uncertain but he was probably answerable to three generations of Pitts—each one a George. The first acquired the Chase in 1714 when Chafin was newly elected as MP for Dorset and had recently built his house at Chettle. This first George Pitt died in 1734. His son, George Pitt the second, died in 1745. It was George Pitt the third who eventually acquired the title of Lord Rivers and in the course of nearly sixty years put the stamp of his personality on the history of the Chase. When he succeeded his father he was a young man of twenty-five. He married a daughter of Sir Henry Atkins in the following year and soon made his presence—and his authority—felt in the Chase.

In 1761 he was appointed Envoy Extraordinary Plenipotentiary in Turin and had to forgo some of the pleasure of hunting, but until then it was his custom annually to entertain his fellow sportsmen every day at Rushmore during the first three weeks of September when they assembled for buck-hunting. In 1749 this convivial gathering witnessed a violent clash between Pitt and the then owner of Gunville Park, Squire Harbin. The Swaynes had failed in the male line when Richard Swayne died in 1725 and the Gunville property passed to his daughter Abigail, who had married a Harbin. Pitt's keepers complained to their master that deer from the Chase were being lured into Harbin's park by pomace—the residue of apple pulp left after cider-making. The scent of pomace can attract deer from considerable distances and once the animals had leapt over Harbin's fence they were unable to escape.

Pitt's response was dramatic. Young Chafin, who was an eye-witness, saw Pitt dismount from his horse at the park gate and call to John Bailey, the keeper of the West Walk, to assist him in pulling down a section of the fence. Other keepers joined in. Pitt then ordered the gate to be forced to admit the carriages in which Bubb Dodington, Sir William Napier and other gentlemen were riding. The inability of the hounds to rouse a buck inside the park must have been a considerable anticlimax.

At the next Dorchester assizes Harbin brought an action against Bailey and another keeper, but not against Pitt himself. There seems to have been an unwritten code that gentlemen did not sue each other, a forbearance which made it possible for one or the other to concede the case without loss of face—by blaming his servants. On this occasion there seems to have been a settlement out of court though Wake Smart and Chafin give conflicting accounts. Smart reports a story that Pitt outwitted Harbin by retaining all the counsel on the circuit, but this seems too good to be true. Chafin's version turns on the unexpected 'discovery' by Harbin of a document in which one of the Frekes (Pitt's predecessors) had either authorized or confirmed the right of his friend Swayne (Harbin's ancestor) to have a park at Gunville.

Whatever the reason, the action was not pressed, but Harbin restored his fence although he was perhaps more discreet in the disposal of pomace. His name has survived on present-day maps and it is not long since I walked along a stretch of earth bank that must have formed part of the boundary of Harbin's Park.

CHAPTER FIVE

The Beasts of the Chase

MANWOOD'S *Treatise on the Forest Laws*, published in 1598, separated the animals that men hunt into three tidy categories. The beasts of the forest were hart, hind, wild boar, wolf and hare. The beasts of the chase were buck, doe, fox, marten and roe. The beasts of warren were lesser game such as rabbit and pheasant. As a system of classification it has acquired the weight of long-established authority but some of the inferences that stem from it are highly questionable. The difference between 'forest' and 'chase' as we have seen is a difference in legal procedures and not in the selection of particular species to be preserved—some in forests and some in chases, or some under forest law and some under chase law. The male (hart) and female (hind) of the red deer were preserved just as closely in Cranborne Chase as in the New Forest. The converse was no less true of the male (buck) and female (doe) of the fallow deer. As for the wolf, there can be no doubt that—so far from being preserved—it was always regarded as vermin, and its slaughter as a praiseworthy deed by whomsoever it was performed.

In the case of the hare it is worth recalling that forest law required a credible account of the death of every single one of a preserved species. The records of the Chase courts show regular presentments by keepers and other officials detailing the numbers of deer killed on instructions, or found to have been killed unlawfully, or simply to have died—as on the occasion in Edward VI's reign when the riding forester had to report that 'there happened a murrain among the deer in the last summer to the number of fifty'. The only place where the hare was the subject of such an 'inquest' procedure was Somerton Forest, and it remains something of a mystery why this particular forest should have such a strangely unique distinction.

In criticizing Manwood, J. C. Cox pointed out in *The Royal Forests of England* that Manwood relied on foreign treatises on hunting at a time when 'forest law had for the most part decayed'. The truth of the matter, in Cox's view, is that the beasts of the forests of Britain were the three species of deer and the wild boar: these were the animals that were considered to be supremely worth preserving. The rest were either vermin or were beasts of warren (excepting only the hares of Somerton). The term 'warren' incidentally calls for some explanation here as it has a second meaning quite distinct from the sense in which we now use the word—a rabbit warren being a place where rabbits are preserved or at any rate permitted to breed. There is the second sense, now obsolete, which indicates an exclusive right to hunt in a particular place. A grant of free warren over demesne land gave to the owner of a property—as distinct from a tenant—the right to hunt over land which was part of his personal domain. Nobody else could do so without his permission. 'Warren therefore meant both the right to hunt and the place where the right was exercised. The right extended to the 'beasts of warren'—that is to say, those which were not protected by forest law and were therefore regarded as 'warrenable'. In effect the lord of the chase was waiving his right to the lesser game in that specific context.

The beasts which were not warrenable were the various species of deer and presumably—when it was available in any numbers—the wild boar. The distinction was important because an act of hunting which started in the wild could not be pursued into 'warren' land if the quarry were a warrenable beast. The Chase keepers therefore could not pursue a hare or a fox on to demesne lands of free warren without the owner's permission, whereas they were at liberty to go anywhere in pursuit of deer. A constant source of friction down the ages of Chase history was the tendency for landowners to abuse their rights of free warren, or for keepers to violate those rights. With the ownership of land changing hands, and tenancies intervening, uncertainty and dispute were at times inevitable.

An appeal to the law, moreover, could intensify confusion rather than dispel it. During the legal arguments that followed James I's gift of the Chase to Lord Salisbury a deposition was made by John Swayne, who asserted that at some earlier time he and Mr Chafin of Chettle had hunted and killed a deer in Littlewood Coppice in the manor of Chettle and were entitled to do so. The matter came before the justices in Eyre, when Mr Chafin—who was lord of the manor of Chettle and also High Sheriff of Dorset—proved his right of free warren. The court thereupon ruled that he might kill the deer there 'and spare not'. If Swayne is to be believed this surprising decision took the deer out of the care of the lord of the Chase—possibly the king himself if the event preceded the transfer to Lord Salisbury—and put them at the mercy of any landowner who enjoyed a grant of free warren, in flat contradiction of the general principle that deer were not warrenable.

There is one exception to that principle which should be mentioned here, though it in no way modifies the Chettle ruling. The exception is the roe deer, which was sometimes thought to compete with other deer and drive them away—a view which found expression in an enactment of 1338 that is considered to have downgraded the roe by transferring it from the beasts of the forest to the beasts of warren. Cox disputes the presumption that, after 1338, the roe was universally rejected although there was an undeniable preference for the fallow in Tudor and Stuart times. As a grazing animal the fallow was perhaps better adapted than the roe to the more park-like landscapes that were emerging as the denser woodlands contracted and thinned. There was certainly no depreciation in the esteem of the roe deer as a huntsman's quarry. In his *Noble Arte of Venerie* of 1576 George Turberville gives this assessment:

> You may hunt him at all times alike, for his venyson is never fat, nor never out of season. . . . All the favour that shoulde be shewed unto the Rowe deare, is unto the Does when they are with fawne, and until their fawnes be able to live without them. They make marvelous good chase and stand up long, and flee farre endwayes, and their fleshe is good meate.

Cox cites cases of roe deer treated as forest beasts after 1338 and we must probably look for additional causes of the steep decline in the roe population before 1800. With all three species of deer it is difficult to find reliable evidence of numbers at different periods, from which to derive any sequential estimate of the way populations may have increased or declined. Where attested totals have survived they were usually prepared with an eye to the proving of a point in a law-suit or a negotiation. To rely on such a census without making a considerable allowance for the motive behind it would be reckless. To give but one example, the estimate of a possible 20,000 deer in Cranborne Chase in 1828 can be taken seriously only as a bargaining figure in the assessment of Lord Rivers's compensation: it has no other connection with reality.

With that proviso it is still interesting to look at such evidence as there is of the animals that were hunted in Cranborne Chase before its disfranchisement. In the case of the red deer the historical evidence is meagre. I have found no reference to hart or hind specifically. The tendency in the Chase court records and legal depositions is to refer generically to 'deer' without distinction of red, fallow or roe. The word 'buck' occurs frequently and there are examples of 'prickett' and 'sore' (bucks in their second and fourth years respectively). Differences of sex and age, rather than of species, seem to have been the prime concern.

The circumstantial evidence is stronger. East of the Avon were the red deer of the New Forest; west of the Stour was the home of the famous white hart of Blackmoor Forest; and on the heath land round Wareham red deer were said to be plentiful in the early 1600s. There is no reason therefore to doubt that Cranborne Chase had its share of red deer even if its chalk downland areas were drier than this species likes. On the western slopes and the heavier and moister soils of the Stour Valley south and west of Shaftesbury the big stags should have found a more congenial habitat until the general decline in southern England confined them to their present strongholds on the high moors of the south-west peninsula, with a small stock retaining a foothold in the New Forest.

In the first half of the seventeenth century there was a stock of red deer in the park at Wardour Castle, to which a brief reference was made in the previous chapter. In addition to the evidence of Aldwell's map there is the testimony of Walter Snelgar who as a young man worked as a keeper at Rushmore and was later employed by the Swaynes in Gunville park. In James I's reign Snelgar, now at the ripe age of seventy, testified that he knew 'the two parks of Red and Fallow Deer, called Wardour Park'. They survived until the Civil War, according to a contemporary account of the siege of Wardour Castle, during which the Parliamentary troops broke down the fences so that the deer wandered at will and were not recovered. In the early 1800s there was an attempt to reintroduce red deer in the chase: seven were brought from Humphrey Sturt's park at Horton. Chafin saw them released but they soon moved away, out of the area.

Historically the fallow deer was the principal species in the Chase, the primary object of preservation for hunting. Prior to the sixteenth century its numbers must remain conjectural but a more reliable picture begins to emerge at the end of Henry VIII's reign, when commissioners were appointed 'for the view and numbering of the wild beasts in the Chase of Cranborne'. The results of this first census indicate a total of a thousand deer, according to the deposition of a keeper. They initiated a regular procedure which yields some later figures from which it is possible to make a continuing estimate. Wake Smart, citing a court roll, gives the following totals—1,170 deer in the year 1620, 1,850 in 1640, 832 in 1645, and 690 in 1657. The first thing to be said about these figures is that the lower totals for 1645 and 1657 are itemized for each of the five named walks of the Inner Bounds, whereas the two earlier and higher figures are bulk totals and might therefore include deer in additional walks—for example, Chettered and possibly Alderholt. In short, the decline from the year 1645 to 1657 is substantiated by exact comparison, but the decline from 1640 to 1645 may be distorted by the inexact comparison of five walks with six or even seven walks.

Fortunately the Salisbury archives at Hatfield preserve a document which gives a useful cross-reference for the earlier period. This is an account of the deer killed during the summer season of 1637 and an estimate of the population as viewed in March 1638. The gross totals are ninety-six deer killed and a population of 1,500 in the six walks—Rushmore, Cobley, Staplefoot, Bursey Stool, West and Chettered. Taking them severally, in detail, Rushmore Walk had twenty-one killed of which sixteen were bucks and three were sores. A doe and a 'greentayle' buck were killed 'by chance'. The March census was 303 of which 87 were in antler. Cobley had twenty bucks and four deer killed—one of the deer having been taken by 'stealers'. The census was 421 of which 91 were in antler. Staplefoot had twelve bucks and two sores killed, and two more sores taken by stealers. Here the census total was 167, including 44 males. Bursey Stool had nine bucks and two deer successfully hunted, while the stealers made off with a buck and a 'tegge'—a second-year doe. The March view was 170, of which 38 were in antler. West Walk returned fourteen bucks killed, and a census of 349 of which sixty-nine were in antler. And finally Chettered had five bucks and three deer killed, and a census of ninety, with sixteen in antler. Lord Salisbury was not pleased with these reports. He considered the deer had 'of late decayed'. In a letter to Sir Charles Berkley in May 1638 he complained of neglect of walking and viewing in certain places, and of killing deer without the proper authority of a warrant.

There is one more piece of testimony worth quoting from this period. John Aubrey, writing from his knowledge of Vernditch Walk only, estimated a thousand or more in 1650, declining to two hundred in Vernditch in 1689. With these estimates, as with any deer census, there must be a substantial margin of error but they do suggest one or two inferences that are worth making. During the seventeenth century any estimate for Cranborne Chase of a deer population in excess of 4,000 or below 1,000 would be implausible; and during the second half of that century the numbers were declining. Since the Civil War and the Commonwealth occupied the years 1642–60 a reduction in the numbers of deer preserved for hunting is scarcely surprising.

During the eighteenth century the fallow deer became increasingly the dominant species as the roe lapsed to virtual extinction in southern England. Efficient keepering and the enforcement of his rights by Lord Rivers may have raised the numbers of deer to new heights by the end of the eighteenth century but it is difficult to credit the figures that were bandied about during the great controversy over the extinction of the rights of the lord of the Chase and the computation of the sum he should receive as compensation. At the start of the campaign it was necessary to show the deer in such menacing numbers as to threaten the livelihood of every agriculturist in the area; but when compensation had to be assessed there was much to be said for playing down the value of the hunting rights— unless you were Lord Rivers. West in 1816 put the figure at 5,000 to 8,000 deer. In 1828, at the time of disfranchisement, a minimum figure of 12,000 and a maximum of 20,000 were uttered and received with apparent seriousness. Against this it is worth setting the evidence of a deputy ranger in the early 1600s that the five walks of the Inner Bounds would feed 2,000 deer: estimates at that period of the actual numbers ranged from 500 to 800. The wooded areas in Lord Rivers's effective control in 1826 would not have been of much larger extent.

Of greater significance are the Rushmore accounts for 1828. This was the year in which Parliament approved the Bill disfranchising the Chase, on the following conditions: that compensation should be payable to Lord Rivers from October 1829 and that his right to preserve deer throughout the Chase should be extinguished in October 1830. What then, one may ask, was to become of the allegedly vast horde of fallow deer? The Rushmore accounts suggest a likely answer. As soon as the level of compensation was fixed, and before his rights were extinguished, Lord Rivers started to clear out the deer in a big way. Since they were doomed he might as well have the benefit of them as leave them to the mercy of others. The Rushmore accounts indicate a grand total of about 1,850 deer killed in 1828, with does outnumbering bucks by more than two to one. In addition 120 live deer were captured and sold off the estate: possibly they went to Mr Drax at Charborough Park, just beyond the south-west boundary of the Chase, where in 1838 there were 600 fallow deer.

Setting aside such herds in private parks, the fallow deer declined sharply in numbers during the rest of the nineteenth century. Those which survived to be 'liberated' on 10 October 1830 from the care of the Chase keepers found little benefit in their liberty. Within days the Chase villages organized local battues during which numbers of the deer perished along with an occasional human being. At Ashmore, for instance, the parish register records that 'Samuel Stainer of Tollard Royal, 50 years, accident- ally shot in Stickway Road on 19 October 1830, died on the 20th, when a party of the parish were assembled to destroy the deer on the disfranchise- ment of the Chase'. The deer had been driven together into Stickway Road, which was a path through the copses.

There is no evidence of deer dispersing into areas beyond the Chase. Henry Symonds, who lived at Milborne St Andrew and hunted to the west of Cranborne Chase, recorded a solitary case of a fallow near Piddlehinton in 1830 and described it as 'a most unusual quarry in that country'. Roe deer, on the other hand, were by then becoming so plentiful that in 1838, near Milton Abbey, Symonds was obliged to stop the hounds 'owing to so many deer being on foot'.

Today there are about 150 fallow deer in the Chase. The present century has seen the arrival of two new species, sika and muntjac. The sika deer probably originate from stocks introduced to Brownsea Island in Poole Harbour in 1896 and to Hyde Park near Wareham after 1900. Others escaped from Rushmore in about 1940 but the sika is an extremely rare species in the Chase. A muntjac is occasionally reported but still remains a rarity despite some increase of numbers. By far the commonest is the roe, and the changing fortunes of roe and fallow make a remarkable story.

We can say with reasonable certainty that, in the three centuries before 1800, the fallow deer prospered in the protected conditions of Cranborne Chase while the roe declined to the point of extinction. In the nineteenth century the fallow lost its last two strongholds in southern England with the surrender of preservation rights in Cranborne Chase in 1830 and in the New Forest, by Queen Victoria, in 1851 under the New Forest Deer Removal Act. Since then the survival of the fallow has tended to rest principally on semi-domesticated herds in park-like conditions. It is the roe which has become the typical wild deer of Cranborne Chase and of Southern England generally.

The turning point for the roe came in 1800 when Lord Dorchester released some at Milton Abbas and started a new trend in hunting. With other species no longer generally available, or only rarely so, the roe became the fashionable quarry. In the early 1800s some were taken to Charborough for hunting, and Lord Ilchester released some in west Dorset. They soon began to appear in hunting records of the period. On a day's run in March 1831 the Mountain Harriers of Puddletown had a mixed bag of one fox, two hares and a roebuck. Five years later their bag for the season included eight roe deer. At about the same time Edmund Morton Pleydell of Whatcombe established his pack of roebuck hounds: in the churchyard of Milborne St Andrew the headstone of Pleydell's huntsman, William Rice, claims that he was the first man ever to hunt roebuck hounds.

In 1857 a remarkable run was noted by Henry Symonds when a roe buck was pursued for four hours in incessant rain from Charborough via Poole to cross the Stour near Badbury Rings and double back to Wimborne, plunging again into the Stour and being taken as it stood under Julian's Bridge, with head and antlers just clear of the water. In the 1870s and 1880s Lord Wolverton's harriers were active in Cranborne Chase. Wolverton, who lived at Iwerne Minster, was a strong supporter of

Gladstone, so he shared political sympathies as well as a hunting enthusiasm with Sir Thomas Grove, MP, of Ferne, and there are several records of the two families hunting deer together; though some, if not all, were 'carted' and released. In 1874 Lady Grove noted in her diary 'Lord Wolverton's hounds. Whyte-Melville and several people came. The Deer was let out in the Park.' Agnes Grove, the young wife of Sir Thomas's son, Walter, wrote in her diary in March 1885, 'I rode grey cob at Gunville. Lord Wolverton hunted a deer but did not catch it.' A week later 'Walt and I rode to Iwerne to the meet. They hunted a deer.' And the following year 'Walter hunted with Wolverton's harriers—stag'.

It is noticeable, however, that such references to deer tend to have an air of novelty about them. The normal quarry was the fox, and had increasingly become so since the middle of the eighteenth century. What stimulated the revival of the roe deer in the long term was not the hunting interest but the commercial policy of modern forestry, with its emphasis on coniferous plantations. These are an excellent habitat for roe deer, and to them must go the main credit for the fact that there are more deer in the southern counties of the second Elizabeth than there were of the first. It is a strange twist of fortune and must seem at first sight to show the folly of expelling one species of deer only to become infested with another. However, that would be a most misleading oversimplification. A study of Cranborne Chase in the 1780s and again in the 1980s will show why.

The complaints of the eighteenth-century landlords were threefold. The preservation of *vert*, of the vegetation that gave food and cover to the deer, rendered impossible the modernization of farming methods. Enclosure, tree-felling, scrub clearance and the like were forbidden, except with the consent of the lord of the Chase. Secondly, where deer roamed over arable land they damaged the crops, but the frustrated farmer was liable to prosecution if he retaliated by harming the deer. And thirdly, there was a moral argument that the Chase laws fostered an atmosphere of violence and crime, in which poaching and smuggling became a recognized way of life.

We shall look in vain for such problems today, and for a variety of reasons. The roe is by its nature less of a menace to the arable farmer. It prefers a more static woodland life than the fallow, which likes to range freely over open ground. Within the woodlands the roe and the forester can co-exist. No longer hampered by a hunting overlord, the owner or manager of a plantation can now determine his own policy and is quite likely to concede a place for the roe in the general ecological balance that he aims to achieve. He may like simply to see a few deer about the place, or he may have a carefully estimated sense of the commercial value of venison and shooting rights. Whatever his motive the modern forester will tolerate deer up to the numerical level where they cause unacceptable damage to the trees.

A particularly interesting development in Cranborne Chase since 1962 is the operation of a Deer Control Society, organized co-operatively by a number of landlords who want to stabilize a properly balanced deer population. A joint census, covering 4,000 acres of woodland and involving fourteen landowners, is prepared annually, in the light of which the next season's cull is decided. In this way a healthy breeding stock is maintained and its existence is justified commercially by the proceeds of the cull. Those beasts selected to be killed are shot with a rifle by a marksman, usually firing downwards from a high seat, and 98 per cent effectiveness is claimed. It is a form of sport much valued by continental marksmen who readily pay substantial sums for the shooting rights, within the agreed limits of the season's cull.

In Britain today conservation of wild life is so often a matter of the careful reconciliation of conflicting interests, particularly when a relatively large mammal is concerned. Even the most unreserved deer-lover must wince with a degree of anguish at the sight of deer in his garden paying a dawn visit to browse off the tender shoots of a bed of roses—and here I speak from experience. Having overcome the historically unrestrained supremacy of the deer in Cranborne Chase it will be a happy sequel if twentieth-century ecology can set the conditions which guarantee the future of these beautiful animals.

We have lost enough already. Chafin, who hunted for seventy years in the Chase, starting in the 1740s, refers to 'martin-cats' as having become nearly extinct because 'their skins were too valuable for them to be suffered to exist'. There were some a century earlier according to John Aubrey, who wrote, 'In Cranborne Chase and at Vernditch are some marterns still remaining'.

Another lost species is the wild boar. It was preserved under Chase law and probably survived into the sixteenth century. There were certainly some on the western slopes of the Chase around 1450. At that time the vicar of Iwerne was prosecuted for killing four wild swine with his bow and arrows in Iwerne Wood. There were some further north in Wiltshire, in Savernake Forest in 1543; and a century later Charles I tried to re-establish them in the New Forest. The most recent introduction in the vicinity of Cranborne Chase was in 1832 at Charborough, where the enthusiastic Mr Drax introduced two pairs, one from France and the other —wilder and more ferocious—from Russia. Their litters averaged ten to twelve and they ran wild with their parents. They were not hunted but netted or shot. Drax wrote later that he bred a lot of them and latterly fenced them inside a wood, but they were savage and troublesome to keep within bounds and he killed them off.

CHAPTER SIX

Keepers, Poachers and Smugglers

IT IS TIME now to look more closely at the people of the Chase: those who preserved the deer, those who hunted the deer by right, and those who did so illicitly. It is they who, over the centuries, gave to the Chase its particular character. Their exploits provide the anecdotes and the legends that still circulate in the Chase villages. A sort of glamour invests the many battles of wits between man and beast, and between man and man—battles in which cunning and ingenuity were often blended with violence and lawlessness. In Sixpenny Handley churchyard may be seen the stone lid of a tomb which bears this inscription: 'When deer stealing was prevalent the deer stealers used to remove this stone to place in the tomb the deer they had taken till they had an opportunity to remove them.'

Sometimes in warm weather their hidden booty would attract flies in a tell-tale fashion, so the deer-stealers paid children to pretend to be innocently at play nearby—but in reality to drive off the flies. One man is said to have been transported for paying children to provide this deceitful service. Such tales are lovingly preserved, along with the legends of the king of the local smugglers, Isaac Gulliver, and the gory details of midnight battles in the woods during which keepers, poachers, smugglers and soldiers suffered broken heads, and occasionally even lost their lives.

To lump together all the Chase officials as 'keepers' is to do scant justice to the variety of their tasks and titles. Between lord warden and under keeper there were foresters, woodwards and verderers, to say nothing of the ranger and the riding forester. Some insight into their numbers and duties are provided by the formal transactions of the Chase court and the orders to keepers that were displayed in the lodges. There is also the evidence of the keeper, Thomas West of Sixpenny Handley, given in the deposition he made in 1594: the earliest first-hand account. Incorporating memories of his father's, who was also a keeper, West speaks of circumstances from the reign of Richard III to Henry VIII and names a succession of wardens appointed by the ruling monarch as his representative, with presumably a general responsibility for the management of the Chase. Under them the day-to-day conduct of affairs was in the hands of the ranger and his staff. Thomas West refers to eighteen keepers and eighteen

B.C.3. – FOUR PART SALES VOUCHER – 7/82
MOORE PARAGON U.K. LTD

4929 833 221 704

D 11/8. 12/93 VISA

H K ALLSOPP

0308113
DEBENHAMS
BOURNEMOUTH

X H.K.Allsopp
CARDHOLDER SIGNATURE

DATE	DEPT.	SALES No.	INITIALS
12-11-83	1741	5625	19.

QTY	DESCRIPTION	UNIT COST	AMOUNT
1	S. WARE T.L.		
AUTHORISATION CODE		TOTAL £	19 95

VISA

PLEASE KEEP THIS COPY FOR YOUR RECORDS

SALES VOUCHER – CARDHOLDER COPY

X H.K UNGSS.

E118080
BOURNEMOUTH

H K ALLSOPP

D 11187

VISA SAV51

404 155 833 4524

SPACE KEEP THIS COPY FOR YOUR RECORDS

INITIALS	SALES No.	DEPT.	DATE
P	2552	1041	25-11-83

VISA

AUTHORISATION CODE	QTY	DESCRIPTION	UNIT COST	AMOUNT
	1	2 MAKE L.T.		
			TOTAL £	2P 0l

SALES VOUCHER — CARDHOLDER COPY

woodwards, whose duties included an appearance at the Chase court which was held twice a year, in spring and autumn.

In the period covered by West's deposition the court proceedings amplify his account. On 25 September 1504, for example, foresters and woodwards attended to report on matters for which each was responsible in his sector of the Chase. The 'locum tenens'—the lieutenant—reported a man who was continually chasing away and disturbing the lord's deer with a couple of dogs: this man was ordered to answer at the next court. The woodwards who spoke on this occasion came from Ashmore and Broad Chalke; at other times there were woodwards from Bowerchalke and Rushmore. The majority of offences were infringements with farm animals—pigs not ringed, sheep grazing illicitly, etc. The penalty was a small fine. Even the riding forester—*Forestarius Itinerans*—was fined for failing to execute one of his duties.

The form of the proceedings followed the same general plan for centuries. The first two presentments were always for what in 1504 were 'Estbokeden' and 'Westbokeden'. This was the traditional division of the Chase or *buckden*—meaning the habitation of the deer—into eastern and western divisions. It was perhaps the way the out-hundred of Cranborne was originally divided. If so, it would account for the separate treatment of Alderholt, which was part of the in-hundred.

How the individual walks were grouped in the two buckdens is not clear, though it is plausible enough to put West Walk and Bursey Stool in the west buckden; and Cobley and Staplefoot, perhaps with Rushmore, in the east. As a boundary guide the word 'buckden' was regrettably overused by our ancestors. On Aldwell's map of 1618 it occurs in three different places which appear to have importance in any attempt to define the inner bounds—thus adding to the confusion that it might have dispelled.

In 1672, when the Chase court had moved from Cranborne to Wimborne St Giles and Lord Shaftesbury's steward now presided, the word 'buckden' had disappeared but the formula was unchanged. The references now were to the ranger or keeper of the east part, and of the west part. There were also chief foresters who were gentlemen of substance and not employees: one was Sir Ralph Bankes of Kingston Lacy and two others were described as 'gent' or 'esquire'. Delegation of the management of sections of the Chase to neighbouring grandees is evident in these arrangements. The keeper of the west part was Thomas Freke of Iwerne who became the next owner of the Chase when Shaftesbury sold it to him in 1695.

In each walk the chief forester had the services of two under keepers.

There is no reference in the proceedings to the woodwards of Bowerchalke and Ashmore, mentioned at the Edward VI court. Care of hedges is the responsibility of verderers, of whom about sixteen were sworn in for a dozen parishes. The general picture of Chase management shows interesting similarities to the New Forest as Celia Fiennes described it in about 1690. There the king was represented, as he had been in the Chase, by a lord warden. There too was the equivalent of the riding forester. Known in the New Forest as 'the Rider of the Forest' he had to 'see about that all things are secure and well done and the Timber kept and Deer, to see they are not spoyled or destroyed; his Right is to all the Deer that are hurt or maimed'. The various lodges, of which there were fifteen in the New Forest, were 'disposed to Gentlemen that have under keepers that takes the care of it . . . its a great priviledge and advantage to be a Cheefe Keeper of any of these lodges, they have venison as much as they please'.

The rules of conduct for the working staff (keepers, under keepers, woodwards etc.) are well documented for the eighteenth century. At the end of that century a detailed memorandum was prepared anonymously but its author was very probably James Webb of Rushmore Lodge, who had the job of supplying Lord Rivers's lawyers with background information. On the topic of the laws concerning the keepers' part in hunting, Webb reported that written instructions were hung up in the steward's room at the lodge. This was a long-established practice. A Chase court in 1713 set out in detail its orders and instructions, and directed that they should be 'sett up in the outward Roome at Rushmore Lodge for all persons to take notice thereof and that coppies thereof be sent by the Ranger to the under keepers of the severall Lodges'. It could well have been a copy of this same document, faded perhaps with age, that James Webb was accustomed to see posted up at Rushmore.

Among its orders was a requirement that the ranger should keep 'a pagg of Doggs', at least seven couple, constantly in hunting condition. No keeper or under keeper could hunt with any dogs except these, and the ranger or his deputy had to accompany them. In circumstances where a deer might be killed by other means than hunting with dogs an under keeper had first to receive a special direction in writing from the ranger or his deputy. The season for hunting was defined in the words 'that no buck be killed after Holy Rood Day and no doe after Candlemas Day in each season'.

To these rules for hunting deer Webb added further details of the keepers' way of life. They were permitted to kill woodcock and rabbits but not game. They could also gather fuel in the copse known as 'Costards' for the use of the kennel—but not, he thought, for their personal use. They might keep two horses, 'or rather one riding horse and a brood mare with a colt at her foot, and one cow—the colt is to be sold when a year old. This however is none of the invariable customs of the Chace but depends on the will of the Lord, and may be altered or abolished if he chuses.' They were also expected to stop gaps in hedges where deer might stray, and to present at the Chase court an account of all misdemeanours that had occurred since the last court.

In daily practice the Chase officials were concerned with the deer and the woodlands in terms of practical husbandry, much more than with 'misdemeanours'. Admittedly the officiousness of minor functionaries is a familiar source of human friction, and so too is the rigidity of systems that are slow to adapt to changing social circumstances: examples of both these human failings are evident in the history of the Chase, but so also are the comfortable adjustments that conflicting interests managed to achieve by a neighbourly tolerance. The traditional picture of harsh laws enforced for the sporting pleasures of a few is too simple. An examination of some of the attested cases of conflict between keepers and malefactors will show how far apart were the extremes of severity and leniency at different times.

The laws of the Norman kings were undoubtedly savage and could cost an offender his life, but one may wonder how many lives were in fact forfeited in this way. The records of Cranborne Chase yield no evidence concerning the harshest period, prior to Magna Carta and the Charter of the Forest, but in the immediately following centuries—when the letter of the law was still severe—the only life recorded as lost was that of the hanged man of Martin, in circumstances sufficiently odd to be worth retelling. There are several versions of the story, which do not precisely coincide, but they seem to spring from two sources—a presentation of the jurors of the Hundred of Domerham, made about 1275 and said by Wake Smart to be preserved in the Chapter House at Westminster, and a complaint made subsequently by the Abbot of Glastonbury and recorded in the Great Book of Glastonbury. The Glastonbury interest arose from the fact that the village of Martin was in the Hundred of Domerham, which belonged to the abbey.

In their presentation the Domerham jurors alleged that two foresters, Walter Brice and Savaric or Savarie, went to the house of John le Bor at Martin and took by force 'a certain man of Forton', accusing him of felony, carrying him off to Cranborne and there hanging him 'without any reason'. The foresters then went to Bridmere and took two of Peter de Skidmere's oxen on the pretext that they were the property of the hanged man. Having impounded these oxen at Cranborne they went on to the house of Richard Martin at Domerham and took a horse, value ten shillings, which they claimed was the hanged man's. This also they detained at Cranborne. 'And they found in the coffer or purse (*loculo*) of him that was hung a mark of silver and a silver *firmaculum* value eight pence.'

The abbot's complaint, which was heard in 1281 by the king's justices at Sherborne, does not name the two foresters but levels its accusation at the head forester, William de Cunnishasele or de Coveshall, alleging that he and other foresters seized the unnamed man, took him to Cranborne on the same day and 'injuste suspenderunt'. There is no further reference to this man or to the event. What follows in the abbot's document is a catalogue of other complaints about different events, the arrest and detention of the abbot's people until they pay fines, the impounding of livestock and so on.

In the outcome the Earl of Gloucester conceded the abbot's case for a new and more liberal code of practice to govern the foresters when they entered abbey territory in future. Evidently this was a period when the high-handed behaviour of foresters and keepers aroused popular resentment. Hutchins cites a case when a thousand sheep were impounded as security for the payment of a fine; and he gives an example of what might be called 'protection' payments, in the modern sense, when foresters were accused of collecting sheaves of corn in the autumn 'from poor men who fear their malice and dare not contradict them'. Then in 1288 there was a charge that certain foresters had been seizing the dogs of freemen in the Chase where they had always been accustomed to hunt hares and foxes.

Not all the accusations against the Chase officials were justified, but when a forester was shown to have exceeded his proper duties he could be fined or imprisoned by the justices. The heightened tension in the latter part of the thirteenth century probably arose from a combination of circumstances. There was the reassertion of the maximum boundaries of the Chase following the judgment of 1280. This greatly strengthened the power of the de Clares as lords of the Chase, who had been making themselves felt increasingly from 1250 onwards after a slack period when the Chase had been held in trust by the Crown during two minorities. Gilbert de Clare, particularly, was a man of great national consequence to whom Edward I was largely indebted for his throne. Until his death in 1295 this Earl of Gloucester was likely to impose the weight of his authority on the Chase. At the same time popular feeling was pressing with some success for a national relaxation of the forest laws, and this mood was certainly reflected in the Chase. The outcome, during the next century, appears to have been a determination to defend sternly the Chase rights respecting deer but to yield concessions, or to act with more restraint, in other aspects of Chase law.

Even when there was poaching on a significant scale the legal process seems to have been slow and less severe than one might expect. The culprit had first to be detected and then 'attached' to appear at the next Chase court where, if the case were serious enough, a prosecution would be started. Such a case came before a jury in the King's Bench in 1359, when John Upton was convicted of poaching deer in several parts of the Chase, including Ashmore, Pentridge, Gussage and Chettle. It had been alleged that he killed and took away ten bucks in 1346, and continued to do much the same thing in the next eleven years. The inference is that he was an experienced habitual poacher and not a man defending his crops or yielding to a sudden impulse. It might be assumed therefore that a severe and brutal punishment would be inflicted on him, but the sentence was nothing more than a fine. The amount, forty marks, was not inconsiderable and Upton had to spend a few months in prison before he was able to raise the sum but he duly paid up and was discharged. Four hundred years later he would not have got off so lightly.

At the time of Upton's offences the Chase was held by Edward I's grand-daughter, Elizabeth de Burgh. On her death it passed to Lionel, Duke of Clarence and third son of Edward III. Five generations later it passed to Edward IV and remained the property of the reigning monarch until James I gave it to Robert Cecil. Such evidence as there is suggests that in the fifteenth and sixteenth centuries the laws of the Chase were applied with enough forbearance to arouse no widespread resentment. If the restrictions were less than popular they were perhaps acknowledged for the most part to have their place in the customary way of life.

The Topp family who farmed at Bridmore seem to have kept up a running battle over several generations, judging by their appearances at the Chase court. Poaching at night 'with nets and other engines' appeared as an alternative to bow and arrows. The killing of a buck in 1535 was punished with a fine and a warning. The only record of a serious clash comes from about 1600 when a young keeper, William Penny, with his father—who was also a keeper—and a youth of seventeen came upon five hunters who had set up buckstalls under cover of darkness. A buckstall was a large net into which deer were driven: sometimes it might incorporate earth ramparts and wattled hurdles. It was a method long established for taking deer. A record of 1322 shows that Edward II paid £5 for cords to make buckstalls. Now, when the two Pennys and their young companion came upon the poachers, there was a fight during which one of the poachers escaped but the others were overcome and taken to Mr Saint Lo

—presumably a magistrate or a Chase official. One of the captured men had a wound in his head from which he subsequently died. William Penny had to appear at the assize in Salisbury and was there 'called in question' for the man's death, but was acquitted and discharged.

It was an ugly incident, foreshadowing the pitched battles of a later period. In the bitterest affrays firearms were used but the usual weapons of offence and defence were wooden staves and a hinged flail-like instrument known as a swindgel or swingel. As a protection from the skull-cracking blows that these weapons could deliver a beehive cap and padded jacket were worn. The cap, as Chafin describes it, was formed with wreaths of straw tightly bound together with split bramble stalks, the workmanship being much the same as that of the traditional beehive. The jacket, or 'Jack', was made of the strongest canvas quilted with wool. So attired, in cap and jack, a man might hope to absorb the heaviest blows with nothing worse than a bruising.

The seventeenth century seems to have brought more lawless attitudes and rougher methods. The legal disputes in which the second Lord Salisbury was involved may have contributed to a more rancorous atmosphere. In 1616 he invoked the legal apparatus of the Star Chamber against three deer-stealers who, 'with other riotous and dissolute persons, being common hunters, spoilers and destroyers of the deer of Cranborne Chase', assembled divers times at Ashmore, armed with long-piked staves, swords, 'privie coats', jacks, guns, crossbows and other weapons, and provided with buckstalls, gapnets, cords, greyhounds, etc., and killed deer and took them away. On one occasion, in night time, they were found hunting by William Budden, a keeper of Bussey Stool Walk and two keepers of West Walk. 'Being required to yield themselves' they assaulted the keepers and shot at them with arrows and bolts out of their crossbows and fled.

In the previous three years this gang was said to have carried away forty deer, and to have been encouraged 'by others of better rank and quality'. This accusation that some of Lord Salisbury's respectable neighbours were secretly involved was repeated in a letter from Thomas Hooper in 1633. He reported that the deer-stealers in Chettered Walk were operating in companies of great strength and well armed; and he added that some of them were 'set on by persons of good rank'. Even more striking was the testimony of one of the rangers at the Chase court in 1649 where he said that he 'desires time till the next court to present hunters, they being persons of such quality, and so many, that he stands in danger of his life to walk the ground, if he should discover them at present'.

This was the period of the Civil War, of course. Cranborne manor house had been looted in 1643 and a dutiful keeper must have felt that there were too many armed men about, with a determination to live off the land. In the more settled conditions of the next century one can identify three quite different kinds of deer-stealer. There was the cottager who, if opportunity offered, would supplement his meagre diet by setting a snare occasionally but would not think of himself as a poacher in a vocational sense. There was secondly the gentleman poacher who enjoyed the excitement of outwitting the keepers and who comforted himself with the knowledge that, if caught, he could avoid prosecution by handing over the recognized penalty of £30 which he carried with him as a precaution. His conscience was easy, moreover, since the land on which he was deer-stealing might belong to one of his friends who was accompanying him, or might even be his own. To such gentlemen the claims of the lord of the Chase to own the deer on other people's land seemed increasingly anachronistic. It was in a spirit of devilment, and from a love of clandestine adventure, that parties of gentlemen went in search of the deer at night and had an occasional skirmish with the keepers.

Sometimes they acted quite openly. Chafin tells an amusing story of a party of noble sportsmen with whom he was enjoying a meal as guests of Sir William Hanham at Ebbesbourne. 'Just as the dinner was over,' he wrote, 'and the cloth removing, a person came into the room in great haste, and said that a buck had been disturbed by the reapers in Ebbesbourne wheat-field; that he had come down near the parish, and was then lodged in the barley not five hundred yards from the house. The company immediately got up from the table, and all agreed with one accord to go and course the deer.'

A couple of brace of greyhounds were quickly obtained, the deer was caught, the gentlemen returned to the house and sat down to their claret, well pleased—until a keeper called to collect the deer and take down the names of those who had killed it. He said he was sorry to offend but was only doing his duty, and would have to report the matter to his master, Mr Jones, at Rushmore Lodge. He was instructed to convey to Mr Jones an invitation to call that evening.

When Mr Jones arrived Lord Castlehaven, as spokesman for the party, said, 'Jones, we all stand here as criminals and plead guilty: what are the damages to be paid?' With notable tact Jones said he looked on the affair as a thoughtless frolic which could be met by a penalty of £30, of which half had to be paid to the poor of the parish. The other half was normally due to the informer but he himself would take on that rôle and would decline the payment. In the outcome, £15 was paid next day to the Overseers of the poor, three guineas were sent to the keeper and Mr Jones was presented with a bottle of claret on condition he did not leave the company until he had drunk it.

As an example of delicate diplomacy by all concerned the story could hardly be bettered. Each one at his own social level—Lord Castlehaven, the keeper and Mr Jones alike—knew how to conduct himself so that the Chase lord's undoubted legal rights were not seriously challenged or neglected, no ill feeling was engendered, no threat or accusation was uttered, and some money moved painlessly from the affluent to the needy. It may reek of social privilege but it displays a code of conduct which could defuse a potential conflict without loss of face.

The third kind of poacher—the hardened lawbreaker—was to be found at the other end of the social scale. He was no gentleman, but nor did he have much in common with casual opportunists like the shepherd of Berwick St John who set a snare in the hedge of his garden to take any deer that came there: for which act he spent three days in the dungeon at Cranborne manor and was fined 3s 4d. At the same time, 1625, the shepherd's wife was in trouble for scrounging firewood but was forgiven on her promise of good behaviour in future. These were petty offenders, quite unlike the gangs that operated later.

The bad name that the Chase eventually acquired as an alsatia of lawless men must be seen as a reflection of changing social conditions. The great upheaval of the Civil War and the Commonwealth would assuredly have left a legacy of rebellious discontent. It was not only the divine right of kings, but of wealth and rank also, that had been called in question. In the following century the widening gap between rich and poor was cause enough for a cynical desperation. The enclosure of common lands and the more ruthless tendencies of the new breed of 'scientific' farmers added to the problems of those who had failed to find any rewarding place for themselves. That they should defy the laws of a society that apparently rejected them is hardly surprising.

After the restoration of Charles II there is an account of an organized gang of poachers whose approach to deer-stealing was different from the typical transgressions of earlier times. Evidence given against Henry Randall of Broad Chalke referred to 'two buckstalls, one iron headpiece, one hat, one jack, one sword and one staff taken from hunters unknown'. This sounds like the booty secured after a battle, and the report goes on to describe the finding of the marks of several deer killed and of a number of men with dogs and nets. The poachers were tracked to Broad Chalke where eight quarters of venison were discovered in the possession of Randall. The inference must be that Randall and his associates were equipped to fight it out with the keepers if they were cornered, and that they were taking deer not for their own immediate family needs but in a quantity that suggests a trading underworld where venison could be bought and sold—or bartered—with no questions asked. In these circumstances a sort of gang warfare between keepers and armed bands of deer-stealers began to develop.

Chafin refers to a Chase tradition, that he is unable to authenticate, of a particularly savage affray in which several lives were lost at Tarrant Gunville. The precise spot came to be known as Bloody Shard Gate, and the wood to which the gate gave access as Bloodway Coppice. Nor was it only under cover of darkness that men were killed. In 1738 a keeper of West Walk, named Tollerfield, was walking back from making his Easter communion at Fontmell Church when he was waylaid and bludgeoned to death. In a similar incident at about the same time one of Lord Pembroke's keepers in Vernditch was beaten to death.

What these cases suggest is a similarity to some of the murders perpetrated by gangs of smugglers in their attempts to intimidate the excise-men. And it is the alliance between smugglers and deer-stealers which gave the Chase its lawless reputation in the eighteenth century. Two favourite ports of entry for the smugglers were the harbours of Poole and Christ-church, both lying a few miles south of the Chase border with largely deserted heathland in between. Richard Warner, whose schooldays were spent at Christchurch and later recalled by him in his *Literary Recollections*, used to see:

a procession of twenty or thirty waggons, loaded with kegs of spirit; an armed man sitting at the front and tail of each; and surrounded by a troop of two or three hundred horsemen, every one carrying on his enormous saddle, from two to four tubs of spirits; winding deliberately and with most picturesque and imposing effect along the skirts of Hengistbury Head on their way towards the wild country to the north-west of Christchurch, the point of their separation.

The romantic view of smuggling tends to concentrate on the risks and adventures connected with landing the contraband, and is apt to overlook the fact that this was only the beginning of the smugglers' problems. The goods had to be moved to hiding places inland and distributed to the towns and cities. For these movements discreet staging posts were necessary, where horses could be rested and fed or replaced with fresh ones. A remote farm was ideal for the purpose, particularly if it had ample cellar-age for the cargo as well as a paddock for the horses. There are several such in the Chase which have traditional associations of this kind, and it is

easy to see how useful the special skills and local knowledge of the deer-
stealers would be to the smuggling fraternity.

A further source of recruitment to this lawless band was the craze
among young men for emulating the exploits of the Waltham Blacks,
a gang of deer-stealers in Waltham Chase in Hampshire who blacked their
faces to escape recognition during their nightly forays. They were imi-
tated by other gangs who called themselves 'Waltham Blacks' and raided
other deer parks and forest areas. In his *Natural History of Selborne* Gilbert
White wrote that, 'towards the beginning of this century [the eighteenth]
all this country was wild about deer-stealing. Unless he was a *hunter*, as
they affected to call themselves, no young person was allowed to be
possessed of manhood or gallantry.' Some of these gangs drifted into
vandalism and unprovoked violence, including murder, until they committed—in White's words—'such enormities that government was forced
to interfere', and in 1722 passed 'that severe and sanguinary act called the
Black Act, which now comprehends more felonies than any law that ever
was framed before'.

The penalty for a second offence was in future to be transportation. The
gentlemen poachers could no longer indulge in their light-hearted attitude
to a possible conviction and they turned their attention to other forms of
excitement. The more timid of casual offenders may similarly have been
deterred by the new severity of the law. Those who stayed in the game
became harder and more bitter opponents. And the young hooligans,
intent on proving their manhood as 'Blacks', must have been ready
recruits for the barons of the smuggling trade.

The best-known handler of contraband in the Chase, Isaac Gulliver,
who was born in 1745, seems to have grown up in the smuggling business.
His father was named by an informer as one of a gang of men who
frequented the New Inn at Downton and were involved in an affray with
excisemen at Canford Cliffs Chine, near the entrance to Poole Harbour.
The young Gulliver married at Sixpenny Handley, his bride being the
daughter of William Beale, who combined usefully the thirst-provoking
and thirst-quenching trades of blacksmith and innkeeper. In the early
years of his marriage Gulliver was the tenant of the Thorny Down Inn on
the newly created Great Western Turnpike road from Blandford to
Salisbury.

By 1778 he was prosperous enough to move to a farm at Longham,
leaving a tenant to run the inn which is reputed to have been one of his
caches. Two years later he acquired Howe Lodge at Kinson, which included among its attractions the fact that it was roughly equidistant from
Poole and Christchurch. Two farms at Crichel—North East Farm and

Thickthorn—are also thought to have been among those owned or occupied by Gulliver; and there is a 'Gullivers Farm' at West Moors. At this time the official estimate was that about thirty vessels were engaged in smuggling along the coast of Dorset.

Gulliver is said to have been known as 'the Gentle Smuggler' and to take a pride in the fact that no exciseman had been killed in any affray involving Gulliver's men—who were known as 'White Wigs' because Gulliver made them grow their hair long and issued powder to them so that they looked like the respectable servants of some noble landowner. There is a suggestion that he was given some freedom in his smuggling because of the intelligence he brought back from France for the government. Colour is lent to this by the granting to him in 1782 of the king's pardon. Thereafter he gave up smuggling tea and spirits, sold his pack-horses and went into the wine trade. Any joy in Heaven over this repentance went unshared by the customs officers at Poole, who remained convinced that the wine Gulliver sold was imported illicitly. However, his gathering respectability was now unstoppable. He became a church warden of Wimborne Minster, saw one of his daughters married to a banker and a grand-daughter to another banker, and left at his death an estate of about £60,000. Two of his great-grandsons were knighted, one of them being the first Lieutenant-Governor of Burma.

Towards the end of the century the campaign to disfranchise the Chase and rid it of its criminal element gained impetus from the ferocity being used on both sides in the conflicts between keepers and marauding gangs. The routing of a party of dragoons in 1779, when they sought to ambush fifty smugglers travelling with packhorses through Hook Wood, has already been mentioned in an earlier chapter. The following year a dragoon sergeant, stationed at Blandford, had thrown in his lot with the law-breakers and was leading a gang of deer-stealers in a night-time raid shortly before Christmas. On Chettle Common they attacked a party of keepers with swindgels, breaking the knee-cap of one and smashing three ribs of another keeper who died later. The remaining keepers drew their cutlasses and inflicted wounds of such severity that the raiders surrendered. The dragoon sergeant lost a hand, severed at the wrist. Chafin, who tells the story, adds that the man was carried—with his arm tightly bound to stop the loss of blood—to the lodge where Chafin saw him next day 'and his hand in the window'.

In a gruesome jest the severed hand was buried in Pimperne churchyard with the honours of war. The captured men were condemned to be transported but, out of compassion for their wounds, the sentence was commuted to a term of imprisonment. The sergeant later opened a shop in London as a dealer in game: encountering Chafin by chance he asked to deal with him, promising to treat him well as he had taken many of Chafin's hares and pheasants in the past.

The catalogue of violence continued with another battle near Rushmore Lodge in 1791. Of the ten poachers one was killed in the fighting and the others were convicted at Salisbury and transported for life. As late as 1816 four armed men were brought to trial and transported for seven years.

Anyone visiting the Chase today is more likely to comment on its atmosphere of peacefulness than its memories of violence. Yet the memories linger, for strong passions are slow to die out completely—even if they fade into garbled legends and imperfect chronicles. And it is not necessarily the bloodiest of pitched battles that reaches out from the past and captures our imagination. One summer's day in 1822 a young keeper named James Barrett, who was in charge of Cobley Walk that afternoon, was going into his cottage to have a cup of tea when he saw two men walking down one side of Stock Copse; although he could not be certain, because of the distance, he suspected—rightly, as it proved—that one of the men was carrying a gun. Years later Charles Penruddocke took down Barrett's account of what happened. Told in his own words the keeper's recollections express with exceptional vividness the deep antagonisms that filled the Chase with such bitterness:

I had thrown off my coat, and had been most of the day in my shirt-sleeves on account of the heat, but in order to disguise myself I put on a smock frock used in hedge trimming and took a trimming hook in my hand. I cautiously followed the men till I saw them disappear through a gap in the hedge, but when I came up to the gap, and was making my way through it I almost struck against a man who was standing bolt upright in the middle with his hands in his pockets. Ah, thinks I to myself, this one stays here to hide the other, so I took no notice of him, but merely passed through by his side as if I was going that way.

For some time I did not catch sight of the fellow I wanted with the gun in his hand, but presently I saw him going quietly along some distance ahead of me. Directly he saw me he started into a brisk walk, which gradually quickened into a run. It seemed as though he knew who I was. There happened to be some sheep folded in the field where we were, and several lines of hurdles which I conceived would have checked his flight, but as he came to each hurdle he went over it like a buck. I thought I knew him then. He was a noted deer-killer and had been pursued by as many as seventeen of my Lord Shaftesbury's keepers, but had eluded them all. His name was Thomas Amy, and such was his swiftness of foot that he boasted he could outrun anybody's keepers.

When I saw it was he I almost gave it up as a bad job, more particularly as he was so far in advance of me, and with the sheep hurdles between us. But somehow I felt that I would not allow him to beat me —and I was a youngish man then, and not easily daunted by anything, so I took a resolution to follow him, come what would. Throwing off the smock frock and pitching away the trimming hook, I bundled through the hurdles, scrambled through an adjoining hedge, and beheld my man some distance away. I followed him smartly, but it was trying work racing over the heavy land. I thought at one time that I should never lessen the distance between us, but by degrees I got nearer and nearer, till I could hear his laboured breathing and puffing. This gave me some encouragement. A short time brought us both to the Blandford Road, having run four miles.

I was gaining on him—I felt it—my blood was up, I would have him, a few minutes more and I should have come to close quarters. Suddenly he stopped and faced me, his body motionless, the gun pointed at my head, and his eye looking along the barrel. 'By . . . ,' said he, 'if you advance another step I will blow your . . . head off.'

I heard his threat, I knew his piece was on full cock, and yet I did not hesitate. I suppose, Sir, that, having run a long way and being in a kind of excited state, I did not think of the danger I ran in bearing down upon him for I continued to move on with my eyes fixed upon him.

Perhaps he feared to fire lest he should be seen. I noticed that he turned his face once in the direction of the Thorny Down public house, about two hundred yards off, when immediately afterwards I was upon him, knocking up the gun. No words were spoken. It became then a matter of strength.

Without any boasting I may say I was a strong man, and it used to be said of me that if I once gripped a man he could not get free. Thomas Amy was a powerful man in his way, and a noted wrestler. He was accustomed to wear iron kicking-plates which projected from the tips of his boots and were filed up sharp. With these he kicked my legs and the bone was cut in notches—took out in chips just as if you had cut it with a hook.

I managed to get him quiet at last, and to take his gun in my left hand while I held him with the other and tried to make him walk with me to Thorny Down public house, where I could rest awhile. I had a job with him. He would not walk. I had to drag him the whole way. Close to the public house he began again and seemed fresher than before. He kicked my shins to such an extent that I could scarcely stand, and finding he could not get away held me by the cheek with his teeth which caused me great agony. To relieve myself I took him by his throat and choked him. I held him there till his face was as black as your hat before he would leave go.

We reached the inn at last, and after giving him into the care of the landlord, who was a friend of mine, I called for some brandy and proceeded to bathe my poor legs with it. So great was the pain I felt almost mad. The flesh was kicked off to the bone. By and by I took my prisoner to my Lord Rivers, who was very kind to me. After hearing my evidence he sent me home in a cart with some soft straw at the bottom, for now that I had given the man into safe custody I could not stand. On my arrival at home I went to bed.

Thomas Amy was sent for trial in due course. He only got six months. Everyone expected he would have been transported.

CHAPTER SEVEN

Down with the Deer, up with the Fox!

IN THE COURSE of his reflections on the Waltham Blacks, Gilbert White expressed a new attitude of mind that was increasingly to prevail in public debate on the future of the Chase lordship. These are his words, in Letter VII of *The Natural History of Selborne*:

> Though large herds of deer do much harm to the neighbourhood, yet the injury to the morals of the people is of more moment than the loss of their crops. The temptation is irresistible; for most men are sportsmen by constitution: and there is such an inherent spirit for hunting in human nature, as scarce any inhibitions can restrain.

He had recognized that the circumstances of eighteenth-century life placed a growing emphasis on the incompatibility of modern agriculture with deer preservation on the grand scale; and similarly on the growth of lawlessness and violence that seemed to have become inseparable from Chase law. One by one the big landowners of Cranborne Chase came to share these views, though perhaps with a difference in priorities. As a clergyman Gilbert White properly rated the injury to morals as more serious than the loss of crops: others might hesitate to go quite as far as that.

In 1618 John Lodge had given his opinion that 'if the deer of the Chase should feed out into the cornfields, meadows and pastures of Bowerchalk, without restraint, the inhabitants and tenants there would be undone'. The Wiltshire villages of the Ebble valley were particularly sensitive to the depredations of deer: the main woodland area lies on the southern flank of the Ebble. As the eighteenth century unfolded the traditional rebelliousness of the Wiltshire farmers against the Chase laws intensified. By the early 1800s the agricultural case against deer preservation was freely publicized and well understood. West, for example, wrote 'much of the woodland and commons is capable of tillage and could be spared for that purpose, were not the conversion forbidden by the Chase-laws. The cultivation of turnips is almost impracticable, unless in very small proportion; which is subject to great damage from the deer. The corn suffers much at times.' Similarly William Stevenson, in his survey of

Dorset agriculture, wrote, 'The Chase is pernicious to the farmers in the neighbourhood, and is the occasion that few turnips are sown, as the depredations of the deer on this crop are great, and cannot be prevented.'

Another sensitive area was to the south-west of Lord Rivers's Rushmore headquarters, in the neighbourhood of Tarrant Gunville and Pimperne, where in earlier years there had been conflict with Bubb Dodington at Eastbury and with the Swaynes and Harbins. After Dodington's death the Eastbury estate passed to Richard Grenville, the second Lord Temple. The close family ties of Grenvilles and Pitts would have made it particularly appropriate for Lord Temple to accept the rôle of spokesman for those who favoured a radical change. In 1786 accordingly he mentioned to Lord Rivers, in a casual and informal conversation, that the time had perhaps come to dismiss Chase law to the lumber room of history.

Lord Rivers did not take kindly to this proposal at first, but he undertook to discuss it with his son and heir. Having done so he authorized Temple to sound the opinion of others. Enough support was forthcoming to justify a public move and on 16 July 1787, a meeting was held at Woodyates Inn for proprietors of land in Cranborne Chase to adopt a course of action: they elected a committee to treat with Lord Rivers. During the following year some ineffectual exchanges made it clear that Rivers had no intention of surrendering a legally impregnable position without compensation on a scale that matched the 'evident, palpable, great and solid' nature of the sacrifice he was invited to make.

In 1789, therefore, the committee of proprietors came forward with the offer of a perpetual rent of £200 per annum—this, being, in their view, a handsome replacement of the value of his lordship's venison, after allowance was made for his costs in keepering and enforcing Chase law. Lord Rivers, however, took a different view. While not opposed in principle to disfranchisement, he had first to be satisfied as to the amount of compensation. By the offer made to him he was unimpressed. One thousand pounds per annum was more like the sort of amount he had in mind.

In this state of deadlock the landowners called another meeting at Woodyates Inn towards the end of 1790. They were now in a more militant mood. They decided to publish a detailed account of the course of the negotiations and to retain counsel to contest any application of Chase law which threatened their free enjoyment of their own properties. In their open letter to Lord Rivers, published in 1791, the committee stressed that their concern was by no means confined to their own interests but saw more significance in the evil effects on the community at large. Like Gilbert White they regarded deer-stalking as a contagious immorality which begot other and graver vices. There was even a note of desperation in the claim that whole parishes had become nests of deer-stealers, where children were taught the black arts of poaching by their depraved parents.

By all this Lord Rivers was unmoved. He retaliated by publishing his own version of the negotiations; and by judicious legal procedures he called the bluff of the landowners in the courts, where their militant zeal tended to be quenched prematurely. The lawyers fed well but year followed year, to the end of the century and well beyond, without a defended action coming to trial. The harsh facts were that Rivers's position was too strong, and his price too high. He lived out his days, to the age of eighty-three, without yielding an inch. It was his son, succeeding him in 1803, who had to deal with the next concerted attempt to negotiate a settlement.

For a dozen years therefore no move was made by either party—a lull during which it is convenient to look at the evolution of attitudes among the big landowners during the four lordships when the Chase was in private hands. The committee opposing Lord Rivers was a strong one but there were some illustrious absentees. The big guns on the original committee were Lords Shaftesbury, Arundell and Temple (who had meanwhile become Duke of Buckingham). A later list of subscribers to the campaign adds such powerful local names as Sturt, Wyndham and Okeden, along with the Marquess of Bath and the Earl of Uxbridge. One looks in vain for a Pembroke or a Salisbury, though Pembroke's attitude is clear enough since he gave a lead by disfranchising his own Vernditch Walk. There were certainly some who supported Rivers, notably the influential Reverend William Chafin of Chettle, whose long family connection with the Chase gave weight to his impassioned defence of the *status quo*. If deer-stealing is to be cured by destroying the deer, he argued, must sheep-stealing be stamped out by the annihilation of the shepherd's flocks?

In its final non-regal phase the lordship of the Chase was held by one or more generations of four families, the Cecils (Salisbury), the Ashleys (Shaftesbury), the Frekes and the Pitts (Rivers): twice it changed hands by purchase, but otherwise by inheritance. During that period of 200 years the area under the lord's effective control shrank considerably; his monopoly was increasingly shared with others; and the advantages of the lordship were measured more in terms of amenity and privilege than of economic worth. It is these factors which in the final stages influenced in varying degrees the owner of the rights, those who sought to extinguish those rights, and those others who were reluctant to do so.

Sir Jack Drummond in his book *The Englishman's Food* has some interesting comments on rural diet in the seventeenth century:

> The owners of the big estates and the prosperous farmers stocked their larders almost entirely from their own lands. Almost every form of wild life from small birds to deer was trapped or hunted; venison was one of the most popular winter meats. There are indications that the prohibition of poaching was less strictly enforced than it was in feudal times. It seems probable that the villagers were able to snare and trap with a certain amount of freedom.

This does not relate specifically to Cranborne Chase of course but to conditions in general. Nevertheless it points a contrast between 1600 and 1800, and suggests a trend from which the Chase was certainly not immune. Self-sufficiency was becoming no longer the imperative aim it had once been: fortified with the wealth of the later eighteenth century the households of the big landowners were not likely to go hungry from a lack of venison—agreeable though it might be to have it. It was the sheer pleasure of hunting that weighed increasingly heavily against economic advantage: and ironically the restrictions governing the deer made the fox appear a more acceptable substitute.

The extreme example of self-sufficiency in the seventeenth century is undoubtedly Henry Hastings, the Squire of Woodlands, an estate adjoining the south-eastern boundary of the Chase and neighbouring the Shaftesburys at Wimborne St Giles. A son of the Earl of Huntingdon, Henry Hastings was born in 1551 and lived until 1650. A graphic and humorous account of him in his old age was written by Sir Anthony Ashley Cooper (later to be the first Earl of Shaftesbury) who described Hastings as 'an original of our age' and added these details:

> He was low, very strong, and very active, of a reddish flaxen hair; his cloaths always green cloth, and never worth, when new, five pounds. His house was perfectly of the old fashion, in the midst of a large park well stocked with deer; and near the house rabbits for his kitchen; many fish ponds; great store of wood and timber. He kept all manner of sport hounds, that ran buck, fox, hare, otter, and badger, and hawkes long and short winged. He had all sorts of nets for fish. He had a walk in the New Forest, and the manor of Christchurch; this last supplied him with red deer, sea and river fish; and indeed all his neighbours' grounds and royalties were free to him, who bestowed all his times on these sports, but what he borrowed to caress his neighbours' wives and

Eastbury House: Vanbrugh's famous gateway with excrescent trees

Pons Petrae: the bridge over the River Allen at Stanbridge Mill

Chettle House

Chettle House, interior

The packhorse bridge at Tarrant Monkton

The beech avenue near Badbury Rings

A hurdle-maker at work

Water crowsfoot flowering in the River Tarrant

Tarrant Rawston church

Ashmore Pond

Crawford bridge over the River Stour

Looking east-
wards over
Cranborne
Chase from
Woodley Down
towards Tollard
Royal

daughters, there being not a woman in all his walks of the degree of a yeoman's wife or under, and under the age of forty, but it was her own fault if he was not intimately acquainted with her. This made him very popular; always speaking kindly to the husband, brother, or father, who was to boot very welcome to his house, whenever he came there he found beef, pudding, and small beer in great plenty; the house not so neatly kept as to shame him or his dirty shoes; the great hall strewed with marrow-bones; full of hawkes' perches, hounds, spaniels, and terriers; the upper side of the hall hung with fox-skins, of this and the last year's killing; here and there a pole-cat intermixed; guns and keepers' and hunters' poles in great abundance. The parlour was a large room as properly furnished. On a great hearth, paved with brick, lay some terriers, and the choicest hounds and spaniels. Seldom but two of the great chairs had litters of cats in them, which were not to be disturbed: he having always three or four attending him at dinner, and a little white stick of fourteen inches long lying by his trencher, that he might defend such meat that he had no mind to part with to them. The windows, which were very large, served for places to lay his arrows, cross-bows, and stone-bows, and such like accoutrements; the corners of the room full of the best-chosen hunting or hawking poles; his oyster table at the lower end, which was of constant use, twice a day, all the year round, for he never failed to eat oysters, both dinner and supper-time, all seasons: the neighbouring town of Poole supplied him with them. The upper part of this room had two small tables, and a desk, on the one side of which was a church Bible, and on the other side the Book of Martyrs: on the table were hawkes hoods, bells, and such like; two or three old hats, with their crowns thrust in, so as to hold ten or a dozen eggs, which were of the pheasant kind of poultry; these he took much care of, and fed himself. On one side of this end of the room was the door of a closet, wherein stood the strong beer and the wine, which never came from thence but in single glasses, that being the rule of the house, exactly observed; for he never exceeded in drink, or permitted it. On the other side was the door of an old chapel, not used for devotion: the pulpit, as the safest place, was never wanting of a cold chine of beef, venison-pasty, gammon of bacon, or a great apple-pye, with thick crust extremely baked. His table cost him not much though it was good to eat at. His sport supplied all but beef or mutton. He was well natured, but soon angry, calling his servants bastards and cuckoldy knaves, in one of which he often spoke truth, to his own knowledge, and sometimes in both, though of the same man. He lived to be an hundred, and never lost his eye-sight, but always wrote and read without spectacles, and got on horseback without help. Until past fourscore, he rode to the death of a stag as well as any.

An 'original' indeed—but differing perhaps in degree only from many another who shared his passion for hunting everything from polecats to yeomen's wives. A devotion to field sports, more strictly understood, was a totally absorbing way of life for those landowners who eschewed politics and preferred the country to the city. The obduracy of Lord Rivers, in clinging to his ancient privilege, would have struck an answering chord in those who believed the arts and pleasures of the chase to be the proper concern of all men worthy of the name. Even those who opposed Rivers had every intention of preserving the game on their own land: all they wanted was the freedom to deal with the deer as they saw fit, and to fell timber at will.

The lull in the controversy came to an end in 1803, when the second Baron Rivers succeeded his father and received a fresh approach from the committee of landowners. If they expected a more liberal attitude from the new lord they were soon disappointed. He repeated his father's demand for an annuity of £1,000 and the committee had to recognize that this was not a negotiable figure. It would have to be paid. What was more difficult to accept was his additional demand for a park surrounding Rushmore. This was valued at £250 per annum, assuming that the land was available. In the event there were serious obstacles to the acquisition of the land, and once more the negotiations languished. However, though no formal progress was made, the temper of the principals was changing markedly. Bowles had good grounds for his suggestion that Rivers's legal advisers had advised the new lord to enforce his rights to the full letter of the law, as a strategy calculated to bring matters to a head. Before 1800, according to Bowles, the rights of the Chase lord had been exercised with much moderation: 'venison was so liberally distributed in presents to those who suffered from the depredations of the deer, that very few persons thought it an object worth enquiring about, as to what indeed were the actual boundaries'. Even when there were good grounds for action the policy was one of restraint. In the 1770s the Rushmore steward, William Salkeld, urged his master to oppose Lord Pembroke's woodmen, who were defying Chase law over the borders of the woodlands—always a sensitive matter. There was a great taking of affidavits, with Rivers evidently anxious to avoid friction. At about the same time Humphrey Sturt was reporting to Salkeld that a coppice belonging to the Poor of Blandford was hunted by a dozen persons with all sorts of dogs till evening: he complained ruefully that 'if this is to be continued unmolested and looked over, there will soon be an end of the Chace in this part, the deer can have no rest and are parted and dislodged from their usual pasturages'.

By 1803 it was becoming clear that the invitation to the Pitt-Rivers family to relinquish the lordship of the Chase had succeeded only in souring the atmosphere. In the following years the conduct of the Chase keepers seemed to be directed towards deliberate confrontations. On Pimperne Down some fences, 'no higher than those which a rabbit could easily have leapt over,' were prostrated to the ground. At Wardour keepers with hounds invaded Lord Arundell's park in pursuit of a deer and killed it there without Lord Arundell's consent and with no apology. Incidents of this kind, combined with the levying of cheminage at Harnham Bridge on all traffic leaving Salisbury, lent colour to the accusation that 'the obsolete and tyrannical laws of the forest were now attempted to be put again in execution'.

For a time it seemed that nothing could check Rivers's intransigence: his legal position looked unchallengeable and the landowners were unable to meet his terms for compensation. However, a relatively minor incident brought forth a village Hampden who, in his wrath, decided to oppose Rivers in what was to become a sensational lawsuit. The conflict began when Thomas King, the tenant of Norrington Farm in Alvediston, was out walking with his dogs. A keeper shot one of the dogs on the grounds that Lord Rivers had not given King permission to walk greyhounds within the Chase. King was so incensed that he determined to provoke a test case. On 12 January 1814, finding deer grazing on his farm, he set two or three brace of greyhounds on to them to drive them away. It was an act of defiance, of bravado almost, that Rivers was in no mood to ignore. A prosecution was started and in the Lent assizes of 1816 the case came before Mr Justice Holroyd and a special jury at Salisbury.

King's line of defence was that the bounds of Cranborne Chase did not extend into Wiltshire, or at any rate not into Alvediston. On the face of it, it was not a very inspiring defence. Attempts to establish the Wiltshire-Dorset border as the northern boundary of the Chase had failed in the past. Rushmore itself, where the Chase courts were now held, was in Wiltshire. In James I's reign Lord Salisbury had established his Chase rights over Lord Arundell's land in Tollard Green and Tollard Park, in Wiltshire, as well as Manwood Copse and—even closer to King—the manor of Norrington.

As for the rights that Lord Rivers was claiming to exercise, it was argued by his counsel that Cranborne Chase—having belonged to King John and subsequently to the Crown from Edward IV to James I—had gained the status of a forest and the appropriate legal apparatus. This apparatus, sanctified by its regal pedigree, was spelled out as courts of vert and venery; a ranger, responsible for the deer; a promoter, to impound sheep feeding in the Chase and promote actions against their owners; the taking of cheminage during the fence month, and so on.

All the weight of precedent seemed to favour Rivers; and yet the jury found for King. What appears to have influenced them was the argument that Rivers's undeniable rights applied in full only to the Inner Chase, and that the Outer Chase was a purlieu or area of *percursus* where keepers might pursue and retrieve deer straying from the Inner Chase, but could not there kill deer or enforce chase law or forest law. Once that was accepted King had merely to claim that Alvediston was in the Outer Chase, not the Inner.

So ended a dispute which, in one form or another, had rumbled on sporadically since 1255 when it was argued that the then lord of the Chase had no forest rights in Wiltshire but only his *percursus* to the banks of the Nadder. For Lord Rivers in 1816 the implications were far-reaching. In the full exercise of his rights he was now confined on his northern flank to the scarp overlooking the Ebble valley. To the east Lord Pembroke had already disfranchised Vernditch. To the south, beyond the Great Western Turnpike, those two earlier lords of the Chase—Salisbury and Shaftesbury—seemed to enjoy a privileged immunity in the running of their estates. The time had come for a dignified and not unprofitable surrender.

It was conducted in a leisurely manner and the second Baron Rivers died before the final papers were signed and sealed. The proposed addition of parkland to Rushmore had to be abandoned. The form of compensation was offered solely in cash, as an annual revenue of £1,800 levied proportionately on the land to be disfranchised by a privately promoted Act of Parliament. The procedure must have been well in hand in 1828 when Lord Rivers died. He had no son to succeed him. His heir was William Horace Beckford, son of Peter Beckford and Lord Rivers's eldest sister, Louisa: in 1828, on the death of his uncle, William adopted the name Pitt-Rivers and became the third Baron Rivers. As a young man William drew heavily on his prospects. In 1807 Lord Rivers had to cope with the massive debts of his nephew and heir: it is quite possible that this financial drain made disfranchisement appear more attractive with its promise of a new source of income. It had apparently become necessary to mortgage the Rivers estate at Arne at this time.

The Act of Parliament, 9 George IV, which disfranchised the Chase, provided for an award dated 29 September 1829 and enrolled two years later by which William agreed to accept £1,800 annually. Commissioner Philip Williams of London had the task of setting out the proportions to be levied from individual landowners. For example Thomas Grove, with 348 acres in Tollard Royal, had to pay £7 6s 4d p.a.—a sort of secular equivalent of tithe which could be bought and sold, or extinguished outright by capital purchase.

The consequences of disfranchisement must seem at first sight to be wholly admirable. The oppression of outmoded forest laws vanished overnight. Farms and villages were freed from the tyrannical rules and actual damage that stemmed from the preservation of deer. In accordance with modern agricultural practice landowners were at liberty to fell trees, clear scrubland, plough up old pastures and fence their properties, without consideration for anything but their own interest. Ironically this proclamation of individual liberty—bringing Cranborne Chase into harmony with the true spirit of nineteenth-century England—was not always so benevolent as the mediaeval customs it displaced. When the Marquess of Anglesey exercised his newly won right to enclose his woods in Sixpenny Handley he did so 'to the extinction of the common feed'. Under Chase law the villagers had rights of pasturage and pannage in the woods at appropriate seasons when they were given access. Lord Anglesey's new fences put an end to those ancient privileges. The commoners responded in no uncertain fashion by suing for damages. The Woodyates Inn, scene of that first meeting to launch the disfranchisement campaign, was now in 1834 to house a trial in which those forces of liberation were opposed and defeated. Mr Serjeant Bompas and a special jury gave the verdict to the people of Handley, upholding their traditional rights.

That it should have been Peter Beckford's son who signed the instrument approving the disfranchisement of the Chase is an additional irony, since it is as the author of the classic *Thoughts on Hunting* that Peter Beckford is remembered. The book was published in 1781 and came to be regarded as the authoritative guide to the breeding, training and hunting of a pack of foxhounds, at a time when the sport in its modern specialized form was relatively new. The pioneer of foxhunting in Cranborne Chase was Thomas Fownes of Stepleton who operated from 1730 until his financial difficulties obliged him to sell Stepleton to Julines Beckford in 1745 for £13,600. The acquisition of Stepleton gave Julines Beckford certain foxhunting rights in Cranborne Chase, and his son Peter grew up at Stepleton with an eagerness to build on Fownes's pioneering efforts. With little to guide him Peter subjected his practical experience to a vigorous intellectual analysis: he was rewarded with two outstanding 'pupils' who carried forward his achievement. One was Thomas Grove of Ferne, the other was Squire Farquharson of Eastbury and Langton Long.

The Groves were an ancient family who had been settled in the vicinity of Shaftesbury since at least the 1520s and represented the town in Parliament during the sixteenth and seventeenth centuries. In 1759 Thomas Grove was born, the eldest son of John Grove who died ten years later. As soon as he came of age Thomas started a pack of foxhounds, and it is probable that he is the friend to whom Beckford's *Thoughts on Hunting* are addressed. At the time of publication Thomas Grove was twenty-two, Beckford forty-one. Three years later Grove had thirty-seven couple of working hounds and a distinctive hunt uniform of a red coat with a large white collar—a uniform later adopted by Farquharson.

The Farquharsons, like the Beckfords, were wealthy newcomers to Cranborne Chase. Originally engaged in shipping in the Aberdeen area they came south when James Farquharson, born in 1728, established himself as a London merchant. He died at Camberwell in 1795 and a memorial tablet in Langton church records that 'By his extensive and correct knowledge of Commerce, he acquired an ample Fortune; His disposition of which has raised many to Opulence'. One of the uses to which he put his fortune was the purchase of land in the valley of the Stour below Blandford. In 1775 he married Anne Staines of Shapwick and established their home at Littleton, between Shapwick and Blandford St Mary. A tablet in Shapwick church records their melancholy losses of eight children in infancy or childhood, but a boy and a girl survived. The girl, Henrietta Anne, married Thomas Grove's son (also Thomas). The boy, James John, was eleven when his father died. Like the elder Grove he was eager to start his own pack of foxhounds when he came of age in 1805. Beckford described him as 'my apt pupil'.

After Eton and Oxford, at the age of twenty-two, 'Gipsy' Farquharson started his career which was to last for fifty-two years as a Master of Foxhounds. His inheritance in land probably amounted to 20,000 acres. Leaving his widowed mother in the family home at Littleton his trustees bought two properties for him: Eastbury, where one wing of Vanbrugh's great mansion had survived, and Langton House standing opposite Littleton on the other side of the Stour. Eastbury he used to accommodate his hunt servants, horses and hounds. Langton he demolished in 1827 and replaced with a new classical mansion; here also he built stables in an oval of Bath stone with a covered ride all round and with oak stalls for thirty-four horses. Eastbury could stable another fifty horses and the kennels at Eastbury housed about seventy-five couple of hounds.

Part of his original pack came from Humphrey Sturt at Crichel, where the Prince Regent had kept some hounds for a time. Some of Beckford's hunt servants joined him when Beckford finally retired, but Beckford's foxhounds had gone to Thomas Grove many years earlier when Beckford, in 1783, gave up foxhunting and went to live in Italy. The French invasion of Italy in 1799 drove him back to Stepleton where he rented a walk from Lord Rivers and established a pack of buckhounds. The feeder of these hounds, John Pettis, was one of the men whose training by Beckford was a valuable recruitment for the young Farquharson.

The historical importance of Fownes, Beckford, Grove and Farquharson is clearly shown by Chafin who speaks with the authority of his long memory of hunting in the Chase. Recalling the days before Fownes's innovation he tells us that 'no hounds were kept and used for any particular sort of game except the Buck-hounds'. It was customary for hounds to hunt casually 'the first that came in their way—all the animals promiscuously, except the deer, from which they were necessarily made steady, otherwise they would not have been suffered at all'. Just how promiscuous a hunting expedition might be is shown by the record of a legal action in 1704, involving some Chase keepers who presumed on their right to pursue deer by invading some enclosed land at Stepleton belonging to Richard Fownes. Fownes sued them for damages and was awarded £11. Evidence was given that their bag comprised forty does, twenty hares, two hundred rabbits, ten pheasants and fifty partridges—taken in a single day. And, to make matters worse, a day in April!

Fownes's specialized foxhounds had been preceded by a pack in Hertfordshire five years earlier but they were the first in the west country. Beckford and his two pupils took their lead from that first effort and gave a completely new character to hunting in Cranborne Chase. With the passing of the great days of the deer it was now the fox which became the favoured quarry of the gentry. In a friendly division of the territory Thomas Grove was recognized as Master of the Cranborne Chase Foxhounds, operating in the north from his estate at Ferne. Farquharson's eyes turned westward across the Stour and deep into Dorset: at Cattistock he established a hunting-box, kennels and stables as temporary accommodation when he was hunting in that area. A benevolent autocrat, 'the Squire'—as Farquharson came to be known—had a remarkable record in several ways. Unchallenged as a master for more than fifty years he claimed with pride that nobody paid to hunt with him: all the costs of the hunt were met by himself. Remarkably he had only two huntsmen in all those years—Jennings for thirty years and Jem Treadwell for twenty-two. In his twenty-one seasons Treadwell accounted for 1,344 brace of foxes, with nearly 100 brace in a single season on one occasion.

According to a hunting journalist, 'The Druid,' writing in *Silk and Scarlet*, the short oaks and hazels of Cranborne Chase were the great Dorset nursery of foxes until, in the second half of the nineteenth century, 'far too many rabbit-traps got set'. Still to come were barbed wire, motor transport and a more commercial approach to land-use in the present century. Foxhunting survives, but the world of Squire Farquharson now seems almost as remote as King John's.

PART TWO

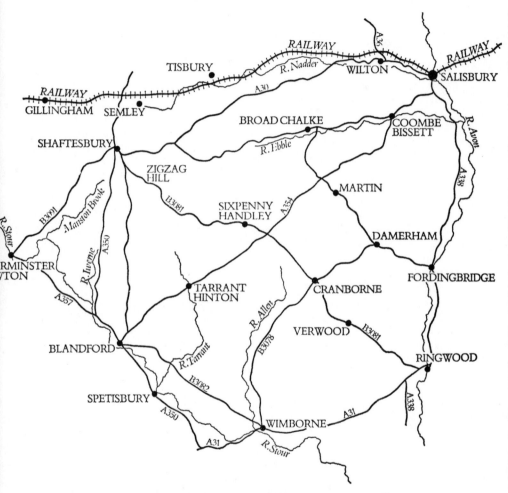

MAP TWO: showing principal rivers—Nadder, Avon, Stour, Allen, Tarrant, Iwerne, and Manston Brook and Ebble.

Railway and principal roads, with modern numbering of A and B roads.

Towns and selected villages.

CHAPTER EIGHT

By Road and Rail

THAT FINE JUDGE of English landscape, H. J. Massingham, once wrote that 'the great way to see Cranborne Chase and to be imaginatively fired by the palimpsest of its cultural continuity is to take the high road from Salisbury to Blandford Forum. A great many people do, but they get from the one place to the other in less than an hour. You want at least a month for the journey.'

That high road, today known prosaically as the A354, came into existence in something like its present form in the middle of the eighteenth century as the Great Western Turnpike. Leaving Salisbury and crossing the Ebble at Coombe Bissett it runs for the best part of twenty miles over expansive downland without passing through town or village street until it reaches the outskirts of Blandford at Pimperne. At either end it starts in a river valley and climbs to the bold exhilarating atmosphere of wide vistas and open skies. The ancient wildness of the surrounding countryside has been largely domesticated but it has still a generosity of scale, an uninhibited linear sweep to its horizons. There is space up here, and to spare, for big flocks of lapwings and rooks. And never far away are the silent witnesses that Massingham had in mind, the symbols of continuity, the grassy mounds of the prehistoric dead, the firm line of Ackling Dyke —the Roman road that struck out from Sarum to Badbury Rings.

The A354 intersects that Roman road and uses a stretch of it—the section from Bokerley junction past Woodyates to Oakley Down. Travelling westwards towards the Handley roundabout you can see how the modern road starts to diverge from the Roman one. If Salisbury cathedral had been built at Old Sarum, instead of New Sarum, the line of Ackling Dyke might have been even more serviceable to the builders of the Great Western Turnpike: they could then have followed it through Stratford Tony and past Salisbury racecourse to Old Sarum.

The positioning of these two roads—the Roman and the eighteenth-century turnpike—suggests that the main line of communication across the Chase was always in an east-west direction. The Ox Drove and the Ridgeway a little further north, and beyond them the Salisbury Way coach route along the northern scarp to Whitesheet Hill, emphasize the point. The big river valleys on either side of the Chase—the Avon and

Stour valleys—provided the north-south routes to the coast. Travellers who ventured out of those valleys on to the sparsely inhabited uplands of the Chase were heading to some easterly destination—London perhaps— or westward to Exeter or Weymouth. And over the centuries they tended to follow one of two general directions running westward from Salisbury: either they continued more or less due westward towards Shaftesbury, keeping to the high ground on either side of the Ebble valley, or they took a more south-westerly course to find a ford or a bridge across the Stour at or near Blandford. The favouring of high ground on the well-drained chalk downs was due to the miry condition of the heavy lowland soils in winter. As late as 1830 Bowles noted that the roads in the Ebble valley 'are impassable for any other four-wheel carriages than those used for husbandry purposes, and are suited only for a *sure-footed* horse': which makes it easier to understand why the mail coaches struggled up White-sheet Hill. The present A30 to Shaftesbury needed modern road-making methods to cope with the 'foundrous' clays that had defied earlier genera-tions of travellers.

When the first trackways were made the general terrain of the chalk plateau would have been woodland of oak and hazel, according to the botanist W. B. Turrill, so the earliest routes probably linked human settlements and clearings in the intervals of following woodland paths. It is also worth remembering that the water table was considerably higher —by as much as fifty feet, according to General Pitt-Rivers. Lesser rivers and streams, like the Allen, the Tarrant, the Iwerne, the Terrig and the Crichel, would have been more formidable obstacles than they are now and would have had to be forded or bridged. If we try to envisage the journeyings over the Chase during the past four or five thousand years we can recognize the justness of Massingham's word 'palimpsest': the lines of roads, different in detail but following the same general direction, are written on top of and across each other by widely different generations.

If we look for the earliest discernible road from Salisbury to Blandford we must follow the line described by Ronald Good in his *Old Roads of Dorset*. West of Woodyates this lies about half a mile to the south of the A354 and runs more or less parallel to it. At its eastern end it probably followed the line taken later by the Romans from Sarum to Bokerley Dyke and Woodyates, but then followed the Neolithic cursus over Gussage Hill to ford the Crichel stream at Veiny Cheese Pond—an im-portant junction with other ancient roads or tracks. From Veiny Cheese Pond the route would be over Launceston Down, crossing the Tarrant at the Tarrant Monkton ford, probably; and so to Buzbury Rings, on the edge of what is now Blandford golf course, and across the Stour at

Blandford itself or at nearby Charlton Marshall. It is impossible to say when this route first began to take shape but, thinking of it as the invading Romans found it, we may designate it in Iron Age terms as the Sarum-Maiden Castle road.

The Roman system of roads in the Chase was governed by the choice of Badbury Rings as the hub from which the main routes sprang. One ran southwards to their new base on Poole Harbour at Hamworthy, one northwards through the Tarrant valley and Ashmore to Ludwell and beyond. Their route eastward to Sarum followed a dead straight line from Badbury to Woodyates, cutting through the cursus on Wyke Down. This intersection of Roman and Neolithic constructions offers a spectacular sight about half a mile west of the B3081 and south of the Handley roundabout. The Roman causeway rises up several feet above the surrounding farmland as it straddles the Handley–Cranborne road and marches through the barrows on Oakley Down until it is absorbed briefly in the A354 as far as Bokerley Junction, where it breaks away and disappears past the woodlands of Vernditch. The cursus is visible for much of its length only from the air but, where the Roman road cuts through it, it is plain to see in the most casual glance. From the point of intersection it follows a course no less straight than the Roman one but on a different axis, across Bottlebush Down and towards Pentridge. The conjunction of these two ancient works is an unforgettable sight. Each is in its way outstanding. The Roman *agger* is judged to be the best example of its kind to survive in Britain. The cursus is the longest yet discovered in Europe.

The next discernible road on the Salisbury–Blandford axis is much later. As the Roman road system decayed there was a revival of the earlier Sarum–Maiden Castle route. The rise of New Sarum and the decline of Badbury made the Roman route inappropriate for such mediaeval travellers as might want to make a journey from Salisbury to Blandford, Dorchester and Weymouth. In the thousand or more years between the Roman era and the beginnings of modern road-making the traffic was mainly of pedestrians, saddle-horses and packhorses. Until the Tudors waggons were of minor importance except in the vicinity of large towns: a packhorse could carry 400 lb. over long distances. Unless a king or an ecclesiastic took the initiative in a longer-range project the creation of roads would be limited to purely local needs. As the waste was enclosed, and the sense of private ownership of land increased, some older roads were closed and others diverted.

When Charles II instructed John Ogilby to prepare a survey of roads in 1675 the route from London to Weymouth ran across Cranborne

Chase on quite a different line from either the Roman Ackling Dyke which preceded it or the Great Western Turnpike which replaced it. Coming eastward from Blandford the route kept close to the Iron Age line over Monkton Down and the ford at Tarrant Monkton to cross the Crichel stream only a few hundred yards from Veiny Cheese Pond. Here the similarity ended as the seventeenth-century road moved further to the south through Gussage St Michael to cross the line of the Roman road and pursue its way via Tenantry Down, All Hallows and Creech Hill to Cranborne. Even in 1675 All Hallows was described as 'a discontinued village.' It was presumably the rise of Cranborne as the administrative centre of the Chase that drew the east-west route so far to the south.

From Cranborne Ogilby showed the road passing through Boveridge to the hamlet of Tidpit at the eastern edge of the village of Martin and then rising over Toyd Down to run in a more or less straight line to cross the Ebble at Coombe Bissett—or alternatively at Homington—and thence to Salisbury. The section from Boveridge to Tidpit and Toyd Down remains today much as it was when Ogilby surveyed it—a narrow minor route which failed to attract any subsequent development but still serves local needs, unlike the section from Cranborne to Gussage St Michael which has disappeared. The two features of this post-Roman road most likely to seize the imagination today are the charming little packhorse bridge over the ford at Tarrant Monkton and the primitive trackway from Tidpit up over Windmill Hill to Toyd Down. To think of these as features of the main road from London to Weymouth is to realize the crude nature of travelling conditions as late as the seventeenth century. Presumably Celia Fiennes cut across from Wilton to Toyd Down when she rode to Bland-ford in about 1690. In her own words she 'went to Blandford in Dorset-shire 18 miles through a haire waring [hare warren] and a forest of the Kings'. Incidentally it is interesting that the Chase could still be regarded by her as a royal forest: the owner of the Chase lordship at the time was the Earl of Shaftesbury.

Charles II's interest in the state of the roads heralded a genuine effort towards improvement. The first turnpike roads were initiated during his reign and produced a widespread revolution in travelling conditions during the next hundred years. The earliest coach to be mounted on springs appeared in the mid-eighteenth century; and at the same time the expansion of trade and increased wealth stimulated the demand for better long-distance routes. The year 1755 saw the start of the Great Western Turnpike Trust which created the direct ancestor of our present A354. It incorporated some existing stretches of road between Dorchester and

Salisbury but in the main it was a newly designed arterial road, linking the larger towns by the most expeditious route and disregarding purely local convenience—much as a modern motorway would do. Significantly it bypassed Cranborne, which was already losing its importance and now saw its decay accelerated when the Great Western Turnpike—and later the railway—ignored it.

The general plan of the Chase section of the turnpike was to get from Blandford to Salisbury as swiftly and efficiently as possible. These two towns bridged the two main rivers, Stour and Avon. In between them the lesser rivers and streams of the Chase, running north-south, had to be crossed—a task which was eased for the road-builders by following a more northerly course than any of the preceding routes. The days of packhorses and fords were passing. From Blandford the new road climbed through Pimperne to cross the Tarrant much higher upstream than ever before, at Tarrant Hinton: over the Crichel similarly, well to the north of Veiny Cheese Pond, whereas the previous road had turned south of it, and then across the Terrig or Gussage stream at Cashmoor.

The next section of the turnpike ignored Sixpenny Handley and Pentridge, driving impartially between them to adopt a useful stretch of the old Roman road as far as the historic gap in Bokerley Dyke. From this point, Bokerley junction, the turnpike again broke new ground in a straight run to the north of Toyd Down, picking up an existing road south of Coombe Bissett and adopting its course into Salisbury. At Coombe Bissett a road bridge was built over the river Ebble for the turnpike, beside the mediaeval packhorse bridge. This new bridge made obsolete the alternative route downstream at Homington.

Between Blandford and Salisbury there were at first two tollgates, Coombe Bissett and Cashmoor. In the 1830s a third toll house was added, at Tarrant Hinton; it is this one which will catch the eye of a traveller today, unmistakable in its design and well preserved. The one at Cashmoor has been demolished: Good located its abandoned garden 'with much lilac and one or two fruit trees' half a mile east of Cashmoor in the angle between the main road and the green lane up to Gussage Hill, where it may still be discerned. The turnpike brought a modest prosperity to the little hamlet of Cashmoor. 'Here,' wrote Hutchins, 'was a noted inn on the London road.' The necessity to halt at Cashmoor probably helped the inn to compete successfully with the Thickthorn Inn a mile to the westward. Both inns were in existence in 1791, but the one at Thickthorn did not survive on the first Ordnance Survey map prepared in the early 1800s.

When the turnpike system was abolished, and main roads passed into the care of county councils in 1888, the noted inn at Cashmoor went into decline. A writer referred to it in 1899 with some disrespect as 'a wayside public'. The windmill that had been Cashmoor's other feature also declined and eventually disappeared. Today Cashmoor can boast of a pub and a guesthouse—both to be recommended—and a bus stop.

An even more noted inn on the eighteenth-century turnpike was the one at Woodyates, where the Chase landowners held their meetings on the disfranchisement issue. It was at Woodyates Inn that George III liked to break his journeys between London and Weymouth. The king's personal room, with its flight of outside steps, was said to be there still in 1899 when the inn bore its later name, The Shaftesbury Arms. In 1919, when Thomas Hardy looked at it in passing, it still retained its genial hostelry appearance although, he wrote, 'now no longer such, to the surprise of everybody since the revival of road traffic'—a comment that emphasizes how completely the railway had come to dominate Victorian and Edwardian travel, to the detriment of roadside inns.

Hardy also noted the connection between Woodyates Inn and the family of the poet Robert Browning. There is a Browning family grave in nearby Pentridge churchyard and some of the poet's ancestors were connected with the inn. In 1902 a commemorative plaque was erected in the church by some of Browning's admirers who wished to record his family connection with the district. Another but more obscure link between church and inn is preserved in Pentridge church bells. Of the four new ones provided in Victorian times three were given by William Day, churchwarden: the same William Day who took over the Wood-yates Inn when the coaches stopped running, defeated by the railway, and the inn lost its usefulness. Kings and important personages no longer stopped at its door. Instead it adopted a new style of life under the guid-ance of William Day.

It was in 1849 that Day arrived at Woodyates to train his horses on the downland gallops leased to him by Lord Shaftesbury. The inn had been taken on by Tom John Hayter in the previous year when it was still a posting house depending on the support of the stage coaches and its own four available pairs of post horses. All the parcels and packets to and from Lord Shaftesbury at St Giles House and the neighbourhood generally had to pass through the inn which functioned as the local post office when the mail coaches called. No longer patronized by royalty the Woodyates Inn now catered mainly for commercial travellers.

Hayter was prepared to let the house and stables to Day. The railway had killed the inn's trade and in Day's words 'it became like a private house'. Day had been born to the turf: his father trained at Danebury for such eminent owners as Palmerston and Lord George Bentinck. At

Woodyates he did well, reputedly winning the best part of a quarter of a million pounds in stake money for his owners. He also engaged in breeding and farming. In his reminiscences he spoke of 'my yearling sales at Alvediston and my sheep sales at Woodyates'. At Alvediston he occupied Samways Farm, once the home of Thomas King; Day's monogram with the date 1861 can still be seen on the grandiose clock tower which rises high above the stables. It is an unusual local landmark. Seen from the top of Whitesheet Hill it looks like an eccentric church steeple. Day is reputed to have built it with the proceeds of a betting coup on the Cesarewitch. He had a brass effigy of the winning horse incorporated in the weather vane, but it was too heavy to operate and has been removed.

In his heyday he must have been a considerable figure in the life of the Chase. He was on friendly terms with the sixth and last Baron Rivers, whose horses he trained and who often invited him to shoot partridges at Rushmore. Day's pen-portraits of local landowners are done with vivacity and humour. He was evidently prone to the ups and downs of fortune that afflict racing men and he found a useful financial supplement in authorship, publishing two books on practical aspects of training and two of reminiscences.

To the later history of the Great Western Turnpike there is little to add. That 'revival of road traffic' which Hardy noted in 1919 has not called the Woodyates Inn back to life but there are some agreeable stopping places for the hungry or thirsty traveller along the way—and still, as Massingham suggested, much to see. It is to the credit of its original creators that the road has been adapted so easily to modern conditions. Very different has been the fate of that other route to the north which used the high ground skirting the Ebble valley to link Salisbury with Shaftesbury and the route to Exeter. What was once a major coach route is now a deserted grassy track, like its venerable companion on the other side of the valley—the Ox Drove.

The two key points in the Chase's northern lines of communication are Win Green and Whitesheet Hill. The general configuration of the Chase is of a plateau rising steadily from south to north to reach its greatest height in a downland scarp, beyond which lies the river Nadder —the Chase's northern limit. That northern scarp is deeply furrowed by the valley of the Ebble, which scores its way therefore between two steep ridges. At their eastern end these two ridges converge in the southern outskirts of Salisbury. To the west the northern ridge culminates in Whitesheet Hill, the southern one in Win Green. It is along these ridges that we can imagine the earliest travellers passing.

Win Green is the highest point in the Chase, with spectacular views on all sides. Here the Roman road from Badbury Rings comes up through Ashmore and passes beside Win Green as it plunges down the scarp to Ludwell. To the west the Zigzag Hill winds down to Shaftesbury, while eastwards the Ox Drove leads along the ridge past Winkelbury Hill. The most open vista is to the north, looking down from the scarp into the furrow which will become, lower down, the Ebble valley. Immediately below Win Green is Ferne House, once the seat of the Grove family. Beyond Ferne and buttressing the opposite ridge rises Whitesheet Hill. It is these two promontories, Win Green and Whitesheet, that stand out as landmarks in the development of travellers' routes along the northern scarp.

The Ox Drove is clearly defined from Win Green to about the point, above Knighton Wood, where the Roman Ackling Dyke would have intersected it. As a prehistoric ridgeway its further extensions at either end are conjectural. Perhaps it continued eastwards past the ford at Stratford Tony to Salisbury along the line the Romans later adopted. Today, with a very slight realignment, the route persists as a green lane between Croucheston Down and Faulston Down to join the A354 near Toyd Clump. As for a westward extension beyond Win Green—it would have had to surmount the obstacle of the Stour, and possibly the Iwerne as well. Good suggests that, from Win Green, it kept to the high ground until it turned south along what was later to be the royal road from Shaftesbury to Blandford, crossing Fontmell Down and Everly Hill to pass along Smugglers Lane and over the Iwerne to Hod Hill. An alternative route would take the later stage to the south of Durweston, below the point where the Iwerne joins the Stour.

This is speculation. What is certain is that for about a dozen miles the Ox Drove is clear, unmistakable and inviting. From Win Green the track follows the scarp above Higher Berry Court Farm to Monk's Down—a summertime haunt of hang gliders. Here the land falls away steeply until, at its eastern end, the down runs into the great headland of Winkelbury Hill which juts out like a cliff overhanging the village of Berwick St John. The Iron Age fort on the hill was excavated by General Pitt-Rivers. It is a naturally strong defensive position, with steep slopes on three sides; on the fourth side additional ramparts separate the promontory from the land mass.

Up to this point the course of the Ox Drove along Monk's Down has a modern road surface. At Winkelbury the Drove parts company with the road, one section of which winds down to Berwick St John while the other twists south to lose itself in the grounds of Rushmore. The Ox

Drove becomes a green lane as it pursues its lonely way eastward, meeting no sign of habitation until it reaches Trow Down and a derelict farmhouse with a barn still in use. The track here is broad and firm enough to carry vehicles without difficulty. The farmhouse itself has the appearance of a reasonable prosperity within living memory. There is a good deal of dressed stone in its fabric, with stone mullioned windows. Its stables and outhouses were of brick and flint in traditional style, but with brick arched doorways. Beside it a lane runs down past Manwood Copse towards Handley.

Bigley Buildings, as this farmhouse is known, is the only house along this stretch of the Ox Drove. The usual practice is to have a barn or hut near the summit of these downland ridges, with the farmhouse on the lower slopes or in the valley. Bigley had house and barn separated by only a short distance, and both adjoining the drove. The height here is 758 feet, with a commanding view of the Ebble valley and the downs rising beyond Alvediston. Flanking the Ox Drove are hedges and grassy verges bright in summer with meadow cranesbill and harebells and scabious. To the south the wide green canopy of the woodlands is a noble sight. The general atmosphere here is one of stillness. Apart from a desultory stirring of the wind there is little movement: the disturbance of a yellow-hammer or a whitethroat from its perch becomes an event.

About a mile onward from Bigley Barn the drove again acquires a modern road surface for a short stretch over Woodminton Down, at either end of which it opens into a road down into the Ebble valley—one to Ebbesborne Wake, the other to Bowerchalk. The latter comes up from Sixpenny Handley to form a crossroads with the drove, passing through a fine avenue of beeches on its northward route. Although it is not on the majestic scale of the beech avenue by Badbury Rings it is a beautiful addition to the landscape. In May any traveller along the Ox Drove will want to stop and admire what Hardy called 'the large limp young leaves of the softness of butterflies' wings'. The delicacy of the young greenery in this beech avenue can be quite breathtaking.

The modern road surface stops at this crossroads and the green lane resumes across Marleycombe Hill and Knowle Hill, passing the sites of two of the Chase's vanished lodges. The first Ordnance Survey map shows Cobley Lodge and Vernditch Lodge as being in existence in the early nineteenth century at locations that can be identified. Cobley Lodge is shown in the vicinity of Cutler's Corner, where the road from East Chase Farm angles at Chettle Head Copse. Vernditch Lodge is shown in the vicinity of what is now Old Lodge Copse, where Grim's Ditch meets the Roman road. On the Ox Drove itself in this area today's map shows

Lodge Farm and 'The Hut' which suggests that here was the only other settlement established, like Bigley, on the verge of the Ox Drove. The Hut is no longer there, however. It has been replaced by the modern building of Hut Farm.

Lodge farmhouse suggests a Victorian rather than a Georgian pedigree but it recalls nevertheless the setting of the keeper's cottage that Chafin described, with its prospect of Chickengrove Bottom. Here, Chafin tells us, the keeper recounted his occasional visits to the parish church and in particular one Sunday when, as he recalled:

> He heard the parson in his sermon talk about a place he called Paradise, which he could not help listening to; 'for', he said, 'by the account he gave of it, it seemed to be a desperate pleasant place; and I thought of it when I got home; but, when I had considered everything, I made up my mind to believe, and I do now believe, not withstanding what the parson said, that if there was but a good trout-stream running down Chicken Grove bottom, Fernditch Lodge would beat it out and out'.

Buildings come and go, or are modified out of recognition, but at least it is certain that along this stretch of the Ox Drove one can share the old keeper's pleasure in 'a desperate pleasant place'. Sometimes tall hedge and woodland embower the drove in a green peace; and then, at intervals, the leafy enclosure opens on to great sweeping vistas of downland. It is one of those remaining places where quietness gathers subtly like mist over the autumn stubbles and it is still possible to be alone with Nature and undisturbed. Often nothing remarkable happens. Flocks of finches gather after harvest along the drove, using its cover as a base for their gleaning sorties on to the arable: their sudden excited dashes emphasize the general stillness. Once in a way there is a rare sight to reward the lone walker—a hen-harrier coming in over Knighton Hill, quartering the ground with that typically confident unstressed flight which eases the bird forward with a few unhurried strokes of the wings, then glides for a similar distance and again punts on with three or four wing-beats.

Look to the north now, across the Ebble valley, and there along the crest of the further scarp is the Ox Drove's companion ridgeway—the Salisbury Way extending eastwards from Whitesheet Hill to Wilton hare warren and Salisbury racecourse. It is a route that must have been used from time immemorial because of its natural advantages. It is high and dry, with no rivers to be crossed, and it follows a line parallel to the two river valleys it looks down on, the Ebble and the Nadder. Its only real drawback as a trunk route is that it terminates at either end in a steep hill.

For a rider on horseback the inclines were unwelcome but endurable; for a coach and horses they must have been a dreaded obstacle. Nevertheless the coaches toiled up and down Whitesheet and Harnham and made the best of a bad job.

The staging point for Whitesheet Hill was the Glove Inn. Here, at the foot of the hill, passengers gathered to await the London coach. The inn survived until about 1880 but its prosperity must have been linked to the coach trade and it had no future in the railway age. It subsequently became Arundell Farm: the present owner has fortunately preserved a crudely painted board showing the Glove emblem above crossed clay pipes.

At the summit of Whitesheet Hill there is a milestone dated 1796. It indicates distances of ninety-seven miles from London's Hyde Park Corner and fourteen miles from Salisbury. It must have superseded an earlier stone which had been erected about 1700 by the Earl of Pembroke, who set up stones at one-mile intervals from the Wilton hare warren to Whitesheet Hill. William Stukeley, writing in the 1720s of Lord Pembroke's enlightened action, commented, 'A traveller is highly indebted to your lordship for adding to his pleasure and advantage, in reviving the Roman method of placing a numbered stone at every mile, and the living index of a tree to make it more observable'. The trees were limes and are shown as 'M. Tree' on a map of 1773, with M. Tree 7 near Compton Hut and number 8—the last one shown—at Chiselbury Camp.

Once the traveller has come—by whatever means—to the top of Whitesheet Hill he can look forward to the cheering expanse of what Stukeley described as 'a fine ridge of downs, continued upon the southern bank of the river Nadder, with a sweet prospect to the right and left all the way'. Landmarks are few. A minor road climbs up from Alvediston and crosses the track to plunge headlong down to Ansty in a precipitous hairpin bend. Fovant Hut, once a stopping place for the coach, is updated and inhabited; Compton Hut has disappeared, and so have the sheep ponds that were to be found along the way. The most striking feature is Chiselbury, an Iron Age camp, jutting out above Fovant village. Here the steep slope of the escarpment displays the well-known regimental badges which were cut in the chalk during the 1914–18 war and have since been preserved as a modern equivalent of the white horses of earlier warriors.

As a green lane the Salisbury Way now terminates where the road from Netherhampton comes up beside the hare warren and turns towards the grandstand of Salisbury racecourse. The association with horse racing is a long established one. As far back as the sixteenth century the second Earl of Pembroke instituted a horse race along the length of the Salisbury Way from Whitesheet Hill to Harnham. This was about fourteen miles and was not run every year. Lord Pembroke also provided a second race, over a shorter course of about four miles, from North Down Farm at Broad Chalke to the hare warren. His lordship's prize was a silver bell, replaced in 1630 by a gold cup. As a race it must have been something like the point-to-point races that the various hunts organize at the present time each spring at Badbury Rings—a popular social occasion locally.

It was in 1859 that the railway began to extend westwards from Salisbury, through Tisbury and Semley to Yeovil which it reached in the following year. This put an end to the coach route, whether along the Salisbury Way or by the more comfortable lower road which succeeded it, the modern A30 via Barford St Martin. The railway stayed close to the course of the river Nadder and scarcely entered the Chase. Similarly the railway development in the south, the Southampton–Dorchester line which began to operate in 1847, did not cross the Chase boundary. Its course ran through Ringwood and West Moors to Wimborne. The only line to operate within the Chase was the connection linking West Moors to Salisbury. Planning for this began in 1861 and the first train ran just before Christmas, 1866. It is the route described by Thomas Hardy in *Two on a Tower* as 'crossing a country of ragged woodland, which, though intruded on by the plough at places, remained largely intact from prehistoric times, and still abounded with yews of gigantic growth and oaks tufted with mistletoe'. This is a somewhat romanticized picture as the line kept to the south-east of the chalk downs and passed over the heathy podsol country of barren undistinguished character through Verwood and Alderholt—a landscape far removed from the Chase woodlands.

The coming of the railway revolutionized the life of the Chase in many ways but it was not a physical presence as the horsedrawn coach had been. It brought paradoxically a deeper stillness to the heartland of the Chase as the tollgates were abandoned and the coaching inns closed their doors. The local grandees with business to attend to in the great cities made their private way to the railway station at Tisbury or Verwood, and the farmers delivered their milk to the new depot set up at Semley station in 1871, the first designed to serve the London market. The bustle and excitement died down along the Great Western Turnpike. Grass softened and covered the wheel ruts on the Salisbury Way. Once inside the borders of the Chase and its surrounding railways you would expect to meet only a scatter of local travellers.

There was once a plan to bring a railway line into the heart of the Chase but it did not materialize. Named the Chalk Valley Railway it was fully described in a handwritten prospectus addressed in 1875 to the Rev.

Tupper Carey of Ebbesborne Wake. The proposal was for a horse tramway or light railway starting from Salisbury to Bemerton and Coombe Bissett, and thence along the valley of the Ebble to terminate at Berwick St John. In addition to the Chalke villages it would, in the opinion of its author, Arthur Pain, serve ten other parishes 'having altogether an area of one hundred square miles and containing eight thousand inhabitants'. The length of the line was to be fifteen miles and the gauge 4 feet 8½ inches, to match the Great Western and South Western Railways with which it would co-operate. The tramway was estimated to cost £1,500 per mile exclusive of land purchase. For goods traffic a light engine could be used, at a speed of about six miles an hour. Where passengers were involved the safety requirements of the Board of Trade demanded that they should be horse-drawn. However, a speed of twenty-five miles per hour would be possible under the alternative plan for a proper light railway using engines up to a weight of twenty-four tons. This would cost at that time £3,500 per mile exclusive of land. To show what could be achieved Mr Pain mentioned the imminent completion of the Culm Valley Railway in Devon for £4,000 per mile—a figure which included land, stations, works and all Parliamentary and other expenses. He added one or two other instances of a hopeful nature to suggest that everyone was doing it; and he volunteered 'to devote a week with you a little later on, to work up the landowners in the district and put the matter in shape'.

It is a matter of history that the landowners were not 'worked up'— and in the 1960s Dr Beeching had fifteen miles less of track to remove.

CHAPTER NINE

The Rivers

IT IS SOMETIMES said that Cranborne Chase has no rivers or streams, and this is true in a limited sense today. No water flows within the Inner Bounds—roughly the central area between the Salisbury–Blandford Road and the southern crest of the Ebble valley. Yet paradoxically the wider definition of Cranborne Chase is largely written in water. Edward I's authoritative warrant rings the Chase with rivers: the Sem and the Nadder in the north, the Avon in the east, the Stour to westward, and along the southern boundary the Stour again with its tributary the Allen. To some extent they lie outside the scope of this survey of the Chase, except as its boundaries. Stour and Avon require a larger perspective, and Nadder is a peripheral interest; even so their influence cannot be ignored, and at least two rivers—the Allen and the Tarrant—belong very fully to the story of the Chase and provide some of its most characteristic and pleasant scenes.

Stour and Avon meet at Christchurch and mingle their waters in the wide lagoon of its harbour. As a schoolboy Richard Warner used to watch the two rivers passing on either side of St Catherine's Hill as they converged; and he later put his observations into a poem:

> See, where fair *Avon* leads her waters clear
> By Catherine's heathy side; and onward speeds
> To meet her *Stour*, a venerable seer,
> Rolling his tide through Dorset's flowery meads:
>
> In vain the married streams their floods unite:
> Old *Stour* still keeps his dark discolour'd face;
> Whilst lucid *Avon* in meanders bright,
> Reflects the spiry reed and nodding grass.

Not the greatest of verse perhaps but it captures the essential difference between the two rivers—lucid Avon, a clear stream from the chalk downs, contrasting with dark discolour'd Stour, turbid with the heavy soils of Blackmoor Vale. Warner also mentions that, in the 1770s, he once saw ninety-five salmon caught in a single draught at a point called Clay

Pool. Salmon-fishing is still a feature of Christchurch, and the rich clear water of the Avon has a long history as an angler's delight, but the river's significance for Cranborne Chase is of a different kind. It was a possible highway to the sea for waterborne trade. In prehistoric times invaders and traders had made their landfall at Hengistbury Head; to them the course of the Avon must have presented itself as a convenient route inland. And so it seemed again, at a much later date, to a remarkable character who followed an unusual combination of trades as Thames wherryman and poet. This was John Taylor whose doggerel verses in the early seventeenth century earned for him a kind of fame as 'the Water Poet'. Two of his cronies, Gregory Bastable and Thomas Estman, were Wiltshiremen; and one of them—Estman—had a brother who was the landlord of the King's Head at Salisbury. Between them they concocted a scheme to sail a wherry in the summer of 1623 from London down the Channel to Christchurch and then up the Avon to Salisbury, as a demonstration of what might be done to develop Salisbury as an inland port.

To complete their party they added a fourth waterman, Arthur Bray of Lambeth. Described as the crew's master gunner, he fired his fowling piece at gulls as the wherry cruised down to Yarmouth on the Isle of Wight and then across to Hurst Castle and Keyhaven on the mainland before dropping anchor at Christchurch. The more serious aim of this boisterous adventure was to explore, in Taylor's words, 'the sands, flats, depths, shoals, Mills and Weares, which are impediments and lets, whereby the River is not navigable from Christchurch or the Sea to Salisbury'; and in so doing to demonstrate that the Avon could be made as passable as the Thames then was 'upwards from Brentford to Windsor or beyond it'.

Taylor's account of the voyage up the Avon has some graphic incidents. Starting their passage through Christchurch harbour they had 'at the least 2,000 Swans, like so many pilots' leading them out of the shallows into the deep channel. At Ringwood some of the King's Trumpeters walked along the river bank as the wherry passed and saluted it with two excellent flourishes on their trumpets. At Fordingbridge the party stopped for a somewhat macabre gossip about a mastiff which had recently killed two men. At Hale they were welcomed by Sir Thomas Penruddock who boarded the wherry and travelled some distance in it.

And so Taylor's wherry entered Salisbury, passing under Fisherton Bridge and tying up at some point convenient for their lodgings with Estman's brother at the sign of the King's Head. All this is narrated humorously in Taylor's typical rough-and-tumble couplets, but for the earnest consideration of Salisbury's maritime future he forsakes his rhyming doggerel:

> Some serious matter now I must compile,
> And thus from verse to prose I change my stile.

Addressing the inhabitants of Salisbury he reminds them that no English town or city which has a navigable river is poor, while scarcely any which lack that advantage are prosperous. And he offers them a telling comparison drawn from their own local knowledge, saying 'You men of Sarum may see what a commodity Navigation is, neerer hand; there is your neighbour Southampton on the one side, and your deere friend Poole on the other, are a pair of hansome looking-Glasses for you, where you may see your want in their abundance'. He then went on to make a promise that—if the Avon were cleared of its impediments to navigation —he would be 'one of the three or four men, which shall bring or carry 16 or 20 Tuns of goods betwixt the Sea and your City'.

The advantages he offered were real and worthy of consideration. They emphasize particularly the problems of acquiring and transporting supplies of fuel, and the consequent effect on, not only the city of Salisbury, but the neighbouring woodlands also. Here is how Taylor developed his argument:

> Now, with extreme toyle of Men, Horses and Carts, your wood is brought to you 18 or 20 miles, whereby the poore which cannot reach the high prices of your fewell, are enforced to steale or starve in the winter, so that all your neere adjoyning woods are continually spoyled by them: which faults by the benefit of the River would be reformed: for the New Forest standeth so neere to the water, that it is but cut the wood and put it into a Boate, which shall bring as much to your City as twenty Carts and fourscore Horses: besides, by this River you might draw to you a trade of Sea-Coale, which would enrich you, and helpe the plaine and inland Townes and Villages where no wood growes.

It is interesting to compare this with the deposition made by Richard Harding in 1618 in Lord Salisbury's Exchequer action five years before Taylor's voyage: 'The country about Cranborne Chase depends chiefly on the coppice woods there for fire-bote, hedge-bote, wattling, hurdling, spikes for thatching; and that the coppice woods are much wasted and spoiled.'

The scarcity of firewood and fuel generally was an increasing problem in the seventeenth century. Supplies of local peat would be in danger of exhaustion. Coal was as yet a luxury. Even 200 years later Cobbett could describe poor families in Salisbury pooling their resources to light a fire by turns in one cottage among four so that all four could boil a kettle on it. In some parishes land was charitably set aside for the express purpose of growing furze to be given as fuel to the poor. Pimperne was one such, twenty acres of land there being assigned in trust for ever for the poor of the parish.

The case Taylor was presenting was sound enough therefore, although he failed to win sufficient immediate support to realize his personal wish to trade up and down the Avon. No positive step was taken until after the Civil War and the Restoration. In 1664 the River Avon Navigation Act was passed and there was powerful financial backing for the scheme. Henry, Earl of Clarendon, subscribed £500. 'Diamond' Pitt was another prominent backer. In 1674 Clarendon instructed a canal expert, Yarranton, to survey the river. Yarranton recommended the construction of a harbour at Hengistbury Head, protected by a fort: he also proposed the building of naval frigates there. In 1675 work began in earnest. A pier and a wharf were built at Hengistbury; and at Salisbury the bishop cut a first ceremonial sod. Navigation in the river was improved by locks and artificial bypass channels. In 1684 two 25-ton barges came up from Christchurch to Salisbury's Harnham Bridge—a triumphant achievement which seemed to justify the issue in 1687 of a code of Tolls and Regulations.

However, these moments of success were short-lived. In the early 1690s severe flooding damaged some of the navigation works and blocked the channels. The difficulty of maintaining an adequate depth of water was evidently going to be costly and there was opposition from such powerful elements as the watermill owners and the farmers who wanted to draw off water into their water-meadows. About this time Celia Fiennes noted that the Avon 'turns many great mills and there have been great attempts to make it navigable which would be of great advantage but all charge has been lost in it'.

For a time Taylor's hopes must have been realized in one respect because John Aubrey spoke of boats carrying wood and corn from the New Forest and judged that it would have been more costly by horse and cart, but the end was in sight when Defoe visited Salisbury in 1722. Navigation stopped two miles short of the city, he wrote, because of 'the strength of the stream'. The high cost of keeping the Avon open to commercial shipping was not justified by results. The corporation of Salisbury could still display a lingering interest in 1729 but the last spark of the enterprise was quenched during the 1730s.

The prospect that Cranborne Chase might have had a great artery of waterborne trade forming its eastern flank seems very remote now. Had it prospered it might have carried the claypots of Alderholt and the watercress of the Allen valley to more distant markets. The Stour, by contrast, offers no such speculations: its winding silt-laden course suggests no thought of navigation in modern terms. It is in the world of prehistory that its era of strategic and commercial importance must be found, in the fortified heights that loom protectively above its valley. Hod Hill and Hambledon, Spetisbury and Buzbury—even Badbury Rings though it stands a mile or two from the river bank—these testify to the value the Stour had for Celt and Roman, as a frontier perhaps or a trade route. In terms of Cranborne Chase it is the stretch of the river from Manston to Wimborne which acts as a boundary to the Outer Chase. North of Manston the boundary follows a tributary of the Stour—the Manston Brook and its feeder stream known as Stirchel, which rises near Shaftesbury. South of Wimborne the Chase boundary again leaves the main course of the Stour to follow another of its tributaries, the Allen.

Above and below Manston the Stour lies in a heavy waterladen countryside where flooding is still today a frequent event. When Thomas Hardy lived beside the Stour at Sturminster Newton he jotted down a short description of the river in flood in November 1877: 'Lumps of froth float down like swans in front of our house. At the arches of the large stone bridge the froth has accumulated and lies like hillocks of salt against the bridge; then the arch chokes, and after a silence coughs out the air and froth, and gurgles on.'

In earlier centuries the sullen floodwaters of the Stour could be more menacing. At Shapwick a husbandman buried in 1708 had been 'drowned in the flood'. Four years earlier two drownings of men in the Stour were recorded. Carrying a greater volume of water then than now the Stour could be a frightening spectacle at such times. Peter Beckford wrote a graphic account of a particularly harrowing occasion in the latter half of the eighteenth century:

> The river Stower frequently overflows its banks, and is also very rapid, and very dangerous. The flood, that morning, though sudden, was extensive. The neighbouring meadows were all laid under water, and only the tops of hedges appeared. There were posts to direct us to the bridge, but we had a great length of water to pass before we could get at it; it was, besides, so deep, that our horses almost swam; and the

shortest legged horses, and longest legged riders, were worst off.—The hounds dashed in as usual; and were immediately carried, by the rapidity of the current, a long way down the stream. The hunstman was far behind them; and as he could go but slow, he was constrained to see his hounds wear themselves out in a useless contention with the current, in endeavouring to get to him. It was a shocking scene; many of the hounds, when they reached the shore, had entirely lost the use of their limbs; for it froze, and the cold was intolerable. Some lay as if they were dead, and others reeled, as if they had been drinking wine. Our distress was not yet complete; the weakest hounds, or such as were most affected by the cold, we now saw entangled in the tops of the hedges, and heard their lamentations. Well-known tongues! and such as I had never before heard without pleasure. It was shocking to see their distress, and not know how to relieve them. A number of people, by this time, were assembled by the river side, but there was not one amongst them that would venture in. However, a guinea, at last, tempted one man to fetch out a hound that was entangled in a bush, and would otherwise have perished. Two hounds remained upon a hedge all night, yet they got together before the morning; when, the flood abating, they were found closely clasping each other, and without doubt, it was the little heat they could afford each other, that kept both alive. We lost but one hound by this unlucky expedition, but we lost all our terriers. They were seen to sink, their strength not being sufficient to resist the two enemies they had to encounter, powerful, when combined,—the severity of the cold, and the rapidity of the stream.

In its gentler moods the Stour can offer several pleasant stretches along the borders of the Chase. Two in particular claim attention, the first being the dramatic sweep that brings the river below Shillingstone to hug the foot of Hod Hill. The western flank of the hill is well wooded and falls steeply to the riverbank. A footpath runs beside the river. In April the coppiced hazel rises from a colourful ground in which celandine, violet, ramsons and bluebells predominate. If anything larger than a bird moves it is likely to be a deer.

The other most inviting stretch of the Stour is below Blandford in the soft green countryside where the river's course is marked by two very fine bridges. The first is Crawford Bridge, a mediaeval span of nine arches, with four massive cutwaters providing a refuge for pedestrians. References to a bridge at this point, linking Tarrant Crawford and Spetisbury, date back to 1235 when Tarrant Abbey was a place of importance. The bridge later fell into a ruinous condition and in 1506 it was repaired or reconstructed. Today it would not be unreasonable to describe it as the handsomest bridge in Dorset but such a claim would be disputed by those who champion its neighbour downstream, White Mill Bridge at Sturminster Marshall. This too is a mediaeval bridge of eight arches, powerfully built in the same reddish stone and heavy style as the Minster at nearby Wimborne. The Stour is wide and shallow here, encircling an island big enough to support a breeding pair of mute swans. The bridge itself is 225 feet long and 12 feet wide. Its long history includes a reference in a will of 1341 to money bequeathed for its repairs.

Between these two bridges lies the village of Shapwick, which has no bridge of its own although it stands at what must have been a crossing-place over the river for the Roman road from Badbury Rings. Shapwick church is set apart close beside the Stour, its grassy churchyard bordering the river. To pause among the headstones in that leafy stillness and watch the steady flow of the Stour is as good a way as any to appreciate the atmosphere of its kinder moods.

At Wimborne the Stour and the Chase part company: one of the Stour's tributaries takes over as the boundary marker. This is the Allen which inspired Michael Drayton to one of his happier flights of fancy in 'Polyolbion' where he described the meanderings and sinuous convolutions of the Stour as it turns and twists past Hambledon and Hod Hill to Blandford and Wimborne. In stately Jacobean couplets he characterized the river as a 'childish wench' who

> looselie wantoning,
> with tricks and giddie turnes seems to in-ile the shore
> Betwixt her fishfull banks, that forward shee doth scour,
> Until shee lastlie reach clear *Allen* in her race,
> Which calmlie commeth down from her dear mother Chace,
> of Cranburn that is call'd;

Today, though Cranborne Chase is certainly not immune to the forces of change, the River Allen can still be justly described as a clear stream, calmly flowing from the almost secret recesses of the Chase to make its unobtrusive entry into Wimborne, where it loses its identity—and its clarity—in the turbid waters of the Stour. Because its course lies away from towns and main roads the Allen is seldom noticed. For most of its length it is out of sight of the Wimborne-to-Cranborne road which lies roughly parallel on its eastern side. The road-bridges that span it—at Brockington and Horton and Witchampton—are on minor routes. Apart from fishermen and an occasional naturalist the Allen attracts few visitors.

An alternative and more appropriate name for the river is 'Winburn'. In the sixteenth century Leland noted that 'Winburn river riseth a three miles by estimation above St Giles Winburne'. A thirteenth-century document refers to the river as 'aquam de Wymborn'; and a glance at today's maps shows that the river is the common element linking together Monkton Upwimborne, Wimborne St Giles and Wimborne Minster.

Its source is in a downland fold, near the point where the Roman road from Badbury Rings to Old Sarum intersects the Neolithic cursus. It is an area uncommonly rich in prehistoric sites. On the northern slope is a long barrow: to the south the Harley Gap leads through the Roman *agger* to the Iron Age settlement on Gussage Hill, and another long barrow. Up here, in the downland solitude, the procession of the centuries easily seizes one's imagination; and the timeless flow of a stream yields an appropriate imagery.

The Allen becomes discernible as a river—or if 'river' be too grand, as a brook—in the vicinity of Monkton Upwimborne. This upper reach is particularly attractive in late spring and early summer, when the redshanks keep up their nervously alert piping and an occasional snipe drums overhead. The cress-beds are a reminder that 'clear Allen' does indeed have the sweetness and purity that traditionally brought the watercress growers to the valleys and surrounding lowlands of the Chase, where the chalk-filtered water springs up.

From the source to Wimborne St Giles the only buildings of any note are farmhouses. One of them, All Hallows Farm, commemorates a church which has long since disappeared, together with its chapel at nearby Monkton. The rise of the earls of Shaftesbury shed a reflected glory on the church beside their great mansion and park at Wimborne St Giles: it too had once been a mere chapel subordinate to All Hallows, but by the middle of the eighteenth century it dominated the upper valley of the Allen and made All Hallows and Monkton both redundant. Today the church of St Giles and its flanking almshouses are a handsome sight: the present church tower dates from 1732, the almshouses from 1624.

Nearby the Allen glides under the road and into the park, where it is connected with the extensive lake which covers seven acres. When Gibbon visited St Giles in 1762 he noted in his journal 'the winding river is beautifull'. Beyond the park's perimeter plantation the Allen straightens its course through soft pastures, with a derelict seventeenth-century farmhouse in the foreground and the ruined tower of Knowlton church appearing above the skyline. Knowlton Circles, close to the Allen's left bank, are another important prehistoric site: it is worth turning aside to see the grassy ramparts of a Neolithic henge encircling the gaunt walls of the deserted Norman church.

A minor road from Knowlton crosses the Allen at Brockington Farm. Here the four arches of the bridge indicate that the higher stream has now attained the style and proportions of a river. And here at Brockington is a trout farm, a recent innovation. Brown trout and rainbow are bred for the table and for restocking the Allen itself and other waters. As feeding time approaches the stewponds suddenly erupt in a turbulence of movement that makes the water appear to boil.

Below Brockington is one of the Allen's most charming stretches, shaded and softened with trees, bushes and reeds, bright on the surface of the river with the flowers of water-crowsfoot, and animated with the calls and movements of reed-buntings and sedge and reed warblers; while beneath the surface appears every now and then the dark thrusting shape of a fish. The trout is pre-eminent here, of course. In 1801 Dibdin described the trout in the Allen as plentiful and also mentioned tench and eel. Hutchins, in his *History of Dorset*, similarly mentions eel; and refers to jack further downstream at Hinton Parva.

Brockington is scarcely left behind before the Allen's main tributary joins it, near Bowerswain. This tributary has been doomed to anonymity by the Ordnance Survey, which is a pity as it might reasonably claim the name of Terrig. Holinshed describes the Terrig as rising south of Woodcutts and running through Farnham. By 1869 it was no more than a winterborne, rising as a spring in winter and dry in summer: however, its course must surely have run past Cashmoor into the valley of the Gussage villages—and there it runs still, until it joins the Allen. This narrow valley terminates beyond Gussage All Saints in a place of tantalizing mystery, known today as Bowerswain Farm but in earlier days as Boroston. Here in 1786 came the antiquarian, Dr Stukely, looking for the site of Vindocladia. From the landlady of The Rose at Gussage All Saints he learnt that Boroston had once been a 'city'; that when she was a girl many old coins had been ploughed up there; and that she believed the place had once had 'seven parish churches which were beaten down in the war time'.

Standing at the junction of Terrig and Allen it is pleasant to speculate on the grain of truth that might be contained within the heady fancies of the landlady of The Rose. But she is departed and so too is The Rose (succeeded by The Earl Haig of a later wartime); and Bowerswain Farm, peaceful and uncommunicative in the sunshine, keeps to itself whatever secrets it may hold. Meanwhile the Allen flows on towards Horton, and more particularly to Stanbridge Mill. The old mill and its sturdy bridge provide a landmark to which a long history attaches. In the thirteenth-century perambulation of the bounds of Cranborne Chase the stone bridge—'pontem Petrae'—marked the point where the Chase boundary joined the Allen and followed the course of the river down to its junction with the Stour at Wimborne. The mill has long been disused but the building is now being renovated. The diversion of the Allen to service the mill channel caused a tendency to flood the adjacent land and this sheet of water has become a welcome staging-post for incoming hirundines and waterfowl. The springtime assembly of swallows and martins is an impressive sight. Coots breed there, and among the more unusual visitors I have noted tufted duck and shoveller.

A few yards away is a staging-post of another sort, the Horton Inn. This is the house that Thomas Hardy described in 'Barbara of the House of Grebe' as 'the solitary wayside tavern called Lornton Inn—the rendezvous of many a daring poacher for operations in the adjoining forest'. The forest in question was Holt Forest, now so sadly contracted that only in the imagination can one recapture the landscape that Drayton described:

Where to her neighbouring Chase the curteous forrest show'd
So just conceived joy, that from each rising hurst,
Where many a goodlie oake had carefullie been nurst,
The sylvans in their songs their mirthfull meetings tell,
And satyrs, that in slades and gloomy dimbles dwell,
Runne Whooting to the hilles to clappe their ruder hands.

Goodly oaks are scarce, but one hill which nourished a remarkable tree was nearby Chalbury. On this steep hill, which overlooks the Allen, grew a very tall elm which was visible from the Isle of Wight until the great storm of 1703 broke off about a third of it. A century later it was described as being still 'a very large tree'. What invites one to climb up Chalbury Hill today is its church, built in the thirteenth and fourteenth centuries, and restored in the eighteenth with box-pews and a three-decker pulpit. It stands in a magnificent position, commanding views on both sides of the hill-top; and to its many endearing features it adds the unique one, in my experience, of having a simple domestic skylight.

Horton offers one other landmark which frequently catches the eye of anyone following the lower reaches of the Allen. This is Horton Tower, built in mid-eighteenth century by Humphrey Sturt as an observatory. It is seven storeys high, with a fireplace halfway up. The building is now a shell and shows some deterioration but the hexagonal top is still intact.

Its presence indicates that at Stanbridge the Allen passes out of the sphere of one great landowning family—the Shaftesburys—into that of another, the Sturts. On both flanks of the river, at Horton and in the Crichel villages, the Sturts lavished their wealth on the improvements that the eighteenth and nineteenth centuries favoured—the construction of large ornamental lakes, and the demolition and rebuilding of churches and rectories. The great lake at Horton covering 280 acres and more than a mile long, well stocked with carp and reputed to yield an annual catch weighing 16,000 pounds, is now dry land; but the comparable lake at Crichel survives and contains a discarded rectory somewhere beneath its placid surface.

The Allen passes very close to the southern end of Crichel Lake but does not join it. Skirting the Crichel woodlands the river throws off some irrigation channels into the watermeadows along its left bank and then enters the paper mills at Witchampton. There is a long history of paper-making on the Allen at Witchampton, associated with the family of Burt. Wallpaper and cartridge paper were prominent among its products, and there was a local saying that 'Burt's brown-paper keeps out the cold'.

Today the paper mill has to adapt itself to modern needs. As part of a large group it now produces paperback covers, packing material and greetings cards, using imported wood pulp.

Witchampton brings the third road bridge over the Allen, and the only 'transportation' one, bearing the familiar warning from George IV's reign that 'any person wilfully INJURING any part of this COUNTY BRIDGE will be guilty of FELONY and upon conviction liable to be TRANSPORTED FOR LIFE'. More pleasant to contemplate is the comfrey which grows in abundance along the river banks in its two customary forms : with creamy-white flowers or with purple. At Witchampton there is also a blue-flowered comfrey, on a roadside bank where its blueness is no match for the more brilliant blue of some adjoining alkanet.

It is a curious fact that the banks of the Allen have retained little human settlement down the centuries: its ancient settlements at Brockington, Knowlton and Didlington are now only names. By contrast the next valley, the Tarrant, has a chain of villages along its course. The Allen today has its scattered farmhouses and an occasional mill, but not much else except Wimborne St Giles—which is a rather special case of seventeenth-century development—and Witchampton. It is therefore worth pausing to explore Witchampton. A Roman villa and what may have been a Roman temple have been uncovered here. The floor designs include a representation of a naked Venus rising from the sea. The Roman road passes close to the village and Badbury Rings is less than three miles away, so a Roman settlement is scarcely surprising. A more unusual find is a Saxon set of whalebone chessmen, of which there are replicas displayed in the church. The original manor house survives only in its ruined thirteenth-century walls. Its successor displays the badges of Maltravers and Arundell, salvaged perhaps from the earlier building: these ancient families owned Witchampton before they gave way to the Napiers and subsequently the Sturts. The population in 1801 was larger than in most of the Chase villages and in 1832 the church was rebuilt, retaining the fifteenth-century tower. It has an unusual dedication, to St Cuthberga who founded Wimborne Minster: and an unusual gargoyle, showing a man playing bagpipes. There are two other churches within a day's march which display a bagpiper—one is at Milton-on-Sea, the other at Hilton below Bulbarrow—which suggests that this may have been the speciality and trademark of a particular mason.

Witchampton has one other notable feature—or rather lack of a feature. There is no pub, no inn, no alehouse: a privation imposing a three-mile journey on the inhabitants and perhaps helping to account for the rather shapeless unfocused character of the village, which lacks a definable centre and tends to be subdued by the adjacent grandeur of Crichel House and the bustle of the Board Mills. Below Witchampton the Allen eases itself into a landscape which becomes increasingly featureless. This is an area of large farms, wide fields and few buildings. Nearer to Wimborne the heavy pastures are gridironed with channels that recall the vanished art of the drowner. The only village on this lower reach is Hinton Parva, also known misleadingly as Stanbridge: here is little more than an idiosyncratic Victorian church, St Kenelm's, which replaces a thirteenth-century one and incorporates a crudely primitive tympanum, probably salvaged from the earlier building.

At Wimborne the Allen flows under Walford Bridge and disappears discreetly in the middle of the town, reappearing just before it joins the Stour at the point where the road from Poole is carried on a bridge over the main river. For much of its length the Allen forms the margin of the Outer Bounds. Its neighbour the Tarrant lies wholly within the Chase, rising in the high ground south of Ashmore and threading a chain of villages on its way to meet the Stour at Tarrant Crawford. Of the two it is the Tarrant which is the more typical chalk downland stream. The Allen's lower course lies along the skirt of the chalk and passes into the clay: the Tarrant runs between downs that lift away gently from the river bottom. Even the steepest part—the Cliff, as it is called, above Tarrant Rawston—is a pleasantly grassy slope, bright with cowslips in season, and moulded in softer style than the more precipitate scarps along the northern limits of the Chase. For the most part the Tarrant winds among pastoral scenes, linking village with village. In its unemphatic way the landscape achieves a harmony with the human settlements of farm, village and church that is deeply satisfying.

Thomas Gerard, writing about 1620, observed that the Tarrant 'in his Course nameth manie little Parishes'. This is no less true today when the roll-call would provide at least eight villages or settlements in the valley bearing the name Tarrant This or Tarrant That. It is a factor which certainly helps to give a unity and an unusually strong identity to the communities which border the waters of Tarrant. Their names proclaim their neighbourliness. From Tarrant Gunville to Tarrant Crawford they unmistakably have one thing in common.

In its upper reaches the river is no more than a winterbourne. It begins to take shape at Stubhampton and streams through Tarrant Gunville, which it can still manage to flood in its more exuberant moments. Here in earlier years it was trained to the special requirements of water-meadows. When the hatches were down and the water was running freely from the higher ground the inhabitants could have a foot or two of flooding to contend with, until somebody raised the hatches and drew off the excess. Nowadays the art of 'drowning' to win an early bite for the cattle has been superseded, and the extraction of water supplies for the towns has lowered the levels of these chalkland streams. The Tarrant has to find its way under the Blandford–Salisbury road and come in sight of Tarrant Monkton before it can claim for itself the dignity of a river.

Where the casual explorer of the valley is first likely to become aware of the Tarrant's presence is at the point where it leaves Tarrant Launceston behind and comes to the outskirts of Tarrant Monkton. Here the stream broadens to provide a ford, and its past importance as a crossing place is emphasized by a packhorse bridge on what was the main London–Weymouth road until the Great Western Turnpike superseded it. Whatever importance Tarrant Monkton had enjoyed as a stopping-place on the road to the capital passed then to Tarrant Hinton, with its toll-house and its roadside inn.

These apart Tarrant Hinton has little to attract attention beyond a fourteenth-century church with handsome arches, unplastered flint walls, and a notable Easter sepulchre of the early sixteenth century. Its neighbour upstream, Tarrant Gunville, is a different matter, for here is one of the Chase's most remarkable sights—or at least what remains of it. Dominating the village is Eastbury House, the eighteenth-century home of Bubb Dodington, the first Baron Melcombe, designed by Sir John Vanbrugh on a scale to rival Castle Howard and Blenheim Palace. His client was an

East Indian nabob and Paymaster to the Navy, George Dodington, who had the misfortune to die when the building work had scarcely commenced. Dodington's nephew, George Bubb, was a rising young politician who, in 1714, became MP for Winchelsea and went to Spain in the following year as Britain's Envoy Extraordinary. When uncle Dodington died in 1720 Bubb adopted his name and inherited a fortune with which to carry on the work at Eastbury and live there in suitable style.

It cost him £140,000 to complete the house. Even in an age of sumptuous and extravagant building Eastbury was spectacular. The frontage of the house was not far short of 600 feet. The grounds were laid out by the man who designed Kensington Gardens: there were canals 'supplied by engines worked by horses', and at the end of the gardens, facing the house, was a Vanbrugh portico which was considered the finest in England. Within the house the principal apartments were hung with velvet and satin. Instead of pictures, large pieces of gilt leather in the shape of a bugle-horn decorated some of the walls. A bugle-horn was Dodington's crest.

It might be standing now as a stately home, with turnstiles clicking as the coaches roll in; but something went wrong. The only bugle-horn to be seen in Gunville today is on the sign of the village pub. The vast mansion that counted Voltaire and Fielding among its guests needed a correspondingly vast fortune to maintain it. When Dodington died in 1762 Eastbury House passed to his Grenville relations and they found it such an embarrassing acquisition that they decided to get rid of it. The first plan was to pay £200 a year to anyone who would take it on. When this failed Earl Temple decided to demolish it. In 1782 John Byng, travelling westwards from London, stopped to look at Eastbury and noted in his diary that the building was then being destroyed.

Today one wing of Vanbrugh's grandiose design is all that remains. According to the present owner Dodington must have lived in 'one of the coldest and dampest houses in England: the walls used to run with condensation'. Mostly it was Chilmark stone that supplied the walls, with some Portland stone introduced into the arches as better able to carry weight without crumbling. It needed gunpowder to dislodge the solid walls when the work of demolition was undertaken. One of the last visitors to see Eastbury intact was Sir Joseph Banks whose aunt, Mrs Grenville, was living there in 1767 when he 'traveld post' from London to stay with her. He would have seen the octagon room with its ceiling designed by Sir James Thornhill; the grand arcade with its flight of steps eleven feet high leading into the entrance hall; and the eight miles of ring

fence which enclosed the estate. The best of the furniture had probably
been sold but Banks commented, 'The inside is fitted up magnificently
with a great deal of gilding and Ceilings painted after the antique. Upon
the whole the inside is much more convenient as well as more elegant
than the outside gives any hopes of.'

Before the Farquharsons acquired the surviving wing of Eastbury in
1807 it was occupied for a time by Josiah Wedgwood's widow. Her third
son, Thomas, who died there in 1805, is remembered as Coleridge's
benefactor and as a pioneer of photography. He was able to make a
photograph but could not prevent it from fading. The fixing properties
of hypo-sulphite of soda were not discovered until later. He is commemorated by a tablet in Gunville church. Also in the church, built into
an outer wall, is a cryptic memorial stone which reads 'Here lieth S.T.D.
Parson. All four be but one: Earth, Flesh, Worm and Bone.' The initials
stand for Sir Thomas Daccomb, a sixteenth-century rector of Gunville.

Inevitably it is the richness of its past that gives a lustre to Tarrant
Gunville, but Tarrant Rushton probably enjoys a wider fame today than
it has known in any previous century. Its airfield was taken over after
the war by one of the greatest of aviation's pioneers, Sir Alan Cobham, to
develop the technique of refuelling during flight—a technique that increasingly preoccupied him and which survives him as a local industry,
while he lies nearby in Rushton church. It is a church that contains one
detail recalling an earlier and nameless pioneer in a different field, acous-
tics. To improve the sound quality, one of our more inventive ancestors
hit on the idea of putting a couple of large earthenware jars on their sides.
By so doing he augmented, one must hope, not only the resonance of the
singing but the impact of the sermon also.

The Tarrant churches merit a chapter to themselves, but if one is to be
singled out for its unusual character it is Tarrant Rawston. Probably
dating from the fourteenth century, this modest little building is mentioned in a document of 1524, was added to in the early eighteenth
century and completely repaired at the end of the century. Its ecclesiastical
functions have long since ceased: the population of Rawston—down to
forty-four in 1901—can now hardly reach double figures. It might have
suffered the same fate as Tarrant Launceston, which lost its church two
centuries ago when someone stole the bells and the building was knocked
down. Rawston, however, has been fortunate in its neighbourly relationship with the manor house. The two buildings stand close together, and
it was the occupants of the house who cared for the little church throughout the eighteenth century. In its modern redundancy it could be nothing
but a burden on the diocese, but in 1973 the present occupants of the

farmhouse bought the deserted church and restored it with a pleasing freshness and simplicity as a private chapel.

Past Rawston and Rushton the Tarrant grows into a useful little trout stream, yielding fish of a pound or more. Occasionally a pike comes upstream from the Stour with unwelcome results for the trout fisherman. Otherwise there is nothing more conspicuous than stone loach and fresh-water shrimps moving in the water. What catches the eye in spring is the profusion of water crowsfoot, its white flowers with butter-golden centres making a carpet of colour on the glistening water as the Tarrant gathers momentum in the last couple of miles.

At Tarrant Keynston the river is crossed by the other major turnpike road that traverses the valley—that wonderful road which runs from Wimborne to Blandford through the seemingly endless avenue of beeches past Badbury Rings. Keynston takes its name from the Kahaynes family, lords of the manor of Tarrant Keynston. About 1170 one of them established a little hermitage for a group of anchoresses or nuns a short distance downstream at Tarrant Crawford. By 1233 they had become Cistercians and soon attracted important patronage. Richard Poore, who as Bishop of Sarum saw the foundations of the new cathedral laid in Salisbury in 1220, had been born at Crawford and elected to be buried in the religious community he had encouraged there. The first lay abbess was King John's daughter, Joan, who had been Queen of Scotland and chose to be buried in the convent church in 1238.

The royal connection gave power and prestige to the abbey that succeeded the first church. In 1252 Henry III, for the good of the soul of his sister Joan, granted the nuns the right of free warren in all their demesne lands in Dorset, Wiltshire and Sussex—evidence of the acquisitions of land already made. Hampshire also bears witness to the abbey's increasing wealth: the village of Hurstbourne Tarrant owes its connection with the other Tarrant villages in their very different valley to its owner-ship by the nuns of Tarrant Crawford. There is an interesting visual link also. A faintly discernible mural in Hurstbourne Tarrant church depicts the parable of the Three Living and the Three Dead—three kings facing three skeletons. The same subject appears on a wall in the little church at Tarrant Crawford.

The abbey seems to have been demolished soon after the Dissolution. Leland says, 'Tarent nunnery, of late days, stood about Crayford bridge, over Stour Ryver'. Nothing of it remained when Gerard wrote in about 1620. Various abbey lands were granted to Sir Thomas Wyat. The buildings that survived are a large barn and other farm buildings with stone buttresses, a fine house which is considered to have been the abbey's guest-house, and a church or chapel consisting of a little square tower, a nave and a chancel only, made of flints with greensand courses and dark reddish-brown corner stones. This must be the chapel referred to in an indenture of 1377, dated at 'Nuns Tarent', appointing Sir Thomas Gilden as chaplain of All Saints, Little Crawford, 'otherwise called St Margaret's chapel'.

The reason why the chapel should be called St Margaret's is immediately apparent when one enters. The south wall of the nave, unbroken except by a single window, is covered with paintings in two tiers. Here are the Three Living and the Three Dead, as at Hurstbourne Tarrant. And here, running the whole length of one tier, is the life of St Margaret of Antioch told in a dozen or more scenes like a strip cartoon. Hers was evidently a violent and painful life, much occupied with being scourged, hung up by the hair and swallowed by the Devil, while occasionally relieving her feelings by taking up a birch and chastising her devilish opponents.

Why this particular saint should be given such prominence is a matter for conjecture. A Turnpike Act of 1765, dealing with a projected route from Blandford to Wimborne, referred to 'Little Crawford or Tarrant Antioch'. Historically Little Crawford was one of the alternative names for Tarrant Crawford, others being Tarent Abbey, Nuns Tarent and Tarent Monachorum (also given, confusingly, to Tarrant Monkton when it belonged to the monks of Cranborne and Tewkesbury). The stabilizing of village names was a gradual process. Hutchins reminds us that fifteen manors or parcels of land were surveyed under the common name of 'Tarente' in Domesday—'very few of which can be ascertained, additional names not being in use until a century and a half after, and then they came in by degrees'.

What, then, of the eighteenth-century reference to Tarrant Antioch as yet another alternative for Tarrant Crawford? It looks as if St Margaret's city came to be commemorated in the name of the place as well as on the wall of the church. However, Hutchins states that Tarent Antioch and Antiocheston were early names applied to Tarrant Rawston, and for a good reason: 'the most ancient lords of this vill that occur are the Antiochs, a family of great antiquity, but of no great note'. In 1303 Nicholas Antioch was mentioned as a witness at Dorchester and in 1316 he was certified by the sheriff as lord of the township of Tarent Antioche. Further, in 1524 the church dedicated to St Mary at Tarrant Rawston was referred to as 'the parish church of our Lady of Tarent Antiocheston'.

We must therefore place the Antioch family at Rawston; and the convent's first patrons, the Kahaynes or de Keynes, at Keynston. It next appears that the Antiochs became important benefactors to the Cistercian abbey: a charter of 1235 refers to land and other benefits given earlier by William de Anteoch and increasingly the Antiochs seem to have displaced the de Keynes as the abbey's local patrons. Hutchins says they were the patrons of the parish church throughout the fourteenth century. Gerard describes Tarrant Crawford as being owned by William de Anteoch and his posterity until the reign of Henry VI. They remain largely anonymous and obscure, however. The latest to be identified is John Auntioche who in 1387 put his signature to a document at Edmondsham.

The conjecture to which all this leads is that the choice of Margaret of Antioch as the subject for such an ambitiously extensive mural should be seen as a compliment to—or even a commission financed by—the chief local benefactor and patron, the lord of Tarrant Antioch. The dating of the mural ascribes it to the first half of the fourteenth century, at which time the Antiochs were already established at Tarrant Rawston. What remains for speculation is the origin of the family name. Should we find in our generation its equivalent in a Montgomery of Alamein? Was the founder of the family a victorious Crusader who distinguished himself on 3 June 1098, at the capture of Antioch from the infidel? And when and where did the last of the Antiochs perish?

Today the little church of Tarrant Crawford wears its weight of history lightly. Beside it the river burbles pleasantly among what seem to be the outlines of a vanished mill, which might have enjoyed a longer life: its neighbours at Keynston and Rushton turned their wheels until the 1920s. The Keynston mill is in fact on the Stour, just above the point where it receives the waters of the Tarrant.

Looking back up the valley it is not unduly fanciful to see an epitome of English rural life in the stories of the settlements that gathered about the sweet water of this fast flowing stream: the Iron Age people in their huts inside Buzbury Rings in Keynston; the Romans in their villa at Hinton; the ancient dead in Launceston's round barrows—at least thirty-seven such sepulchres; the life of austerity at Crawford and of luxury at Gunville. The Tarrant valley is full of such memories, of ghosts perhaps —and yet to outward seeming so uneventfully serene.

CHAPTER TEN

Landscape with Figures

BY A PROVISION in the will of the rector, John Gane, who died in 1746, the great bell of Berwick St John church was to be rung for fifteen minutes at eight o'clock every night from 10 September to 10 March as a sort of aural lighthouse, a beacon of sound, to guide benighted travellers who had lost their way on the broad rolling uplands of the Chase. This friendly gesture was still performed in the early 1960s, after which the bell fell silent for lack of an experienced bell-ringer to undertake the nightly duty. Gane's legacy, now worth about £12 a year, is still available if a competent volunteer comes forward; but it must be admitted that a resumption would be welcomed mainly as the preservation of a pleasant custom rather than as a practical aid to navigation.

In Gane's day, however, it was easy enough to lose one's way on the downs, particularly on a dark night. Even by day the course of a trackway could be uncertain. Where it passed between banks or hedges it was simple to follow but when it came to open downland there would be an ambiguity of alternative ways for getting from one landmark to the next: in such circumstances it was not difficult to wander off course. The best guides one could hope for were what were known as *Dorsetshire milestones* —heaps of gravel or chalk, and preferably chalk because it showed up better at night. Surtees gave an interesting account of these artificial landmarks and their value as late even as 1830, when the turnpike roads were well established. As soon as the traveller left the turnpike and set off across country he could still be in trouble.

Surtees left the Great Western Turnpike at Blandford where he hired a yellow postchaise in which he was soon 'passing through divers fields, commons, and opens, and wandering about the tortuous byroads, which all countrymen delight to follow' until he found himself on a trackless open down. To his anxious enquiry the postboy replied, 'It be all right—the House be just over the hill before us; these 'ere white heaps you zee marks the road—they be what we calls Dorzetshire milestones.' In recounting his adventures Surtees commented, 'Of all the countries I have ever been in, Dorsetshire is the most difficult for a stranger to find his way about. Fingerposts there are none; downs, with their "Dorsetshire mile-stones", stretch about in all directions, and the cross-roads, over the bleak and barren heaths, are puzzling beyond description.'

Far worse must have been the dangers and tribulations one or two centuries earlier. An eloquent witness is Daniel Defoe, over a hundred years before Surtees. The route Defoe followed was from Shaftesbury to Salisbury along what later became the regular course of the London–Exeter coach, following the line of the scarp which overlooks the Nadder valley from Whitesheet Hill to Salisbury racecourse. Although it has long since fallen into disuse the turnpike track is easy to follow, bordered as it is today by hedges or boundary fences: yet Defoe, who was a traveller of wide experience, asserted that 'the road often lyes very broad, and branches off insensibly, which might easily cause a traveller to lose his way'. Even more surprisingly he says that along the whole fourteen-mile stretch there was 'neither house or town in view all the way'. For today's walker one of the pleasures of the journey is the frequent glimpses of villages and farms in the valleys on either side of the ridge. If Defoe enjoyed no such reassurance he did, however, have what he describes as as 'a certain never failing assistance upon all these downs for telling a stranger his way'. This was the shepherds who tended their flocks on these lonely uplands. Ever present along the route they were glad enough of a chance conversation with a wayfarer to distract the day's monotony.

In this sparsely inhabited landscape, then, one of the first figures to be identified is the man Andrew Young described so graphically in his poem, *The Wiltshire Downs*:

> As still as a windhover
> A shepherd in his flapping coat leans over
> His tall sheep-crook
> And shearlings, tegs and yoes cons like a book.

Chalk downland is traditionally a place for sheep. In Thomas Huxley's words it has the character of 'a peacefully domestic and mutton-suggesting prettiness'. There were certainly sheep in the Chase in prehistoric times but the earliest indication of numbers comes from the year 1086 when there were 1,037 sheep at Cranborne and 826 at Ashmore. At about the same time the density of human population on the chalk uplands of Dorset was about eight per square mile. The downs were no longer well wooded when the Domesday Book was compiled and would have settled to the open appearance that we think of as traditional—though without the roads and hedges and boundary fences that now parcel out the broad expansiveness of the pristine landscape. On these swelling heights and steepsided combes the shepherd was king.

With the men of the woods, the foresters, the hurdle-makers and their like, the shepherd had a complex and intimate relationship centring on the hazel coppices. From them came his hurdles. Within them his sheep could sometimes graze, and sometimes not. The customary practice with regenerating hazel was to protect it with fencing for about five years and then to permit farm animals to graze from Old May Day to Martinstide, though sheep might be excluded at times when cattle and pigs were permitted. The rules were not always the same in every century and at every place. Chafin, for example, describes cows being milked in the woods but says categorically that sheep were banned. In the reign of James I, Robert Topp of Bridmore was brought before the Chase court on a charge of grazing sheep in Whitehazel coppice and Costards coppice: perhaps he did so out of season or while the young hazel was still fenced. Sometimes sheep were forfeited as a penalty in kind rather than cash. For example in the next reign, Charles I's, twenty sheep were taken from Edward Topp as part of a distraint for unpaid dues. In general the shepherd had to respect Chase law and the forester's fences, but sheep and deer could co-exist without great friction.

The association of shepherd and hurdle-maker in their heyday is well shown by John Claridge in the survey of agriculture he published in 1793. He estimated that fifteen dozen sheep hurdles—these were 4 ft 6 in long—would enclose an acre and accommodate twelve to thirteen hundred sheep. They were moved every morning. The cost of the hurdles was 7s 6d per dozen, and this included the stakes and the bonds or ties known locally as 'wriths'—pronounced as 'wreaths'. The equivalent price in 1980 would be upwards of £35 per dozen.

Today's hurdles are more likely to be made for gardens and other semi-ornamental uses than for sheep. The hurdle-maker's trade declined in the present century with the general decline in sheep husbandry. By the 1960s sheep began to reappear more numerously in the Chase where they were regarded as marginally economic. In more recent years they have become once again a familiar sight, but no longer handled in the traditional way nor in the traditional numbers.

Fortunately there is still enough demand for hurdles of various types and for the associated trade in thatching spars to keep this ancient craft alive and incidentally to justify the retention of some of the hazel coppices. A description of the hurdle-makers' technical skill, as exemplified by Douglas Judd of Sixpenny Handley, may not be out of place here. He uses two tools: a spar hook and a nobby hook. The spar hook is a light billhook used for splitting the gads or rods. The nobby hook is a heavier tool with the hook taken back and rounded off: it is used for trimming off the woven ends and for any heavier chopping. The hooked tip of the spar hook is also useful for picking over a heap of rods and selecting a particular one.

The only other piece of equipment is the lathe. This is a curved billet of wood drilled with holes at regular intervals, into which the upright rods—called 'zales'—will be inserted. The lathe is lashed to pegs driven into the ground so as to hold it firm and give leverage. It inclines towards the maker for ease of working. An upright rod standing separately serves as a marker for the height of each zale as it is prepared.

The making of the hurdle starts with the end zales—unsplit rods which are inserted into the extremities of the lathe. To make his intermediate zales, which provide the vertical framework, the hurdle-maker trims off a rod, slashing away twigs, leaves and knots, splits it with his spar hook— which he twists from side to side as he eases it downwards—and sharpens to a point the end that goes into the lathe.

When all the zales are in place, vertically, the horizontal cross weave starts with four stout unsplit rods at the bottom for strength, woven in and out and twisted back. Split rods are then introduced, woven in with enough overlap to be twisted back and woven in reverse. It is important that the rods should be pliable enough to stand vigorous twisting, and with no knots at the twisting points. The rods may not be long enough to go right across and overlap at each side: they finish within the hurdle and any projecting tip is cropped off. And not every one has to be twisted back at the end zale—it can be trimmed off there with the nobby hook. The important rule, in Douglas Judd's words, is to 'keep your middle up—the same as when you're making a haystack'.

As the weave builds up it is pressed down with the knee or beaten down with a billet of wood, to consolidate it. When the weave is completed there is a final beating down and every unwanted projection is trimmed off. The finished hurdle is curved, following the line of the lathe. When it is stacked this curve will be pressed out, thus adding an extra tautness to the weave. The weather side of the hurdle will show the outer rind of the rods, with the inner split sides showing creamy white on the reverse aspect of the newly made hurdle. And it is the boast of a good hurdle-maker that it would take you a longer time to pull his hurdle apart than it took him to make it.

Until 1970 it was customary to hold an annual auction on the Rush-more Estate at which the hurdle-makers bid for those copses which were ready for felling. Beyond a certain age the hazel rods become too coarse and brittle, and are then said to have 'got overstood'. The auctions were similar to those held in the Sedgemoor area of Somerset when the withy-beds were auctioned to basket-makers 'buying for work'—buying and gathering the raw material of their craft. However, the hazel auctions were suspended after 1970 owing to the decline in the trade and matters are now arranged by individual negotiation with each of the hurdle-makers—of whom there are probably no more than half a dozen working regularly. The Rushmore Estate has 800 acres of productive hazel which is felled and regenerated in the traditional cycle.

In about 1950, when the auctions were in full swing, this is how a hurdle-maker described the procedure:

The woods are put up for auction once a year, in the autumn, and we do buy the timber by the lug. Ten strides wide and ten strides long is four lugs—what we call lugs. And we bid so much a lug. We look round the hazel copses first, to see if we can get the best pieces. We bid for 'em, and sometimes we get 'em, and sometimes we get the rough. Depends on the price. You want about three or four acres for a year's work.

When the auction's over you pay five shillings in the pound for what you've bought and the rest before the next auction.

The old rule was to have all your wood cut by the end of March and all out of the woods by June—but now we work in the woods all year round.

There are few more agreeable ways of spending a morning than in the company of a hurdle-maker at work in his copse. The air is sweetly scented as the flakes of hazel fall from his hook like flower petals. With luck there may be a nuthatch near to whistle in that bright exultant tone which, to human ears, sounds so full of cheer. And the men who spend their days in these green solitudes seem to store up a wealth of local history and local pride, of ancient anecdote and song. One I know has a fine edition of William Barnes's poems among his most cherished possessions and speaks the poems as Barnes intended, in the Dorset vernacular. Another, long since dead—old Buffer Lucas—taught me one of the loveliest of all folk songs, 'The Pricketty Bush'. The work itself has a rhythmic character, interlacing the pliant wood in structural patterns of prosody and harmony.

In the clearing from which the cut rods have been removed a little miracle takes place. During the summer the ground vegetation takes on a generally yellow sheen as the wood cow-wheat pushes up its narrow tubular flowers with their golden entrances. This is a phenomenon first recorded at the beginning of the nineteenth century by Chafin in his *Anecdotes* and it is one worth retelling in his own words:

A gentleman shot in the Chase a brace of pheasants of that year's breed which were most remarkably fat, and he brought them to me as curiosities on that account. We knew that they were taken so far distant from any cornfields, that it was impossible for them ever to have tasted any common grain; we therefore opened their crops, in order to discover what food they could have met with of so nutritive a quality as to make them so immensely fat. We found them full of the pods of some plant unknown to us, and in each of these pods were four seeds resembling pearl barley, but more oblong. To satisfy our curiosities, we took the liberty of sending one of the plants, with the pods, to an eminent physician and learned botanist of Salisbury.

This good friend informed us that the plant was the *Melampyrum Sylvaticum*; that he had known that common fowls had been fattened with the seeds, but that the rareness of the plant and *habitat* of it were so uncertain, that it would not answer any purpose of economy to adopt the use of them in that way. These plants are by no means plentiful in the Chase, and are to be found only in the copses of one year's growth, which are hedged round; the seeds, therefore, must lie dormant in the soil fifteen or sixteen years, until, by some of the wonderful works of Nature, the earth is prepared to cause vegetation.

Much that Chafin records has gone for ever, but this 'wonderful work of Nature' was there to be seen in Hoe Coppice, in Garston Wood, in the summer of 1977—to be repeated, we may hope, in about 1993 when the time comes to clear-fell the hazel once again.

It is the head forester's task to mark out the area of coppice that is ready to be turned over to the hurdle-maker: after which he presides over the process of regeneration. A memorandum written at Rushmore Lodge at about the same time as Chafin was writing his *Anecdotes*—the early 1800s —gives some interesting details of the traditional management of hazel. After noting that the copses of the Chase are generally felled at fifteen or sixteen years' growth the author comments, 'Lord Pembroke's are kept till 20 years and indeed it would be better if the Rushmore copses were to stand as long, tho' during the four years interval the yearly income would stop, as the increased profit of the wood would more than compensate for the delay.'

The memorandum goes on to describe the method of regeneration:

For *three years* after a copse is cut the owner has a right to fence out the deer and all other cattle, (In some parts of the Chase this term has *by encroachment* increased to five years,) in order to improve the growth

of the wood which if fed by the deer at so early a period, would be of
little or no value. At the three years end the keepers have a right to
make *Leaps and Creeps*, and at five years end, sometimes at seven, the
fences are taken up and the woods laid open to the deer.

There were thus three stages—the first, of total enclosure; the third, of
free access; and a second, intermediate stage when the keepers could make
a few places suitable for an adult deer to leap over or for a fawn to creep
through. In Tudor times, however, there seems to have been less concern
to protect the young hazel shoots by fencing out the deer completely in
the early stages. A copse of first growth springing up from old stools was
called a *spring*, and Turberville tells us that 'Harts do go to their layre
commonly in the springs': for which reason he advises the huntsman 'to
choose some standing in some tree on the border of the spring, from which
he may behold all things that feed therein'. Presumably hazel was more
abundant then, and less valued.

In the case of domestic animals it was the practice at Rushmore in 1800
to exclude them at all times. If there had previously been any commoners'
rights they were extinguished. The rule was expressed unequivocally—
'In the woods of Rushmore and Staplefoot Walks no cattle are allowed
to feed but by permission of Lord Rivers. It is the business of the Rushmore
Woodman, on the part of Lord Rivers, to preserve the outside bounds
of the Rushmore Woods and thereby to save them from the depredations
of sheep and black cattle.'

Mention of the bounds and borders of the woods leads to the other
species of trees that made up the woodlands of the Chase, besides hazel
and oak and yew. The Rushmore memorandum tells us that:

> the borders are preserved exclusively for the benefit of the deer and are
> not to be cut by the Woodmen. The Keepers alone have the right to
> shroud them for the maintenance or browsing of the deer. They con-
> sist principally of evergreens and berry-bearing plants, of which the
> following are most common—Holly, Ivy, Thorn, Crab or Wilding,
> Whitebeam or Whiting Tree and Maple. The two first—the Holly
> and the Ivy—are called Vert, and are of most service to the deer. The
> others are generally named Berry, and the deer in the season resort to
> the trees in great numbers for the fruit, particularly to the Whitebeam.

The value of maple in the borders was simply as standing trees in which
the keepers chopped steps to make a high seat from which to observe and
sometimes to shoot deer.

Pre-metric signpost to Sixpenny
Handley

The Grove Arms inn sign, Ludwell

Toll-house on Tarrant Hinton Down

St Giles
House,
Wimborne
St Giles,
from the
south-west

Wimborne
St Giles:
church and
alms-houses

Left: Colonel Augustus Lane Fox, who became General Augustus Pitt-Rivers, as a young man

Below left: Statue of a Chase keeper in Cranborne manor gardens

Below right: General Pitt-Rivers

Traditional Chase use of brick and flint in building

Larmer Tree Gardens, Tollard Royal, c. 1895

The Cross
Roads Pottery,
Verwood, in
the 1920s

Aside from the requirements of the deer and the practical uses of hazel the Chase timber was not of outstanding value. The claim is made that some of the finest oaks in Dorset today grow in the vicinity of Edmondsham but this is not typical Chase country. Edmondsham lies on the border of the Chase where the chalk gives way to heavier clayland. A more representative view historically is West's, in about 1816—'In the woodlands, though the soil is favorable for ash, and produces a little oak, the quantity of timber is very small. The young saplings are generally broken or damaged by the deer.'

In spite of disfranchisement the Victorian landowners did not direct their improving zeal towards forestry except in terms of ornamental planting and fox coverts. Where they grubbed out derelict woods it was not for replanting but for the plough. It is probably no great exaggeration to say that, by 1900, the woodlands of the Chase were degenerating into little more than a miscellaneous breeding place for pheasants, rabbits and foxes. The hazel still retained a commercial value while the shepherd needed hurdles; but as the sheep disappeared, and the old woodcrafts declined, many of the copses were allowed to grow on untended. The general agricultural depression intensified the atmosphere of neglect and apathy.

The impact of two major wars, conducted under siege-like conditions, had a great effect on the Chase. The threat to our imports of food and of softwoods revived agriculture and engendered the Forestry Commission. Much of the old deciduous woodland was swept away to be replaced by either newly broken arable or by coniferous plantations. For example, on the Farquharson lands north of Tarrant Gunville the woodlands became derelict during the 1930s and were increasingly infested with rabbits. In the second war and afterwards 700 acres of this woodland were cleared, using a variety of heavy machinery which included demobilized Sherman tanks. Lower down the Tarrant valley Ashley Wood above Tarrant Keynston is another good modern example of contracting woodland and expanding arable. The same story can be told of many another part of the Chase.

There is another side to the coin, however, for not everyone wanted to banish the woods. One remarkable family in particular, the Gardiners of Fontmell, pioneered a creative attitude to forestry in the 1930s when few landowners considered it a subject worth thinking about. Balfour Gardiner showed what could be done to bring overgrown and generally neglected coppices back into production and his work was carried on by Rolf Gardiner—hence the appearance on recent Ordnance Survey maps of Balfour's Wood, Rolf's Wood and Gardiner Forest. In 1938 Balfour

Gardiner gave Vernditch and Stonedown Wood to the Forestry Commission, which has continued to develop ways of bringing neglected woods back into production. By 1966 nearly all the 1,750 acres controlled by the Forestry Commission within Cranborne Chase had been replanted with a mixture of hardwoods and conifers.

In the other big woodland area, the Rushmore Estate's 2,500 acres, the only hardwood planted is beech, set in a matrix of Norway spruce: Douglas fir and larch get up too quickly and would kill the beech. Ash is not planted, but when any appears in regenerating hazel it is preserved. Incidentally ash is acquiring an unexpected rôle with the elimination of elms by Dutch elm disease: in at least one place in the Tarrant Valley a community of rooks, deprived of their traditional rookery in a group of elms now felled, have colonized half a dozen ash trees.

There are a few other indigenous materials that provide employment or have done so in the past. The nut harvest has already been described in an earlier chapter. To it may be added the roots of valerian which were much sought after by London druggists in the eighteenth century. Cranborne Chase was famous for this commodity which, like wood cow-wheat, was to be found only in year-old hazel coppices. The roots were gathered in October and November when other casual employment was scarce. The valerian trade has gone but moss is still gathered and sent away to be used as a packing material.

Figures of greater prominence in the Chase landscape are the cress-growers and—historically at least—the potters. Watercress is a flourishing industry and you will not travel for long in the outer zone of the Chase without coming across the deep green rectangles of the beds. Holwell, Monkton Upwimborne, Fovant and Ludwell are four locations that immediately come to mind. The mineral-rich chalk streams were par-ticulary favourable for cress-growing in the past. Nowadays there are problems of water pollution and of transport facilities to be set against some of the old traditional sites.

The pottery industry died out about thirty years ago but many examples of its products are still to be seen in the Chase villages, as well as in local museums. In the nineteenth century it found employment for a substantial number of men and boys: in 1841 the figures were a hundred men and ten boys. How far back it dates is uncertain but the local archaeologists who have been making an intensive study of the industry can show a sequence of records from the late fourteenth century. Old kiln sites are still being uncovered and earlier documentary references may yet come to light. Bearing in mind the importance of the New Forest as a source of Romano-British pottery it is tempting to speculate on the possibility of a continuous tradition, since the mediaeval industry was sited in the south-east corner of the Chase—separated from the New Forest only by the river Avon. A Romano-British kiln near Rockbourne lends some substance to the possibility.

The clay deposits on which the industry was based extend from the area between Fordingbridge and Rockbourne south-westwards to Wimborne. Where the chalk is replaced by the tertiary formations of the South Hampshire basin a narrow band of clay separates the chalk from the sandy heathland. The proximity of the heath is important as a source of the two other materials the potters needed—sand and firing-wood. Cranborne Common and Alderholt Common contained both in abundance, and precious little else. They were therefore well placed in relation to the village of Alderholt, which seems to have been the earliest centre of the industry.

As the vein of clay was worked out the potters moved south-westwards to exploit new supplies. The expansion of the industry in the seventeenth and eighteenth centuries was associated with new kilns in Daggons, Eastworth, Edmondsham and Horton before 1700, and at Crendell and Verwood soon afterwards. By 1750 there were at least fifteen kilns working, with Verwood increasingly becoming the main centre. In the nineteenth century the older centres declined, though in 1841 Wake Smart mentioned Daggons and Crendell as still important sources of the potter's clay. The threat to the industry came from improvements in transport—particularly of course the railway—which made the mass-produced pottery of the Midlands available in southern England. However, Verwood persisted into the present century and the last kiln there did not close until 1952.

In the 1920s the clay was dug at Holwell near Cranborne and brought by horse and cart to Verwood, where the potters used to tread the clay with their bare feet. A variety of pots of simple utility were made—kitchen pans, costrels, jars and the like. These were hawked by horse and cart round the district and in the big coastal towns, such as Bournemouth and Poole. Sturdy rather than elegant, Verwood ware is usually of a dull yellow colour and has a distinctive appearance. Specimens of it are displayed at the Salisbury Museum and the Red House Museum in Christchurch.

Shepherds and foresters, farmers, cress-growers and potters—these are historically the typical figures of working people in the Chase landscape. To them must be added the village tradesmen, the cobblers and bakers and blacksmiths together with one or two more unusual callings. Donhead St Mary in 1885 enjoyed the services of a dealer in tea and a maker of rakes.

A century or more earlier Berwick St John contained the workshop of a clock-maker of some renown, William Monk: the mechanism of the clock he made for Sherborne Abbey in 1740 is preserved and displayed at the abbey. The church clock at Broad Chalke is also his.

Such men are an exceptional minority, however, and there is a further large body of people to be accounted for. In 1801 the census for Farnham showed a population of forty-four males and the same number of females: of these eighty-eight only sixteen were chiefly employed in agriculture and a further twelve in trade, manufacture or handicraft. Similar proportions are found in the census returns for other Chase villages during the nineteenth century and leave unanswered the question of what the remaining sixty persons were doing. One or two would follow a profession, a few might be infirm or child-bearing, but we can assume that the large undefined remainder was made up of servants of various kinds—domestic servants in the great mansions of the local grandees, outdoor servants in the stables, the kennels, the game preserves, the hothouses and the gardens. Being one among that great army of footmen, chambermaids, game-keepers, coachmen and the rest was a major occupation in the Chase until recent times.

In her diary for 1896 Agnes Grove, a daughter of General Pitt-Rivers, described her journey home from Bayreuth—where she had been to hear *The Ring*—as being 'without incident beyond Giovanni the footman being left behind'. One has the impression that a footman more or less was considered expendable. From the dissolution of the religious houses to the end of Edwardian England it was in the palatial establishments of the aristocratic dynasts that the dynamic of Chase life was to be found. Intermarrying, sometimes feuding, sometimes making defensive alliances, wheeling and dealing among themselves, outshining each other, the great landowning families were the policy-makers, the universal employers, the arbiters of laws written and unwritten—little less than kings in their petty kingdoms. And if one family is to be selected as the most representative of the Chase in its heyday it must be the last lords of the Chase—the Pitt-Rivers of Rushmore—who are the subject of the next chapter.

CHAPTER ELEVEN

Pitt-Rivers of Rushmore

———————————

IN NOVEMBER 1858, Lord Stanley of Alderley paid a visit to Rushmore. How the visit came about remains a mystery, but the motive for it is easier to discern. It was not in the cause of friendship, nor did it spring from a disinterested love of the countryside, although the letter he wrote to his wife opens with an interesting description of Rushmore at that time:

> This is, I believe, the only place in England 18 miles from a railway station. It takes as long to come from Salisbury as from London to Salisbury. The road is all over a down country and the house here is situated at the top of the highest hills on this high downy country, 800 feet they say above the sea. Immediately within sight of the house the country is bleak open downs, but below these is an immense extent of beautiful wild wood, the remains of old Cranborne Chase, and rough ground with old thorns scattered on the open downs. The estate goes for 20 miles, with no neighbours.

What was of greater concern to Lord Stanley was the wealth of his host and the health of his host's children. His host, the fourth Lord Rivers, was in his late forties. His host's wife, the eldest daughter of Earl Granville, bore her husband thirteen children in all, so the succession seemed safe enough—until it was noticed that nine of those children were girls, and of the four boys two had died. Lady Stanley would have been well enough aware of these circumstances to read between the lines as her husband's letter continued:

> He is poor and gets comparatively a small income from the estate, but it is improving every day. I saw the eldest son carried out by a servant and put into a little carriage—he cannot walk at all and is not likely to live; they say the younger one is better than his brother, but I suspect not much.

It was an accurate estimate. The boy in the little carriage died the following year. His only surviving brother had but eight more years to live. All four boys perished in their late teens, as if some malign destiny were at work. But of course what is malign for one may be benign for some other—and in this particular instance Lord Stanley had no tears to shed for the sorrows of the Rivers family. His thoughts must have been concentrated on the possible benefit for his daughter, Alice, and the man she had married five years earlier, Augustus Henry Lane-Fox. The link between Fox and Lord Rivers was that they were second cousins—their paternal grandmothers had been sisters. When Fox first presented himself as a suitor for Alice Stanley the prospect that he might one day inherit the Rivers estate seemed so remote as to be discounted totally. Lord Stanley had rebuffed the young officer and refused his consent. Imperceptibly, however, the odds against the outsider had shortened, while Alice became visibly less attractive to others. Somewhat grudgingly the marriage took place, in 1853. Now, five years later, Lord Stanley judged that it might be prudent to make a personal inspection of Rushmore: accordingly he took the train to Salisbury and rode those eighteen miles over the downs to satisfy his curiosity. As he concluded the letter to Lady Stanley he was evidently intent on returning to London without delay. Only one thing remained to be said—'Is there anything you want from Fortnum & Mason?'

The male succession in the Pitt-Rivers line broke for the first time in 1828 when the second Lord Rivers died without a direct heir and was succeeded by his sister's son. It broke for the second time in 1880, when the title was not renewed and the estate passed to Lord Stanley's son-in-law. Before we come to the events of 1880 it will be appropriate to look briefly at the family background to the Rushmore that came so unexpectedly to Augustus Henry Lane-Fox, subsequently to be known as General Pitt-Rivers. House and family both have a long and varied history.

Of the four families who held the lordship of the Chase, after it passed finally from the Crown, the Pitts held it for longer than the others combined. Their association with the Chase goes back at least to Elizabethan times when Sir William Pitt, a Commissioner of the Navy, lived at Iwerne Stepleton and his brother, Thomas, was a physician at Blandford. Soon after he was knighted in 1618, Sir William purchased Stratfieldsaye in Hampshire. Thomas the physician had a son, John, who became rector of Blandford St Mary and fathered the more eminent line of Pitts in which 'Diamond' Pitt, the Earl of Chatham and Pitt the Younger are illustrious names. With them we are not concerned, however; our attention must be concentrated on one of Sir William's grandsons, George, who was born at some time after 1620 and died in 1694.

This George Pitt and his son—also George—had in common a talent for marrying well. George senior married in 1657 Jane, widow of Lord

Chandos, Baron of Sudeley, and daughter of the second Earl of Rivers—
titles which reverberated down the years in the minds of her Pitt descendants. George junior married twice, less aristocratically than his father but
perhaps more profitably. His first wife was Lucy Lowe, the widowed
daughter of Thomas Pile of Baverstock. Pile had another daughter,
Elizabeth, who was married to Thomas Freke; and it was to the Freke
family that Lord Shaftesbury sold the Chase and its lodges in 1695.

The Frekes were a distinguished and wealthy family who had prospered
under the Tudors. They acquired Hinton St Mary and rebuilt the manor
house when the nuns of Shaftesbury were expelled, and they owned
property in Iwerne Courtney and Hannington. By Thomas Freke's will
George Pitt had a reversionary interest in the Freke estate after the lives of
Freke's wife, her father and her sister (Mrs George Pitt). In 1714 only one
of the four was still living—George Pitt. The rich inheritance was his.

Thereupon he went one better, taking as his second wife Lora Grey,
heiress of Kingston Maurward in Stinsford. She outlived him and saw him
buried at Stinsford, where he is commemorated by a portrait bust. On his
behalf it can fairly be claimed that he was the effective founder of the Pitt
fortunes. From 1714 onwards the Pitts were a force to be reckoned with.
They sat in Parliament; they exercised their lordship of the Chase; their
acreage and their influence put them on level terms with the most illustrious of their neighbours. It was said that they could ride to the Channel
coast without stepping off their own land. Even if this were not the
absolutely literal truth it is not far out: in a county of large estates they
could compete with the Wingfield Digbys as to which of them was
Dorset's greatest landowner.

That they should enter the peerage during the eighteenth century must
have seemed inevitable. The fourth successive George Pitt, born in 1720,
emphasized his suitability for a barony by his career as a diplomat in Spain
and Italy. At home he sat in Parliament for Shaftesbury for five years and
for the county for a further 27 years. He was also Colonel of the Dorsetshire Yeomanry: in Edward Gibbon's diary we have a glimpse of Colonel
Pitt in his tent, entertaining the Duke of York to breakfast.

Pitt's wife drew from Horace Walpole the complimentary reference
that she was 'all loveliness within and without', but Pitt himself was
described in 1771 as 'her brutal, half-mad husband'. Be that as it may, he
was well enough esteemed to become, four years later, the first Baron
Rivers of Stratfieldsaye. In 1802 he acquired an additional title as Lord
Rivers of Sudeley Castle. His choice of titles tells us something about the
man because the name 'Rivers' and the reference to 'Sudeley Castle' seem
quite capricious—until one recalls his great-grandmother, who died

exactly a hundred years before George Pitt the fourth became a baron. She was the only member of the nobility in the Pitt lineage; her Sudeley and Rivers connections were still remembered, evidently. The Rivers earldom had expired in 1728. As for Sudeley Castle in Gloucestershire, the Pitts had acquired it at some stage. In 1810, no longer needing it, the second Lord Rivers sold it to the Duke of Buckingham.

He also sold Stratfieldsaye to the government so that a grateful nation could present it to the victorious Duke of Wellington after the final defeat of Napoleon. By contrast Rushmore became more important as a Pitt establishment. In 1760 George Pitt replaced the existing building, converting some of the old structure into offices. In 1794 an Enclosure Act made it possible to add 776 acres of pasture and woodland so that it became—in Bowles's words—'a most desirable residence for any nobleman or gentleman who may be fond of retirement and rural sports'. In fact it was mainly used as a summer residence and hunting-box.

The first Lord Rivers lived to be eighty-three, and things were never quite the same again after his death. Of his four children his only son, succeeding at the age of fifty-two, was childless and remained so: it was from the three daughters therefore that an heir had to come. Penelope was married, at the age of seventeen, to Viscount Ligonier: Louisa, also at seventeen, to Peter Beckford. Marcia, adventuring more cautiously into matrimony, was thirty-three when she became the bride of James Fox-Lane, MP for Horsham and a friend of the Prince Regent. In her case prudence was rewarded as her more impetuous sisters were sadly matched.

If the eldest, Penelope, had any children they are not recorded. She was deleted from the family records because of her naughty behaviour. As Lady Ligonier she had an affair with Count Vittorio Alfieri. Her secret was betrayed to her husband by a groom, who confessed that he was jealous of Alfieri because he too was granted the privileges of a lover by Penelope. In a blaze of public scandal Ligonier fought a duel with Alfieri and divorced Penelope. When last heard of she had married Trooper Smith of the Blues, in 1784.

Louisa's marriage followed a similar course but stopped short of disaster. In six years she bore five children, of whom three died in infancy. Meanwhile a flirtation with her husband's young cousin, William Beckford of Fonthill, grew into an acknowledged love affair of passionate intensity. The family elders invoked the customary device of travel to separate them, her husband was tolerant, and in any case Louisa's health began to deteriorate alarmingly: she died at Florence, aged thirty-five. Her only surviving son succeeded his uncle as the third Lord Rivers, and the fact that he had two sons and thirteen grandchildren should have made the history of the third and youngest of the sisters, Marcia Lane-Fox, irrelevant.

It was a suspicion to the contrary that prompted Lord Stanley's journey to Rushmore. The last of the sickly teenage boys he saw there survived his father for only a year. At the age of eighteen the fifth Lord Rivers died and his childless uncle Horace became the last of the Rivers. Until that moment, in 1867, Major the Hon. Horace Pitt had had his ups and downs. Described as 'not a provident man' his tastes were unsuitably extravagant. He kept a string of racehorses at Pimperne, trained by 'old Mr Percy', until his financial difficulties obliged him to retire to what he called a fisherman's hut in a remote part of Scotland. When he inherited Rushmore he was having problems with moneylenders but he vowed that he would never leave the estate worth a shilling less than it was when he came to it, and he is reputed to have kept his word. In 1880, at the time of his death, the income from the estate that his successor, General Pitt-Rivers, could expect was put at over £27,000 a year. Twenty years later when the general died the estate was valued for death duty at more than £400,000.

There is one last thing to be said about the extraordinary passage of the Rivers fortune into the hands of Marcia Pitt's grandson. Even though the beneficiary had to be a Lane-Fox as a result of her marriage, the odds were still against Augustus Henry because he was the younger son of a younger son. What carried him over the final hurdle was the thought that whichever Lane-Fox inherited the estate of Lord Bingley (their family title) might acquire the Rivers estate also—with the danger of its becoming a subordinate dignity. When the second Lord Rivers made his will he was determined to carry on the family's name and independence although he had failed to beget an heir. He therefore incorporated in his will the condition that 'my own estates and the estates of the late Lord Bingley shall never vest in or belong to the same person so long as there shall be two sons of my said sister Marcia Fox or any issue male of such two sons in esse at the same time'. And there was the further requirement that the succeeding Lane-Fox should take the name of Pitt-Rivers.

What manner of man was the general? We can form some impression from a variety of sources—the correspondence and reminiscences of his wife's family, the diary of one of his daughters, the memories of his employees and neighbours, the testimony of his professional colleagues. He was in the first instance a soldier, commissioned into the Grenadier Guards when he was eighteen and evidently intending to make the army his career. He fought in the Crimea, went on half-pay in 1867 but returned to full duties in 1873; he was promoted to major-general in 1877 and finally retired as an honorary lieutenant-general after his inheritance of Rushmore.

He was twenty-two when he first proposed—unsuccessfully—to Alice Stanley, twenty-six when he married her. Her father held government office and had earned for himself the nickname 'Sir Benjamin Backbite'. An arrogant ambitious man, he soon made it plain that Fox was not an acceptable son-in-law. Lord Stanley's wife and his mother were sharp-tongued and vivaciously witty in their letters to each other, and the collective correspondence usually treats the young soldier with malicious humour or withering contempt. Alice was presented to the queen at a Drawing Room in 1846: her first two seasons were unsuccessful and her grandmother commented to Lady Stanley, 'I am afraid you will be obliged to bring her again out of Town without a husband. You had better make up your mind quickly, expect nothing'. Three years later she wrote, 'I do wish Alice had a husband of some kind or other—she would be *so* well with a child every year I have no doubt.' Next year it was 'poor Alice . . . does anything amuse *her*? Was she ever very amusable?'

Perhaps not, but she perked up later that year when her rebuffed but not discouraged suitor visited her home at Alderley. Her mother wrote to Lord Stanley, who remained in London, describing a family evening— 'Maude played on the pianoforte, and the young major and Alice laughed at each other's jokes'. Lady Stanley was sufficient of a realist to know that a more eligible husband for Alice might be extremely hard to find. In the following year the prospect of marriage was being actively canvassed. Fox's widowed mother had said that he would have an income of ' £1,000 easily and eventually £1,500'. Anxiously Alice hoped that her father would give her as much as he gave her sister Blanche as a marriage settle-ment. Her mother put the matter squarely to Lord Stanley. He replied with a terse note about other matters, and a dismissive postscript—'No time about Alice now'.

Fox's financial prospects had benefited meanwhile from the death of his elder brother, in 1852, and there was a noticeable softening in the Stanleys' attitude: it would be pleasing, but extremely difficult, to regard this as as a mere coincidence. Grudgingly Lord Stanley conceded, 'If Major Fox has 2,500 besides his commission it is probably not a case to refuse one's consent.' It was now the turn of Fox's mother, Lady Caroline, to be difficult. She put off the marriage indefinitely. When Lady Stanley met her she was 'not cordial'. Her statements and those of her son, according to Lady Stanley, 'rarely coincide. They are odious people'. It was a time of tension all round. In December 1852 Lady Stanley wrote to her husband, 'Nothing can be more touchy than Fox and he complains of the silliest things—such as you never having said you were glad to see him.' Nevertheless, two months later, Fox and Alice were married. With the least possible delay her pregnancy was announced and her grandmother commented grimly, 'As they are poor, cubs will come thick and fast—don't tell Mr Reynard, pray, as he don't understand a joke.'

The first child was still-born and almost at once Fox was involved in the Crimean war. He took part in the battle of the Alma, after which he was unfit for further active service and returned to his regular duties as a musketry instructor. His uncompromisingly perfectionist and intellectual approach earned him some hostility and he evidently felt that his talents were inadequately recognized. His belief that his father-in-law should use his influence on his behalf did not please Lord Stanley who referred to him as 'the discontented Field Marshal' and wrote, 'Fox seems of a discontented and querulous nature and expects some high post will immediately be offered to him and if not that he is ill-used.'

It was not in Fox's temperament to suffer fools gladly or to underrate himself. The monotony of peacetime soldiering in depots or training camps could not satisfy the ardent energies of an enquiring mind, which had discerned in the evolution of weaponry a pattern of progress that could be applied to other human activities. His examination of prehistoric weapons, tools, coins—indeed of any artefacts that survived—convinced him that they could be put in a sequence of continuity, so that a history of material culture could be deduced from them. This science of 'typology', as he called it, had features in common with Darwin's concept of biological evolution; the publication of *On the Origin of Species* in 1859 had a powerful influence on Fox. As his biographer M. W. Thompson observes:

> What for Fox had been a hobby—albeit a very serious one—now by analogy with Darwinian evolution took on quite a different status. The linear series of the development of artefacts might be arranged in a great family tree to reveal the course of the evolution of human material culture as a whole. For a man with the sense of dedication of Fox this was a challenge that had to be taken up. It was this change in status of his studies that was the most important influence of Darwinian evolution upon him. Much of his later life, including the Cranborne Chase episode, is unintelligible unless this is realised.

In the 1860s and '70s he began to make a name for himself in scientific circles and to enjoy the personal regard of such eminent men as Huxley and Lubbock. When he was elected a Fellow of the Royal Society, in 1876, one of his sponsors was Darwin. In the same period he began to excavate archaeological sites as an extension of his enquiries into prehistoric sequences of material culture, until increasingly his work as an archaeologist became an end in itself.

In 1880 Horace, the sixth and last Lord Rivers, died. Augustus Henry Lane-Fox entered Rushmore in his new identity as General Pitt-Rivers: now fifty-three, he had twenty years of life ahead of him in which he was free to pursue his scientific interests to the full. While his six sons and three daughters were growing up he must have stayed on the army's payroll from necessity. With the inheritance of his fortune it was no longer necessary. In addition to Rushmore the family had their London residence in Grosvenor Gardens. Ranging in age from twenty-five to fourteen the young Fox-Pitts, as they were now styled, brought an unaccustomed ebullience to their new surroundings.

Looking back, seven years later, on the opportunities that his inheritance presented to him General Pitt-Rivers wrote, 'Having retired from active service on account of ill-health, and being incapable of strong physical exercise, I determined to devote the remaining portion of my life chiefly to an examination of the antiquities on my own property.'

The nature of his ill-health has been shown by M. W. Thompson to be diabetes, with the further handicap of recurring bronchitis. His mental vigour was unabated, however, and he went to work with a will on the prolonged archaeological campaign subsequently recorded in the four privately printed volumes of his *Excavations in Cranborne Chase*. To describe them in detail is beyond the scope of this present book. They include the Iron Age hill fort at Winkelbury; the Romano-British settlements at Woodcutts and Rotherley; Bronze Age camps at South Lodge and on Martin Down; and the Neolithic long barrow known as Worbarrow near Handley Hill. To these must be added what is perhaps his best-known work—the excavation at Bokerley Junction.

The linear earthwork known as Bokerley Dyke runs for about four miles from Blagdon Hill to the vicinity of Woodyates. Just north of Woodyates it intersects the Roman road from Badbury at Bokerley junction; the significance of that meeting point was one of the general's most striking discoveries. His interest was aroused when a farmer discovered some Roman coins while extracting topsoil from the dyke. For two years Pitt-Rivers excavated on a massive scale, uncovering part of a Romano-British settlement at Woodyates and gradually piecing together a fascinating story. In its original form Bokerley Dyke was constructed probably in the early part of the fourth century and did not extend as far as Bokerley junction. The Roman road was open and in use, the Woodyates settlement was inhabited, and the reason for constructing the great earthwork is uncertain. Whether or not it was conceived as part of a military defensive system it was seemingly developed later as a rampart against some danger from the north-east. By careful dating Pitt-Rivers was able to show that Bokerley Dyke was soon extended over and beyond the Roman road, blocking it, but that a way was cut through to restore the road temporarily. In its final stage the road was again blocked and Bokerley Dyke straddled it permanently.

There could be no finer tribute to the care and thoroughness of the general's methods than the fact that, in 1947, Professor Christopher Hawkes was able to reinterpret the account of the excavation in the light of more recent knowledge and to correlate the decline of the Woodyates settlement with the first closing of Bokerley Junction in the period AD 367–69 and to date the final closure in about AD 405. Thereafter the Roman withdrawal from Britain must have emphasized the importance of Bokerley Dyke: with woodland at each end to obstruct attempts to out-flank it the great rampart would have been a formidable obstacle to the new invaders. Certainly the Saxon penetration from Southampton Water seems to have skirted Dorset in its northward drive.

Long after his death 'the Old General' was remembered with affection for the employment provided by his excavations at times when other employment was scarce. Some believed that he arranged the work as a matter of policy to counteract what would otherwise have been seasons of poverty and local distress. The available labour was of course unskilled and without experience of archaeological work; Pitt-Rivers employed permanent assistants to supervise and record the excavations, engaging young men whom he could train for the tasks he delegated to them. These clerks, augmenting the retinue at Rushmore, were not always appreciated by the family. In 1882 one of the general's daughters, Agnes, confided to her diary, 'A whole heap of clerks etc. came yesterday. Three —and the money the Man gives them and the food they eat, if only we could have it we should be quite rich. Oh it is a wicked waste of money and they do no good. Drawing old stones and bones and skulls etc.'

'The Man' was a frequently hostile name for her father, and 'the Minor One' for her mother. It was a turbulent and quarrelsome family life, in the Stanley tradition. Writing of the generation of Stanleys to which the general's wife belonged, Nancy Mitford commented that among them 'there was not one quite ordinary human being'. They all had 'a sort of downright rudeness, a passion for quarrelling'. Thomas Hardy, recalling his experience at a Stanley family party, wrote, 'An exciting family dispute supervened, in which they took no notice of us guests at all.'

The younger generation at Rushmore emulated their elders with explosive scenes, savage quarrels and dramatic reconciliations. Agnes's diary is full of such emotional occasions, and Bertrand Russell—a Stanley nephew of Mrs Pitt-Rivers—has preserved a malicious picture of a visit to Rushmore in his *Autobiography*:

> With the exception of the General, most of the family were more or less mad. Mrs Pitt-Rivers, who was a Stanley, had become a miser, and if visitors left any of their bacon and egg she would put it back in the dish. The eldest son was a Guardsman, very smart and correct. He always came down late for breakfast and rang the bell for fresh food. When he ordered it, my Aunt would scream at the footman, saying there was no need of it as there was plenty left from the scrapings from the visitors' plates. The footman, however, paid no attention to her, but quietly obeyed the Guardsman.

In his thumbnail sketches of his 'more or less mad' cousins Russell lampoons them with a vindictive relish; but there was undoubtedly a strong vein of eccentricity among them, and the general's youngest son, Arthur, was certified as insane and confined in an asylum in Scotland.

While the archaeological excavation proceeded General Pitt-Rivers was engaged simultaneously in other local activities which at first glance might seem unrelated to his main work but were in truth an integral part of it. In the Victorian manner he felt he had a mission to educate the generality of people, the ordinary folk. 'The improvement of the masses' was a phrase that came naturally to him. It was his aim to display publicly the continuity of history and prehistory, the step-by-step evolution of the natural world and of material culture. In his own words, 'The knowledge of the facts of evolution, and of the processes of gradual development, is the one great knowledge that we have to inculcate, and this knowledge can be taught by museums, provided they are arranged in such a manner that those who run may read. The working classes have but little time.'

The knowledge which he pursued in his excavations he offered to share with others in his museums. His earliest anthropological collection, displayed at the South Kensington Museum in the 1870s, was later given to Oxford University where it grew into what is now the Pitt-Rivers Museum. In Cranborne Chase he put two collections on permanent display. One, devoted to the visual arts and containing works by Cuyp, Cranach, Breughel, Poussin and others, was housed in the thirteenth-century building known as King John's House. Characteristically the general excavated round the building and dated its earliest part—a little after King John, but the name persists.

The other collection was devoted to a miscellany of folk art, panoramic models of his excavations, agricultural implements, pottery and more unexpected exhibits which reflected the general's wide interests—ranging from an historical display of locks and keys to bronze figures newly acquired from Benin. This was housed in the old gipsy school which he expanded as Farnham Museum. The idea of a gipsy school had been inspired by John West, rector of Chettle from 1820 to 1846, who had previously had missionary experience in Canada and saw a fresh evangelical opportunity in the Christianizing of the Chase gipsies. The school was built by voluntary subscriptions, to give free education to gipsy children, but West died before the building was completed and the project languished without him.

Admission to the Farnham Museum and to King John's House at Tollard Royal was free. And as if to demonstrate that a pilgrimage of self-education did not have to be an unrelievedly solemn affair the general also provided, free of charge, the pleasure gardens at the Larmer Tree. He began work on the gardens in his first year at Rushmore and continued to add to them until almost the time of his death. The temple was the first building to be erected, in 1880; the half-timbered cottage in 1881 and the bandstand in 1886. A theatre was added in 1895 and a dining-hall seating two hundred in the following year. The Oriental buildings came in the late 1890s—the lower and upper Indian houses in 1897 and '98, the Indian Room in 1899. A Moultan chimney-piece from the Viceroy's Reception Hall at the Lahore Durbar in 1894 found a permanent home at the Larmer Tree Gardens.

Those who made their way to the seeming obscurity of Tollard Royal and nearby Farnham could certainly look forward to a day of varied pleasures. If they wanted to picnic in one of the arbours at the Larmer Tree the general provided crockery, knives and forks, tables and chairs, and even cooking stoves and utensils. German skittles, bowls and swings were available in the shrubbery. For a diversion they could look at some of the general's strange menagerie of animals that he was trying to acclimatize and in some cases hybridize with British species—the Mesopotamian deer that he crossed with fallow, the yaks that he crossed with Jersey, Pembroke, Highland and Kerry cattle, the reindeer that succumbed to a hot summer, the Australian bower bird and the unsuccessful South American parrots. There were llamas and emus, prairie dogs that bred but failed to survive, impeyan pheasants and sheep from Aden. Here, as in all his interests, the general's zeal as a collector can only be described fittingly as cornucopious.

If the visitor wished for music he could start an impromptu singsong—

having first asked the caretaker for the keys of the piano and American organ—or he might hear the general's private band performing. The band was yet another of the general's creations aimed to broaden the interests of the villagers and to enliven the Victorian Sabbath. Some of the bandsmen were Rushmore estate workers, others lived and worked in Tollard Royal like Ted Coombs, the village postman. They were given a uniform based on Romney's portrait of a Chase keeper—'big felt hats and swallowtail coats, breeches and gaiters' is how Mr Coombs described it. To train the band General Pitt-Rivers called in the bandmaster of his old regiment, Mr Godfrey—a name of more than passing interest since his son was Sir Dan Godfrey, the founder of the Bournemouth Symphony Orchestra.

Adjoining the Larmer Tree Gardens was a racecourse with lawn tennis courts inside its perimeter. Here also were the first tee and the last green of an eighteen-hole golf course which extended across Minchington Down to Rushmore Park. The charge for a day's play was sixpence for men and threepence for ladies.

The general's enjoyment of his inheritance and the bold initiatives it permitted lasted for only twenty years, which were latterly clouded by failing health. As early as 1892 his daughter Agnes noted 'Papa very weak and ill'. By the summer of 1899 the end was in sight, when she wrote 'P. very ill' and added characteristically 'at loggerheads with the nurse'. The following spring on 4 May 'Papa died quite peacefully at 1.45 this morning. I drove over to Rushmore and saw him. He looked quite beautiful.'

In death the general had one or two novel and idiosyncratic ideas yet to express. He favoured cremation at a time when it was regarded with horror by many, including his wife if we may believe the story that, when she declared her determination to be buried in the normal manner, the general retorted, 'If I say you'll burn, woman, you'll *burn*!' She was spared that fate, however, as he predeceased her. As to the disposal of his own corpse, he exemplified his scientific objectivity by indicating that:

if it could be done without inconvenience and without jarring upon the feelings of those that I leave behind, a post-mortem examination should be made of my body, and the particulars of my physical constitution recorded by a competent anatomist for the information of my descendants, more particularly the form and peculiarities of the cerebral convolutions and I should even think it reasonable if it were practicable to preserve the skeleton for comparison with those of any of my progeny who might be similarly minded to have it done.

As a last act he wished to place himself in the long continuity that

Ferne Tennis Club, 1879: Ladies' Committee

Horace Pitt, the sixth and last Baron Rivers

A stone curlew

Veiny Cheese Pond, Long Crichel

Typical downland coombe near Win Green

Martin Village

Ackling Dyke, the Roman road from Badbury to Old Sarum

stretched back to the earliest inhumations he had excavated—as if to record and date and 'typologize' himself for the benefit of some future archaeologist studying Victorian England. His grandson, Captain George, quoted the general as saying, 'What the people lack is history. They must learn the links between the past and the present.' It was the study of those links that were his life's work. When he was appointed, in 1882, to be the first Inspector of Ancient Monuments he inaugurated a new era in which the physical testament of prehistory became a national concern, where hitherto it had been at best the subject of an antiquarian hobby.

Today Rushmore House is a school, King John's House the private residence of one of the general's great-grandsons, the contents of the Farnham Museum are dispersed and the Larmer Tree Gardens closed except for some special occasion in aid of charity. Times change—even in Tollard Royal the nineteenth century has been displaced by the twentieth. But if the general's visible impression on the local scene is less apparent than it was in 1900 there is no gainsaying that his name is written indelibly —if invisibly—on the landscape of Cranborne Chase, at Winkelbury and Worbarrow, at Rotherley and Woodyates and many another place where, in Sir Mortimer Wheeler's words, 'From the miserable scraps of ancient humanity which his spade was constantly bringing to light information had to be wrung drop by drop by sheer intellectual grasp, by an imagination that found its exercise in an enlarged understanding of the manifestations and processes of ordinary, unheroic human destiny.'

CHAPTER TWELVE

The Villages of the Chase

SOME OF THE Chase villages have already been described in their particular contexts, but others have still to be given the attention they merit. This chapter is to make amends to them; not in any special order, rather in the desultory wandering way that one explores the Chase over a period and gradually accumulates a personal hoard of impressions and memories. Yet, having said that, it must none the less be appropriate to choose Cranborne itself as the starting point. It gave its name as an identity to these secluded and uncertainly defined hunting grounds and was for centuries their administrative centre. Whatever else it may have lost, its aura of historical consequence is certainly not extinguished. The Chase of Cranborne will not disappear from the map of England for many years to come.

The River Crane, from which Cranborne takes its name, flows down from Pentridge and passes through the grounds of Cranborne Manor, providing a pleasant waterside stroll for today's visitors to the manor gardens. It is a vicinity that must have attracted human settlement at an early stage. About a mile downstream there was a Roman building; by AD 930 the Saxons had established a priory in what later became the vicarage garden; and half a mile to the south-east of the village the Normans fortified Castle Hill. Domesday records *Creneburne* as one of the king's manors and there was already a hunting lodge here when King John acquired the Chase. During his reign money was spent on repairs on four occasions between 1198 and 1207. In addition, during 1207–8, the lodge was either rebuilt or considerably enlarged. Sixty-seven pounds, six shillings and four pence—a substantial sum at that period—was spent on 'building the King's houses of Cranborne'.

In the early fourteenth century the then Earl of Gloucester rebuilt the house entirely: this in turn was transformed into the present manor house, created by Robert Cecil for the entertainment of his royal master, James I. Described by one authority, Arthur Oswald, as 'the loveliest manor house in Dorset' Cranborne was never the seat of the heads of the family, who preferred Hatfield House. The rôles it has filled have been those of hunting-box, administrative centre for the Chase and the Salisbury estate, and seat of the eldest son. When it housed the Chase court it had its dungeon equipped to receive prisoners detained by the Chase officers. The ringbolts, to which prisoners' chains were locked, survived until the early 1800s when the prison was converted into a larder.

The traditional importance of Cranborne lay in its combination of Chase court and manor house, priory, market and road centre. More than any other Chase village it might have grown into a town, providing a diagonal focus point between Ringwood and Shaftesbury in one direction and between Wimborne and Salisbury in the other; yet somehow the advantages it seemed to enjoy crumbled away. The priory originally had Tewkesbury as a subordinate priory, but when Tewkesbury was rebuilt in 1102 the rôles were reversed: Cranborne's abbot was transferred to Tewkesbury and Cranborne became the subordinate house. Even so Cranborne retained some local importance as a religious centre, its church having four outlying chapels. Decay eventually afflicted them, the one at Verwood being in ruins in 1666; the one at Alderholt was in use as late as 1650 but fell into disuse about 1670 and was demolished about 1690.

Lord Salisbury's sale of the Chase to his neighbour, Lord Shaftesbury, automatically transferred the business of the Chase court to Wimborne St Giles and incidentally ended the long chapter of royal hunting trips to Cranborne. As a commercial and trading centre Cranborne had two annual fairs and its weekly market. The weaving of ribbons was an established local industry in the eighteenth century and there were tanners, glovers and seven innkeepers, as well as the usual crafts and trades appropriate to a largely self-sufficient community that numbered a population of 1,402 in the census of 1801. By then, however, any hopes of rising commercial prosperity must have been fading. In 1815 the market was described as 'nearly lost' and in 1828 the market house was pulled down because the weekly business had declined so much.

The reason for its decline must lie in the way Cranborne was bypassed by road and rail. Its ancient nexus had brought together routes that radiated to Wilton, Salisbury, Ringwood, Blandford and Wimborne—routes of great importance in earlier centuries when the main road from London to Weymouth and Poole issued through Salisbury to Cranborne, and the north–south route across the eastern half of the Chase was the Wilton Way to Cranborne. The makers of turnpikes and railroads had new criteria, however. They were looking for the quickest and easiest passage spanning rivers and linking towns. Cranborne is not a bridge-town and it failed to develop a satisfactory route of its own eastwards. Fordingbridge might have been the key to Cranborne's problem but any hope of a Cranborne–Fordingbridge thrust across the Avon disappeared from view in the depths of the New Forest. From Blandford on the Stour to

Salisbury on the Avon the turnpike swept to the north of Cranborne, which lacked the commercial magnetism to deflect the road builders from their ideal course. Similarly when the railways extended westwards from London it was through Salisbury and Ringwood that they passed, to Tisbury and Wimborne respectively. Even when a rail-link between Salisbury, West Moors and Wimborne was planned and constructed in the 1860s it avoided Cranborne, preferring to set up stations at Alderholt and Verwood.

A contributory factor may have been the inactivity of the Poole, Wimborne and Cranborne Trust, set up in 1755 as a potential rival to the Great Western Turnpike. It acquired the existing road from Wimborne to Cranborne and was intended to modernize the traditional route from Cranborne via Tidpit and Toyd Down to Coombe Bissett and Salisbury. Swift and energetic action might have saved Cranborne but for some reason the Trust did not take over this section at first. A later Act did so expressly but no repairs were ever done and an Act of 1835 formally abandoned the project. The Great Western Turnpike had won the day and the only remaining move was for Cranborne to join it. Here too the inactivity of the local turnpike Trust was to lead to the abandonment of its projected road from Cranborne to Sixpenny Handley. It was forestalled by Lord Shaftesbury who built his own new road from Wimborne St Giles across Bottlebush Down to meet the Great Western Turnpike at what is now the Handley roundabout. The traveller from Cranborne joins Lord Shaftesbury's road—the B3081—at Creech Hill Farm.

In spite of these setbacks Cranborne's population nearly doubled in the first sixty years of the nineteenth century, to 2,656 in 1861, but this is mis-leading since it was a parish total and Cranborne was the largest parish in Dorset, embracing Verwood, Edmondsham and Alderholt. Wake Smart puts the population of Cranborne itself, considered as a 'town' or large village, at 721 in 1841, which makes an interesting comparison with the 1901 census—taken seven years after Verwood and Alderholt had been detached from Cranborne as separate parishes. Cranborne's 1901 popula-tion of 687 confirms the general impression that Cranborne stood still and gradually atrophied during the nineteenth century. Today its quiet charm will please the casual visitor, and its air of undeniable respectability gives the lie to the old belief that the world will end 'when Cranborne is whoreless, Wimborne is pooriess and Harley is hareless'. Fortunately one can still see an occasional hare up by the Harley Gap.

Since their emancipation Verwood and Alderholt have gone their separate ways, turning their backs on Cranborne. Alderholt looks to Fordingbridge as its urban centre, Verwood looks to Ringwood—for the present, at least. If the planners' unlikely dream of Verwood as a sort of poor man's Swindon by the year 2000 is realized it will not need to look outside itself for anything—except sympathy maybe. The churches of the new parishes were in existence before the separation from Cranborne. Verwood's church was consecrated in 1829, Alderholt's was built by the Marquess of Salisbury and consecrated in 1849—an act of generosity somewhat soured by his lordship's subsequent enclosure of part of Alderholt Heath, which provoked much opposition in 1858 as an invasion of common rights.

The heathy nature of much of these new territories emphasizes their alienation from the characteristic ambience of the Chase. Cranborne is on the edge of the chalk downs at a point where a topsoil of gravel, composed of water-rolled flint pebbles in sand, begins to overlie the chalk. Almost immediately, to the south and east, the chalk gives way to the Eocene clays and sand. The narrow belt of potter's clay provided Alderholt and Verwood with their era of local industry: beyond the clay the acid heath extends to the borders of the Channel coast. The sweet water of the tributary Crane is lost in the peaty mainstream of the Moors river. The land at Verwood was rated by Hutchins as 'of a wild and heathy character and sterile nature'. Surtees, describing this area of heath and moor along the southern border of the Chase from Horton tower to Ringwood, warned that 'it is necessary to ride to a leader who knows the country, to avoid the unpleasant predicament of floundering in a bog'. Nothing could be more different from the dry and bracing heights of Win Green and Whitesheet Hill than the point on the outer bounds south of Verwood where the Ebblake stream crosses Black Moor to join the Crane in the swampy valley of the Moors. Here the downland flora is replaced by bog asphodel, cotton grass, sundew and the superb blue flowers of marsh gentian; and here, according to Trelawney Dayrell-Reed, bitterns still boomed in the 1930s.

Another aspect of Verwood in the early years of this century was described by Ralph Wightman in *The Wessex Heathland*, where he gave this account of the colonization of the area:

Even before the 1914–18 war the railway made it possible for retired people to live a suburban life on the line which runs through the heath to West Moors and Verwood. The motor-car, between the wars, made it possible to branch out beyond the railway and there are hundreds of little villas all over this part of the heath. There is a strange mixture of modern brick houses with an occasional old cottage which once got a living from the poor soil. Most of these old houses are very small, built of crumbling cobb and with thatched roofs. They stand on a half-dozen acres of sandy soil, hardly won from the waste, and there are very few native inhabitants. Almost every holder is a stranger who was tempted by the relative cheapness of the land.

Beyond Alderholt and Verwood lies the Avon valley. The river's western bank is technically within the Chase but it is difficult to see the great riverine estates of Somerley and Breamore as having much kinship with the rest of the Chase. The higher ground above the valley is extensively planted to conifers, with the newly named Ringwood Forest surrounding the sand and gravel quarries that are one of Verwood's modern industries. There is an impersonal quality about these standardized plantations, extending northward to the commons of Alderholt and Cranborne, which provides a suitably negative border to terminate the south-eastern corner of the Chase.

What is true of the Avon valley applies equally to the Nadder. The northern boundary of the Chase follows the course of the waters of 'Noddre', as the Saxons named it, but the villages on its banks and those of its tributary, the River Sem, played no great part in the history of the Chase. In some degree they lay outside the effective application of Chase law: at most they were in the purlieu or percursus extremity of the Chase territory. It is indeed tempting to find a natural frontier in the great scarp from Whitesheet Hill to Salisbury and to dismiss the vale below. To do so, however, would be to ignore Wardour Castle and Wilton, the homes of two of the most influential families in Chase history—the Arundells and the Pembrokes.

Wardour Castle was built in 1392 and severely damaged in the Civil War, after an heroic defence by Lady Blanche Arundell. It is now in ruins. In 1770 Henry, the eighth Baron Arundell, built a new castle, which is now a school. In *Jude the Obscure* Thomas Hardy gave an interesting description of the castle—particularly its picture galleries—at the end of the last century when it was still occupied by the family.

The fortunes of Wilton have been very different. Of all the great houses in the Chase it is the one that conforms most closely to the general concept of a 'stately home', visited annually by great crowds who marvel at its historical splendour. It is indeed a national treasure. The little market town of Wilton lies just outside the Chase, on the north bank of the Nadder, and the same is true of the other settlements along the river—Barford St Martin, Dinton, Teffont and Tisbury. It is the villages clustered about the A30—Ansty, Swallowcliffe, Sutton Mandeville, Fovant and Compton Chamberlayne—that represent the Chase's northern fringe. Historically they looked southwards. Each of them had its down or its *iver*—a dialect word for a steep slope—running up to the cliff-like crest of the Salisbury Way. The farmsteads developed on the heavy lowland soils and the sheep flocks grazed up the southern slopes.

The A30 between Barford St Martin and the foot of Whitesheet Hill is comparatively modern. It does not appear in Tunnicliffe's *Topographical Survey*, published in Salisbury in 1791, but it is shown in the early Ordnance Survey maps, so it can be dated at about 1800. What it did was to link together two existing main roads and largely supersede them. At Barford St Martin it diverged sharply from the road to Hindon, Mere and the West, which declined to its present condition as the B3089. At the foot of Whitesheet Hill the A30 met the Salisbury Way coach route. Those steep hill climbs had been unavoidable when the lowlands had been too boggy in winter for the eighteenth-century roadmakers to tackle: the new lower road from Salisbury to Shaftesbury, represented by the A30, must have been hailed as an important advance. Doubtless it invigorated the villages through which it passed, though their origins are ancient enough. Sutton Mandeville's church has Norman elements; so has Fovant's; and in the chancel of Compton Chamberlayne a tablet records the members of a single family, the Penruddocks, whose mortal remains during four centuries have been accumulating there.

The most celebrated of the Penruddocks was Colonel John, who in 1655 led a rising to restore Charles II. With the support of another colonel, Hugh Grove of Chissenbury, he marched into Salisbury with 200 men, broke open the gaol and proclaimed Charles as king. Popular support was not forthcoming, however, and the force moved westward in the hope of winning recruits. It was to prove an ill-timed adventure. At South Molton the rebels were easily overcome by a detachment of cavalry sent out from Exeter. After sentence of death at Exeter an appeal to Cromwell to act mercifully brought the grim concession that Penruddock and Grove should be spared hanging and be beheaded instead. Penruddock's final letters to his wife, Arundell, are eloquent and moving. A man of undoubted personal courage, he wrote, 'The greatest conflict I have had in this extremity was my parting with thee; the next encounter is to be with Death, and my Saviour hath so pulled out the sting thereof that I hope to assault it without fear.'

Compton Chamberlayne today is a fine example of the traditionally integrated unit of manor house, park, church and village. The house, originally built in the reign of Henry VIII, was later Italianized. The park is reputed to have been a deer park in 1100. In 1885 it held about 300 deer and the two lakes were well stocked with wildfowl.

Climb up the track from Compton village to the top of Compton Down, cross the Salisbury Way and look down into the next valley, and you will see one of the pleasantest stretches of the Chase countryside. This is the valley of the River Ebble or—as it is sometimes called—the Chalke Valley. A single minor road runs the length of the valley, not intending to do more than lead you to one of the villages, to Alvediston or Ebbesbourne Wake, Broad Chalke or Bowerchalke. The valley retains a discreetly private atmosphere, minding its own business in the deep fold between the Chase's two highest ridgeways—the Ox Drove from Win Green and the Salisbury Way from Whitesheet Hill. Wayfarers of many centuries must have paused on the heights to look down speculatively on this thread of human settlements.

The Ebble begins to acquire form and presence at Alvediston, tracing its course—choked with watercress—past the church. Anthony Eden lies buried here, his tomb lettered with elegant simplicity and placed in the front of the churchyard where it overlooks the little valley of what Leland called 'the Chalke bourne'. 'Stowford river' was another name that the Ebble once had and later discarded. Standing apart from the village, under Gallows Hill, is Norrington Farm—once the home of the Gawains or Gawens, who bought it and built their mansion in 1377 and in 1658 sold it to Sir Wadham Wyndham. Several large marble tablets in the church commemorate the Wyndhams. In its heyday Norrington must have been a fine place, with its gardens, stewponds and bowling-green, but it declined when William Wyndham built a new mansion at Dinton. By 1830 Norrington was dilapidated and being used as accommodation for farm labourers. Happily it is now restored to something like its original splendour. Its fourteenth-century origins are unmistakable—even to a recently discovered wallfixing for rushlights—and it can again challenge comparison with the best of the manor houses and country houses in which the area is so rich.

At Ebbesbourne Wake and at Broad Chalke the only roads out of the valley run southwards. Between Alvediston and Throope the northern slopes—with one exception—offer nothing better than farm tracks and bridle ways. The exception is at Fifield Bavant, where a minor but adequate road climbs to the top of the scarp, crosses the Salisbury Way near Fovant Hut and makes a spectacular descent to join the A30 beside Fovant village. At first glance Fifield Bavant may not seem to have much to offer. In 1825 it had seven houses with forty-nine inhabitants and nothing that has happened since in Fifield Bavant could be described as a boom. Its church was dismissed by Bowles with the words 'nothing to recommend it. It has the appearance of a barn.' Nevertheless it is worth a visit, if only from curiosity because it must be almost the smallest church in England. Its dimensions are given as thirty-five feet long by fifteen feet wide. Claimed as a thirteenth-century foundation it is now largely hemmed in by the modern industrial buildings of the manor farm. Its walls are of stone, its roof tiled and surmounted with a little louvred bell-turret in which a single bell summoned, one February Sunday recently, a congregation of two.

To find a church that Bowles admired one need go no further than the next village, Broad Chalke, where he judged All Saints to be 'certainly the handsomest church in the vale'. It is a chunky foursquare building with a foursquare tower and an attractive interior. A memorial brass commemorates the novelist and poet, Maurice Hewlett, who died in 1923 after twenty years in the parish. A more celebrated author, John Aubrey, was one of the churchwardens here in 1659: the other was George Penruddock. Aubrey inherited the tenancy of a farm in Broad Chalke from his father in 1652 and kept it for about fifteen years. During his time as churchwarden he saw the last of six bells installed in the tower and he described them as 'one of the tunablest rings of bells in Wiltshire'. The years he spent at Broad Chalke are reflected in his *Natural History of Wiltshire*.

The Ebble runs on through Bishopstone and Coombe Bissett and Odstock to join the Avon below Salisbury, near Longford Castle, but the essential character of the valley scarcely extends beyond Stratford Tony. At Coombe Bissett one joins the main Blandford–Salisbury road and the city of Salisbury begins to gather its suburbs about itself. Odstock's claim to attention nowadays is its district hospital rather than its gipsy curse or its two uncommonly durable rectors who between them served the parish for 137 years. Bishopstone draws back from the valley road and prefers to remain undisturbed, and it is at Stratford Tony that one is tempted to stop and watch the Ebble burbling gently over pebbles where a rough track fords across to climb the downs above the village. It is a small and unpretentious place—just a few houses clustered about a little squat-towered church of stone, brick and flint, in what amounts to a cul-de-sac. In spring there is a wild profusion of daffodils round the churchyard. High up on the downs forget-me-not grows in the lane beside Throope Hill.

That shallow pebbly fording place across the Ebble is of little consequence today, but the Romans used it when they made their road from Badbury to cross the stream here and continue up the road to what is now Salisbury racecourse but was once the Roman route to Old Sarum. The modern road out of Stratford Tony in that direction is exactly on the Roman line. And when the Saxons and their successors travelled south from Wilton they came past the hare warren on top of the hill and down to the ford at Stratford Tony, to follow the Wilton Way over the downs to Tidpit. It is not difficult to imagine Celia Fiennes pausing to let her horse drink from the Ebble stream here before riding up to Toyd Clump on her way to Blandford in about 1690.

If we now return to the head of the valley and look westward from Alvediston we enter a new landscape lying well below the heights of Whitesheet, Win Green and Winkelbury but having no substantial river valley and none of the marshy or heathy character that surrounds the chalk margins elsewhere. From Berwick St John through to Shaftesbury the landscape lacks any striking feature. The Nadder rises between the Donheads but it is of little consequence until it meets its tributary, the Sem. The villages and hamlets along the A30—Birdbush, Ludwell, Charlton and Coombe—are undistinguished. Yet there is enough of interest to detain us. In this north-western corner of the Chase there is an element of Dissent, of nonconformity, which makes a welcome contrast to the strongholds of the Establishment elsewhere; and there are the sad remembrances of one of the principal Chase families, the Groves of Ferne House and Berry Court.

Charlton strikes a puritanical note, with its church so vehemently scorning beauty that one suspects a blunder in the architect's office—the winning design for the frontage of a Victorian gaol being used in error for the west end. The interior has an attractive austerity, very bare with white walls and the atmosphere of an early Congregationalist chapel. There are three good modern stained-glass windows which would surely have pleased Herbert William Bryans, whose headstone in the churchyard makes the grave seem a friendlier place. The youngest son of a youngest son he wrote his own epitaph thus:

> For ten years I made tea in India
> For two I made wine in France
> For thirty stained glass windows in England
> And bad puns all the time.

He died in 1925.

The Donhead villages—St Mary and St Andrew—are ancient settlements on the fertile greensand. St Mary's church has Norman walls and pillars, and a font that has served the parish for 900 years. St Andrew's has the arms of Shaftesbury Abbey in its east window and a chantry founded in 1327. At Ludwell, a hamlet in Donhead St Mary, the Grove Arms preserves the name and the badge of a family which once dominated the Donheads and the neighbouring parish of Berwick St John, distributing its patronage and its dead between the three churches impartially. The Groves played no great part in our national history but their story is an important thread in the social texture of the Chase.

They originated from Buckinghamshire, from John de Grove of Chalfont St Giles, who died in 1353. One of his descendants, Thomas, was High Sheriff of Bucks in 1434. Thomas's younger brother had a son, John, who settled in Wiltshire—perhaps immediately at Berry Court, which is half in Donhead St Mary and half in Donhead St Andrew and was certainly the residence of the Groves in the early sixteenth century. When the religious houses were dissolved Berry Court was under lease to one of the Groves and remained the family seat until 1563, when Ferne House was acquired. In 1560 Robert Grove was described as of 'Dunhead Andrew' when Clarencieux King of Arms authorized the Grove arms for him to bear, so we can confidently locate him at Berry Court. He was one of two commissioners appointed in 1563 to make a survey of Lord Pembroke's lands; previously he had been Sir Thomas Arundell's Steward.

It was Robert who started the rise in the Grove fortunes. He became MP for Shaftesbury and Feodary for the county of Wiltshire. His son William, trained as a lawyer, followed his father as MP for Shaftesbury, married an heiress, purchased Ferne in 1563 and Sedgehill—north of Shaftesbury—in 1582. In the next generation a second William married the heiress daughter of a Shaftesbury MP and through her he acquired a fine house in Shaftesbury. A description of the town in about 1620 says 'the greatest ornament of the town is a fair turreted house of the Lord Arundell's of Wardour, which as it were shrowdeth under the high walls the dwelling of—Grove, a very worthy gentleman'. A map of Shaftesbury in 1615 identifies both these houses—Arundell's at the corner of Bimport and Tout Hill, Grove's on the northern side of Bimport and its first side turning. They are the only two private residences named on this map, which implies that Mr Grove—identified as William in a second map of a few years later—was already an important citizen. The house itself has been immortalized by Thomas Hardy as 'Old-Grove Place', the home of Phillotson and Sue Bridehead after their marriage in *Jude the Obscure*.

The Grove connection with Shaftesbury and with Parliament persisted into the troubled years of the Commonwealth and its aftermath. That great nonconformist, Richard Baxter, provides an interesting picture of Ferne as a sanctuary for dissenters during the lifetime of Thomas Grove—described by Baxter as 'that learned, humble holy Gentleman, Mr Thomas Grove, an Ancient Parliament-Man, of as great Sincerity and Integrity, as almost any Man I ever knew'. Their acquaintance dated from 1643 when Grove was appointed a member of the Westminster Assembly, in contemplation of which Baxter asserted that 'the Christian world, since the days of the Apostles, had never a synod of more excellent divines (taking one thing with another) than this'. It held 1,163 meetings, designed to replace bishops with presbyterianism and generally to purify the forms of public worship. As religious controversy intensified, while the political pendulum swung between the puritan ascendancy and the restoration of the Catholic Stuarts, Thomas Grove's own involvement became more militant. The partisanship of civil strife was keenly felt in the local community. In 1645 the aged rector of Donhead St Mary, George Pope, was ejected because of his royalist sympathies and replaced by Peter Ince. The royalist colonel, Hugh Grove, who was executed in 1655 for his part in Penruddock's Rising, was Thomas Grove's close kinsman—though in the opposite camp. In 1660 it was the turn of Peter Ince to be ejected from the rectory of Donhead St Mary and to be given sanctuary at Ferne House by Thomas Grove.

During the 1660s, according to Richard Baxter, the diocese of Salisbury was 'more fiercely driven on to conformity by Dr Seth Ward, their Bishop, than any place else'. Ferne became an illicit meeting place for dissenters as the spirit of resistance grew: it is significant that Dorset can claim eleven 1662 foundations of Congregationalist churches, and Wiltshire nine of 1662 or 1670. The Conventicle Act of 1664, which forbade the assembly of more than five persons for unauthorized religious purposes, brought matters to a head. Grove was involved in a lawsuit or prosecution of some kind and seems to have gone into exile. In a reference to Peter Ince as a member of the Ferne household, Baxter wrote that Mr Grove himself 'is now driven out of his Country for receiving and hearing such in his House'. At some time prior to 1669 Ince was imprisoned at Dorchester.

In 1671 Thomas Grove returned to Ferne, to be reunited with Peter Ince. In 1672 the ejected rector of Sutton Mandeville, Thomas Rosewell, was invited to Ferne. He was a friend of Peter Ince who had preached at his ordination at Salisbury in 1654. Another member of the group, then or later, was Samuel Wells, the son of an ejected minister. Bred up to the ministry Samuel became Grove's chaplain, married his daughter Elizabeth, and is buried at Berwick St John. The Declaration of Indulgence in 1672 made life easier at Ferne, which was now licensed as a meeting place. Peter Ince became the first minister and founder of Birdbush Congregational church, though the church building was not completed until 1723. Either Ferne or Berry Court probably continued for some time to be used as a meeting place—perhaps until Thomas Grove's death in 1691.

Birdbush, on the A30 east of Ludwell, is about a mile from Ferne. That

first church of 1723, with its rather elegant rectangular leaded windows
and its austere farmhouse squareness, has gone—replaced in 1871 by a
more consciously church-like design. Writing of this latter building in
1936 the author of *The Story of Peter Ince* declared his belief that 'So
important is this church . . . that it may well become for future years a
famous shrine for Free Churchmen from all parts of the country'. Alas for
such high hopes—by 1973 it had outlived its purpose and its surviving
activities were transferred to a smaller adjoining chapel served by a
minister from Shaftesbury. When I visited the church in 1975 it was
apparently abandoned and neglected for lack of funds to maintain it.
There can be no victorious carousal by the old Enemy, however, in the
Lamb Inn which for long stood brazenly in front of Birdbush church. The
last pint has been pulled, the sign has disappeared, and the house is now
a private dwelling.

The Groves of the eighteenth century were no less men of their time,
though the two periods could hardly be more different. As the memory of
'that excellent, humble, holy, learned Gentleman', Thomas Grove,
recedes into the past we must turn to his namesake four generations later
in Romney's portrait of him as Master of Foxhounds, painted in 1788.
Besides this portrait two other Romneys hung at Ferne. One was of
Thomas's wife, Charlotte, whom he married in 1781: her sister, Lady
Shelley, was the mother of the poet—a relationship of some consequence,
as will shortly appear. The other portrait was of Thomas Grove's sister,
Elizabeth, who in 1776 married her cousin William Chafin Grove of
Zeals. Another Romney portrait of Elizabeth hung at Zeals, with one of
her husband, who incidentally preserved a Grove tradition by being MP
for Shaftesbury.

They were grandees indeed, the Groves, in the days of George III and
the Regency. According to Colt Hoare, a contemporary of Grove, 'The
present proprietor of Ferne has much improved his estate by considerable
purchases, and by high cultivation and extensive plantations. The old
mansion-house having fallen into decay, he rebuilt it on an enlarged scale
in the year 1811, on the site of the old structure.' Berry Court was still his,
and he bought Ashcombe Farm from the Arundells in 1814. Ashcombe
stands on the downs above Berry Court and beside Win Green: Grove
pulled down the old mansion and converted part of the stables into a
farmhouse. He had his London house, of course, and also an establishment
in Weymouth which must have been on a tolerably lavish scale, judging
from a report in March 1819 that 'Mr Grove gave a grand dinner to the
Gentlemen of the Farquharson Hunt at his house Loyal Terrace at
Weymouth'.

His approach to fatherhood was no less compendious, there being eleven children of whom eight survived childhood and enjoyed the occasional companionship of their Shelley cousins. The Groves visited the Sussex home of the Shelleys, and the families also met in London. At seventeen Harriet Grove was in love with Percy Bysshe Shelley. In her 1809 diary brief entries record almost daily correspondence with the young poet and it is thought that she had some collaborative hand in his first novel, *Zastrozzi*. Her elder brother John had a flat in Lincoln's Inn Fields which seems to have been a useful rendezvous and lodging for young Groves and Shelleys visiting London. When Harriet and Percy Bysshe coincided they met daily to go shopping and theatre-going. Their parents regarded them as an engaged couple and left them alone together. In one of her diary entries Harriet wrote, 'All the Party went out save me and Dearest P.'

The intensity of this cousinly romance persisted through 1809 and into 1810, but by August Shelley was expressing in poetry his sorrow at the loss of Harriet. It seems certain that the wildness and vehemence of some of his beliefs and opinions disquieted her. She must have confided her misgivings to her parents, for there was a spell of coolness between the families. Quickly any thought of a marriage faded away. On Shelley's side, however, his friendship with Harriet's brothers was unimpaired. In July 1811 he was staying with young Thomas Grove and his wife in Wales; and a few weeks later it was Charles Henry Grove who accompanied Shelley on his visits to another Harriet—Harriet Westbrook—and who went with the eloping pair to their departure on the London-to-York coach. That same autumn Harriet Grove married William Helyar and retired into a life of rural obscurity. 'All those fine capabilities will moulder' was Shelley's last sad comment.

The Victorian prosperity of the Groves was crowned with a baronetcy in acknowledgement of those generations of political service: the latest Thomas, Member of Parliament for South Wiltshire, became Sir Thomas Grove. His son and heir married one of the daughters of General Pitt-Rivers in 1882 and this alliance of Ferne with neighbouring Rushmore was a great social event, drawing the two families closer together in their pleasures and sporting pastimes. They danced, hunted, and shot together in traditional style; and they pursued the latest craze, lawn tennis. General Pitt-Rivers laid out a tennis court in the Larmer Tree Gardens and the daughters of Ferne went one better by forming a ladies' club, with a uniform playing suit and a club emblem—appropriately a frond of fern. Their photograph, taken in 1879, is the earliest extant of such a group anywhere in Britain.

While the young ones played, Sir Thomas had his problems to face. The cost of his Parliamentary elections was ruinous. The agricultural depression was already threatening those who lived improvidently. His pleasure-loving son was unemployable, except as a magistrate. The Romneys disappeared from the walls of Ferne, to be replaced discreetly by copies. When Sir Thomas died in 1897 Ferne itself passed into other hands. The new baronet, Sir Walter Grove, continued to reside in the smaller house at Sedgehill until his death when that home also—the last of the Grove establishments—was sold with its contents by the heir, who worked in Hollywood as an adviser on the manners and customs of the English upper classes: an ironical destiny.

The great mansion at Ferne was demolished during the present century. Only the stables remain, forming the nucleus of an animal sanctuary in the derelict park. So far as Cranborne Chase is concerned one of its most eminent and durable families has disappeared as if they had never existed. It is a story of rise and fall worth recalling over a glass in the Grove Arms at Ludwell beside the carved coat of arms with the family's motto of decent pride, *Ny dessus, ny dessous:* neither above nor beneath, not superior but not inferior either.

Beyond Ludwell the A30 leads into Shaftesbury and the north-west boundary of the Chase. The town itself lies outside, as the boundary marker was St Rumbold's church on the eastern outskirts. Rather surprisingly there is another church dedicated to St Rumbold in the Chase, the one at Pentridge. A reason for this local attachment to Rumbold is not immediately apparent. His father was King of Northumberland, his mother a daughter of the King of Mercia. Rumbold himself lived for only three days: what he did in those three days to achieve sainthood defies imagination.

The town of Shaftesbury has not yet fulfilled Thomas Hardy's prophecy that it would one day become a health resort, but it is an attractive and salubrious place commanding splendid open views from its hilltop position. In 981 the corpse of Edward the Martyr, murdered at Corfe Castle, was brought to Shaftesbury Abbey for burial. As a result of the cult that developed the town was known for a time by the alternative name of Edwardstowe. When the abbey ruins were excavated during the 1930s the remains of the martyr, in a lead coffin, were exhumed.

From St Rumbold's the Chase boundary passes into the next parish, Cann, to follow the course of the little Stirchel stream from its source to its junction with the Manston Brook and then with the Stour itself at Manston. The area between this water boundary and the A350 is low-lying and sparsely populated. Its landscape of streams and brooks and isolated farmsteads suggests that it was a marshy wilderness until comparatively late in local history and was not cleared, drained and cultivated until the settlements on the higher ground to the east were established. Faringdon or Farrington is a little hamlet that had a chapel of ease and now has a church, rebuilt in 1839. The only house with any real pretension to be regarded as a mansion or country seat in this vicinity north of the Stour is at Fontmell Parva where the central block of the manor house was probably built in the late seventeenth or early eighteenth century by Admiral St Loe, who is said to have brought the mahogany panelling from Honduras. The wings are nineteenth-century additions. In the entrance hall there is a fine shell alcove carved in wood, and in the grounds there are some mighty lime trees. A survey of 1771 shows a tucking mill here.

The A350 traces its line along the skirt of the Chase's western scarp. Like the A30 at the foot of the northern scarp it was a late developer. On the first Ordnance Survey map it appeared as only a minor route and it did not achieve the status of a turnpike until the 1820s. The traditional route from Shaftesbury to Blandford was by the higher road along the crest of the scarp. Here, as at Whitesheet Hill, the choice was between a hard scramble up to the good going of the chalk downland or the wintry risks of boggy conditions on the lower clays. The A350 would have begun modestly as a chain of local routes linking one village to the next, before better drainage and improved road-making techniques developed it as a main road between towns.

Its villages look east and west—east to the downland, west to the vale. That is the classic stance of many of the Chase villages, exemplified here in Compton Abbas, Fontmell Magna, Sutton Waldron and Iwerne Minster, to name four: each has its individual line of communication running east-west. The downland for wool and hay, the vale for milk and corn—that was the old balance. And in these villages the air of a long established well-being is undeniable. Iwerne Minster is perhaps foremost among them, recorded in Domesday as a substantial settlement. Its minster, with its chapelries of Sixpenny Handley, Gussage St Andrew, East Orchard, Margaret Marsh and Hinton St Mary, was given to the Abbess of Shaftesbury in 956 by King Eadwig. The present church has an impressive Norman arcade, a fourteenth-century tower with a shortened stone spire, and an atmosphere of modern zeal misapplied. It contains Wolverton memorial tablets, reminders that Iwerne Minster House was the principal residence of the lords Wolverton, a branch of the Glyn family: it is now Clayesmore School.

The River Iwerne or Ewern rises near the minster and gives its name to two other villages—Iwerne Stepleton and Iwerne Courtney, otherwise known as Shroton—on its course as it threads its way along the eastern flank of Hambledon Hill and Hod Hill before joining the Stour. In Iwerne Courtney church the elaborate and colourful Freke monument recalls the forebears of one of the lords of the Chase; adjoining the church a thatched barn of massive proportions is also notable. Stepleton was an early Pitt possession and passed to the Fownes before Julines Beckford bought it and it became the home and hunting headquarters of Peter Beckford. His marriage to Louisa Pitt brought Stepleton back to the Pitts; the last generations of the Rivers barons are buried here in the family vault that Beckford designed for himself and his descendants in the little Norman chapel. Once it was the parish church of a village long since vanished. Now the great house stands alone in its park and seems uncertain of its rôle in the twentieth century. The kennels that Beckford described in *Thoughts on Hunting* are converted into cottages; the stables are empty.

The A350 follows a twisting course with sudden bends round the park of Stepleton House. The legend that Peter Beckford got the surveyor drunk in order to prevent the road from crossing the park is a plausible explanation for the vagaries of the present road but is probably apocryphal. In its windings the road follows the lower contours of Hod and Hambledon and throws off a minor road between the two hills which clings to Hambledon's southern and western slopes, where Hanford and Child Okeford lie. Hanford House, once the home of the Seymers, is now a girls' school. Child Okeford's church, dating from the thirteenth century but virtually rebuilt in the nineteenth, has a special place in the history of English hymns. A Tudor rector, Sir William Kethe, wrote two enduring favourites—'All people that on earth do dwell' and 'O worship the King, all glorious above'; and the church choir was the first to sing the tune by Sir Arthur Sullivan to which 'Onward, Christian Soldiers' is sung. Sullivan composed it while he was staying with the Seymers at Hanford House.

Of the villages north of Iwerne Minster it is Fontmell Magna that stands out. Here are some fine houses, a mill, a dismantled brewery, a church with some unusual sixteenth-century carvings and a local centre of cultural activities at Springhead, the home of the Gardiner family whose representatives over three generations—Balfour, Rolf and John Eliot— have in their various ways won a more than local reputation. Fontmell's mid-Victorian population was about 700, compared with 250 to 300 in the twelfth century. In his history of the county, *Dorset*, J. H. Bettey cites two surveys made for Shaftesbury Abbey which give quite a detailed picture of Fontmell Magna in the twelfth century. In about 1130 there were sixty-five abbey tenants. Twenty-two were villeins holding a yardland—

roughly equivalent to thirty acres; nineteen villeins holding half a yard-land; and twenty-four cottagers farming smaller areas, usually about four acres. Forty or fifty years later the number of tenants had risen to eighty, the new totals in the respective categories being twenty-eight, twenty-seven and twenty-five, with the implication that an additional 300 acres had been brought into cultivation. This in turn suggests that strict forest law concerning the preservation of vert for the deer was not being enforced very rigorously in these villages beyond the western scarp and adds some weight to the argument pressed against de Clare in 1280, that the proper western boundary of the Chase was the royal road along the crest of the scarp from Shaftesbury to Blandford.

Up here, along the length of the higher road, there are no villages or settlements between Melbury Abbas and Pimperne. Melbury lies in a hollow on the outskirts of Shaftesbury: through the village the road climbs by a one-in-six gradient to Cock Hill and the promontory of Melbury Beacon. It was a splendid place to be on the night of the Coronation bonfires, with Melbury and Win Green both ablaze; but at any time it is an impressive vantage point with a wide prospect westward to Blackmoor Vale. For half a dozen miles along the road only single farms appear at intervals in the solitude which divides the Iwerne valley from the brooding Chase woodlands above Stubhampton and Tarrant Gunville. The eastern side of the road is as secret and withdrawn as the west is open and panoramic: it is indeed a natural boundary in that sense.

As a reminder that we are flanking the true heart of the Chase the road passes the most westerly, and incidentally the best preserved, of the Chase lodges. This is West Lodge, a mansion of the eighteenth century primarily, but with an earlier history. In depositions made by keepers in the early 1600s West Lodge was said to be one of the two oldest lodges. Walter Snelgar, whose memory went back to the early years of Elizabeth, asserted positively that when he first became a keeper 'there was one only ancient lodge, called West Lodge'. Under the new régime of Lord Salisbury this old West Lodge was apparently abandoned and a new West Lodge was built in about 1610 on land leased from Robert Swayne, who owned the manor of Tarrant Gunville.

After the Chase with its lodges passed to George Pitt he had three sons to provide for. Shortly before his death in 1734 he bought Encombe in the Isle of Purbeck for the youngest, John, who also became ranger of West Walk; and it was this John Pitt of Encombe whose architectural skill and taste created the elegant style of the present lodge. Both Encombe and West Lodge are transformations and extensions of earlier buildings, and Edmund Marsden has drawn attention to the similarities in their architectural treatment. A more general influence from Vanbrugh is interesting in view of the proximity of Eastbury, designed by Vanbrugh and recently completed for Pitt's friend, Bubb Dodington. In 1749 Chafin was one of a hunting party which included Dodington at a 'sumptuous repast' at West Lodge where, Chafin wrote, John Pitt 'had made great improvements in the Lodge Mansion'. The church at Stratfieldsaye is another building for which John Pitt is thought to be responsible.

He may also have had some responsibility for the new building work at Rushmore which his great-nephew George Pitt, later Lord Rivers, put in hand about 1760, but there is as yet no evidence for this though the presumption must be strong: if John did indeed design the church for George Pitt at Stratfieldsaye, completed in 1758, it is certainly likely that he would then have taken charge of the improvements required at Rushmore. As for West Lodge, after his death in 1787 the mansion was apparently not acquired by his son, William Morton Pitt, who inherited Encombe. The occupier of West Lodge in 1791 was George Damer, later Lord Dorchester, who also held the office of ranger of West Walk. After the disfranchisement of the Chase West Lodge became part of the Wolverton estate and it continues to be a private residence.

CHAPTER THIRTEEN

The Heartland

TO SAY THAT the heart of the Chase lies to the east of the upper road from Shaftesbury to Blandford is to recognize the appropriateness of the Inner Bounds, which made this road their western limit. West Lodge commands the western scarp of the chalk and takes an eagle's view of the Stour valley and the Vale of Blackmoor. Behind and around West Lodge the woodlands gather, the downland slopes climb and fall, the villages stand apart and were not easy to approach until comparatively recent times. A messenger sent from Cranborne or Ringwood to Shaftesbury by road 250 years ago would probably have had to travel by way of either Salisbury or Blandford. Not until after 1832 did the Cranborne Chase and New Forest Trust extend its turnpike system north of the Horton Inn. The Zigzag Hill road north of Ashmore was an admittedly difficult feat of road-making and—on the evidence of maps—seems not to have been in use until after 1879. Sixpenny Handley similarly had to wait until 1822 for a through link to the Great Western Turnpike. The decisive opening of the Inner Chase came with the general intention to improve communications from the Bristol Channel to the Hampshire coast. Within the Chase the modern B3081 is the fruit of that endeavour by the Cranborne Chase and New Forest Trust.

This is the route that, leaving Shaftesbury, climbs the Zigzag and runs across Charlton Down to meet the road—originally a Roman road—from Ashmore to Ludwell. It is a point to linger at. Win Green stands nearby, a reminder that the prehistoric ridgeway came over the crest from the Ox Drove to find a landmark in the barrow here. Now one road forks away to the airfield at Compton Abbas, and another to Ashmore village. As the B3081 skirts round Woodley Down above the two Ashgrove farms it sends away yet another fork road, towards Farnham, and pursues its own course down into Tollard Royal and up again to Sixpenny Handley. In a severe winter drifting snow can quickly bury the hopes of travellers in the deep downland folds.

This quartet of villages—Ashmore, Tollard, Farnham and Handley—displays the historical qualities of the Chase more vividly than any others. They provided the inner citadel of the deer, the hiding places of smugglers and poachers, the headquarters of the keepers and foresters. From West

Lodge to the furthest eastern lodge, Vernditch, these are the only four churches you will pass as you travel from the Zigzag to the Great Western Turnpike. In general they occupy the highest slopes of the Chase, lying in the dry zone between the Ox Drove and the sources of the south-flowing streams—the Tarrant, the Crichel and the Terrig of the Gussage valley. Underground rainwater tanks and wells were until recently the only source of supply and in a dry season within living memory water had to be carted three or four miles and was sold for £2 per thousand gallons.

All of which gives a symbolical splendour to Ashmore's famous pond, which nobody quite understands but which is there for all to see covering three-quarters of an acre at an elevation of about 700 feet; and was reputedly there when the Romans were constructing their road nearby. Is it a swallet-hole, as one writer has suggested? Is it an outsize dewpond? To say that it never dries up is an exaggeration, but not a great one. On average it happens only once in twenty years. At such a time the ancient custom was to hold a feast. Cakes were baked to be eaten round the margin and in the bed of the pond. Local farmers hauled out the hundreds of cart-loads of mud which had accumulated on the bottom and spread it on their fields. A feast of this kind happened to coincide with the celebrations of Queen Victoria's Golden Jubilee in 1887. In the present century the pond dried out in 1911 but has not done so completely since: not even in the drought of 1976, when a little moisture remained in the middle. In 1971 the sludge was cleared out to give the pond its full maximum depth of sixteen feet.

Historically Ashmore is said to be the only pre-Roman village settlement in Dorset which has survived on its original site. Older patterns of life have certainly been tenacious here. The open fields of mediaeval agriculture were not enclosed until 1859. To protect the crops from the deer a five-foot fence had to be maintained for a length of nearly 5½ miles. The village with its cultivated land was contained within this palisade while the woodlands and the down beyond had to be left open to the deer, except for copses less than three years old. The deer constantly attempted to creep through into the cornland and nooses were hung in the hedge to snare them. Visiting keepers tended to be entertained lavishly—even improperly, according to some stories—while local men hastily removed the snares and any victims.

There is no pub in Ashmore today but there used to be two, before 1800. One was the Three Horseshoes, the other The Stag's Head—this being the crest of the Barbers, for long the local squires. The theme of stag and deer is ever present, and most attractively in the church where a group of carved bosses by John Skeaping represent the theme of 'As pants the hart': in six scenes the hart escapes from a mounted huntsman and his hound. The church was largely rebuilt in 1874, incidentally, when the churchwardens by some happy chance were Mr Hare and Mr Rabbets.

Ashmore had an unusual squire for a time in the eighteenth century. This was John Eliot, a London merchant and a member of the Society of Friends. An enlightened and public-spirited man, he started a school in the village in about 1770 when he paid Dinah Newhook 6s 4d a month for teaching ten children. A Quaker was not such a novelty to Ashmore as might be supposed. In his journal George Fox describes how, in 1663, he attended a meeting of Quakers near Ringwood and then 'took horse, having about twenty miles to ride that afternoon to one—Frye's house, where a meeting was appointed to be held next day'.

The Frye in question was William Fry, and his house was Higher Ashgrove Farm, north of Ashmore village and on the eastern side of the county boundary and the B3081. The meeting to which George Fox was riding was illegal and narrowly escaped from being raided. In the words of Fox's journal, 'The officers had purposed to break it up, and were on their way in order thereunto. But before they got to the meeting, word was brought them "There was a house newly broken up by thieves", and they were required to go back again with speed, to search after and pursue them; by which means our meeting escaped disturbance.'

The Frys had been at Ashgrove since 1607. William first met Fox in 1657 and became a Quaker immediately, refusing to pay tithes in the following year and being imprisoned in 1660. Despite persecution he set aside a piece of his farmland at Chevicombe Bottom as a burial ground for the Society of Friends. In a deed assigning the land to his son, Thomas, he stipulated that 'the people called Quakers shall have free liberty without lett or disturbance to come to and from the burying-place by the way now used'. William himself, at the age of eighty-six, was buried there in 1708 and the practice continued until 1775. In later years it became customary to preserve the right of way by organizing a procession of Quakers to the burial ground at the start of each decade. This is still done.

Ashgrove is north of Ashmore, linked in spirit with Fry's Congregationalist contemporaries who showed an equally defiant courage on the other side of Win Green, at Ferne and Birdbush. South of Ashmore the falling slopes take on pagan and pantheist qualities. At Washer's Pit and along the flanks of Stubhampton Bottom the old woodlands reassert themselves. Names that the Elizabethans used for individual coppices and wooded areas, names such as Elden, Broderidge, Bokeldean, Moris and Stonedeane, survive on our maps today as Elderen, Broadridge, Bossleton, Morris and Stony Bottom. In this context a Forestry Commission sign announcing 'Wareham Forest' must be presumed to be part of some cunning plan to confuse and mislead an invading enemy.

Stubhampton Bottom is in effect the headwater valley of the River Tarrant, which does not nowadays appear to view until lower down. It is popular with naturalists for its profusion of wild flowers, its butterflies and its occasional sighting of a deer. To wander down the minor road through Fontmell Wood to Washer's Pit is to experience the enchantment of Nature in its most appealing forms. Here, too, old legends and super-stitions gather. By Folly Hanging Gate there used to be a barrow where wild spirits of the air, called Gappergennies, were sometimes heard wailing. A cross was always kept cut in the turf opposite the barrow, until the day when the making of the Ashmore–Fontmell road levelled the barrow and the bones it had contained were removed to Ashmore churchyard; since when the voices of the Gappergennies, or Gabbygammies as they were sometimes known, have been silent. You may however still hear the hunting horn, held to no human lips, which signals the escape over Spinney's Gate of the unfortunate lady who had been hanging by her hair from an ash-tree over the well at Washer's Pit. Her rescuer was inspired and led to the spot by a thrice repeated dream. If you fail to hear the ghostly hunting horn you may be compensated by a chance encounter with a woman in white who has been seen by travellers, and felt brushing against them in the darkness, between Washer's Pit and Spinney's Pond.

It is an area charged with ancient memories that seem to fade as the valley inclines down to Tarrant Gunville, and Ashmore is left behind in its upland fastness. The B3081 meantime swings eastward over Woodley Down, away from Ashmore in the direction of Tollard Royal and Farnham. According to General Pitt-Rivers, Tollard took its name from the local landowner, Toli, in Edward the Confessor's reign; and it became royal when King John acquired a knight's fee here by his marriage to his first wife, Hadwisa. The royal connection is a slender one, however, as there is no evidence that John or any other king maintained a residence here, and the suffix 'Royal' does not appear to have been used before 1535. The manor became Crown property in the fifteenth century as part of the Yorkist estates, and it was during Henry VIII's reign that Tollard passed into the possession of Sir Thomas Arundell and was retained by the Arundells until George Pitt, the first Lord Rivers, bought it. It was the rise of the Pitts which brought Tollard Royal into prominence: under them the administrative centre of the Chase moved from Wimborne St Giles to Rushmore Lodge and Tollard Royal. Although Rushmore itself is now a school the Rushmore Estate still has its headquarters in Tollard.

The village lies in a narrow cleft with a long avenue of beech trees. In early spring the churchyard is white with a profusion of snowdrops. Here lie the fourth Lord and Lady Rivers, almost exact contemporaries who died within forty-eight hours of each other in 1866. In the previous year one of their daughters had been married in the church, had gone on her honeymoon to Switzerland and there been killed by lightning—another tragedy for these parents who had seen three sons die and knew the fourth and last would barely survive them. The legend of a gipsy's curse put upon the family does have an awesome plausibility.

To look for Tollard's famous Larmer Tree is to court disappointment. In the 1930s H. J. Massingham came looking for

a Wych elm under whose spreading boughs were held the mediaeval Chase courts. I went to see it, [he wrote] for I love an old tree almost as much as I do an old barrow. But the monarch was invisible and all I could see was a turnstile. I asked the custodian where the tree was, but she would not tell me until I had paid sixpence to go through the turnstile. Still I could not find the tree and finally she conducted me to a sapling oak that was growing from the roots of a dead tree-butt. 'But where's the Larmer Tree?' I asked her. It was the butt, the sapling had been planted to replace it.

The sad truth is that, after a lifetime of three or four hundred years, the old wych elm just failed to survive into the twentieth century, although the butt was still visible in 1943. As a gesture of continuity General Pitt-Rivers had an oak planted in the hollow centre of the decayed elm and this sapling is alive and well today. The 'mediaeval court' that Massingham mentioned was not the Chase court but the manor's own court leet which continued to be held under the Larmer Tree until well into the nineteenth century. It was an annual event, on the first Monday in September, and it had become customary to relax Chase law while the court leet was in progress, to the extent of permitting the lord of the manor with his stewards and servants to hunt and kill a deer started within the precincts of the manor. This one day's liberty is what has become known as the Tollard Hunt. Sixpenny Handley claimed a similar privilege 'from time immemorial'.

Charles Bowles who became the steward of Tollard Manor in 1799 speaks of the annual Tollard Hunt as 'an high holiday for the esquires, gentlemen and yeomen of the neighbourhood'—a view which is difficult to reconcile with the fact that Lord Rivers, as lord of the Chase, contested these 'immemorial' rights. Arguing that the sitting of the manorial court provided no exemption from Chase law he secured a verdict against the

Tollard Hunt in 1789, as his son did against the Handley Hunt in 1817. Such a strange contradiction prompts one to read between the lines and suggest that these special occasions had got out of hand. Men who were not servants or tenants of the lord of the manor were probably taking the law into their own hands and embarking on a day's hunting under the pretext of the ancient custom. It was against a man who was not one of Arundell's tenants and who had ignored Arundell's 'express prohibition' that Rivers directed his action to terminate the Tollard Hunt.

What then was the 'high holiday' that Bowles enjoyed a decade or more later? The answer seems to lie, as so often in Chase history, in a spirit of neighbourly accommodation. On the day of the court leet Lord Rivers made it a practice to have the Chase hounds meet at Tollard Royal and kill a brace of bucks, which were presented to Lord Arundell: and we may presume that Lord Arundell's steward and his lordship's principal tenants would have a day's hunting and some share in the venison. The Tollard Hunt may have ceased to exist legally in 1789—but what's in a name?

Tollard Royal is the only Chase village south of the Ox Drove to lie in Wiltshire. The county boundary makes a southern loop as if to gather Tollard in with the Chalke villages. In the Larmer Tree Gardens a boundary stone stands, part in Wiltshire and part in Dorset. On the Dorset side the land begins to fall towards Farnham, and beyond to Chettle and the rising of the Crichel stream which flows into Veiny Cheese Pond and the Crichel valley. Farnham has lost its modern momentum with the closure of the Pitt-Rivers museum, for it has few other resources. Historically it lay just inside the Lesser Bounds and its woods formed a large part of Bursey or Bussey Stool Walk. Bussey Stool Lodge was 'new' around 1600 when it replaced an 'ancient' one. It was replaced again early in the eighteenth century with a building mainly of brick, which fell into disrepair in modern times but has lately been gutted and restored.

What Farnham lacks most conspicuously is such a house as its southern neighbour, Chettle, can boast of. Designed, in all probability, by Thomas Archer, Chettle House was the home from about 1710 of George Chafin and his descendants. His father, Thomas Chafyn, had fought against Monmouth at the battle of Sedgemoor and was for some years ranger of Cranborne Chase until his death in 1691. George followed in his father's footsteps, holding the title of head ranger: he also represented Dorset in Parliament for over forty years. His marriage to a daughter of the wealthy Sir Anthony Sturt may have been the immediate motive for the building of Chettle House, which took twenty-five years to complete. As with the church designed by Archer in London's Smith Square all corners are rounded. The doorways in the east and west halls have tympana ascribed to Alfred Stevens and the drawing-room ceiling is thought to be the work of Stevens's father. The house is open to the public, and the objects on display include a 'beehive' cap and a swindgel of the type used in the encounters between keepers and poachers.

George Chafin and his Sturt bride had five sons but none of them produced a successor. The last Chafin to live at Chettle was the youngest son, William, who was born about 1732. Although he was the eleventh child seven had already died. His father attributed these losses to 'the nursing of them too tenderly' so he had young William baptized immediately and despatched to a shepherd's cottage where he spent his first five years. William's elder brother died in 1776, ten years after their father, so William lived on alone at Chettle for over forty years. He hunted until he was over eighty and then settled down to write his *Anecdotes*. While doing so, under the glass cupola that used to surmount the house, he was struck by lightning, so it is said, but survived to complete his book. He died in 1818 and the house became a subject of legal disputes for some years. After a period of neglect it was taken in hand by the Castleman family. The two castles, which stand like chesspieces on the parapet, were added as a sort of architectural pun on the new owners.

The last of the Inner Chase villages is Sixpenny Handley—a name which, in the form of '6d Handley', has brought many a camera to focus on local signposts and which inspired a new crop of merry quips when the introduction of decimal coinage prompted an inevitable call for a change to 'Two-and-a-half New P. Handley'. The name is in fact a corruption of Saxpena Hanlege. The village itself has no air of antiquity, for it was largely destroyed by fire in 1892. The inhabitants seem, in the main, to have been prudently insured: their compensation inspired an envious local saying that, since the fire, 'Handley men wear two waistcoats'.

Handley is the largest of the Inner Chase villages, with two pubs, a guest-house and several shops. Its church is one of the few man-made landmarks in the area, visible at a distance in several directions. In the seventeenth century the village was a meeting place for local landowners who rode over for a game of bowls. The first Earl of Shaftesbury mentions some of those he used to meet on these occasions. Among them were Henry Hastings, the eccentric squire of Woodlands; Mr Ryves who had an eight-mile ride from Ranston to Handley; and Bampfield Chafin who, according to Lord Shaftesbury, was 'a personable well-carriaged man of good estate, wanted neither understanding nor value for himself and was an enemy to the Puritan party'.

Those games of bowls were a deceptive interlude before the Civil War. Some who played there had their lands sequestered later. Some fought on one side, some on the other. Bampfield Chafin was captured by Parliamentary troops and died a prisoner in Exeter. Time smooths the scars of violence but there are memories in Handley that do not easily fade. And it was not only an underworld of poachers and smugglers who were caught up in the later outbreaks of violence, but decent labouring men made desperate by the starvation wages after the Napoleonic wars. When the agricultural riots swept southern England in 1830 a magistrate, with better judgment than some, commented that 'had we committed for participating in and aiding the burning of machinery at Sixpenny Handley, we might have committed two thirds of the labouring population of the district'. Threshing machines were burnt in many of the Chase villages; and in Martin the Coote household was besieged at West Park, until Lord Arundell came to their relief with a troop of yeomanry. A threatening note to one landowner read, 'The Handley Torches have not forgot you'.

Scattered about Handley are a number of little settlements—Deanland and New Town, Woodcuts and—going eastward—Cobley and Woodyates. The 'next village' that one might expect does not materialize. The Inner Chase peters out against two barriers—the modern main road, A354, and the ancient Bokerley Dyke. Combined, they separate Sixpenny Handley from Pentridge and Martin. For all practical purposes today the Inner Chase lies between the Ox Drove and the A354, with the upper road from Shaftesbury to Blandford as its western boundary. Here is the heartland of what was once a vast hunting ground, where the requirements of vert and venison overruled everything else. It keeps still much of its distinctive character, even though the long strange history written over its landscape begins to fade in the harsher light of twentieth-century economics.

To be classified as an **Area** of Outstanding Natural Beauty has a fine ring to it. If that is to be the Chase's destiny one must hope—without much ground for doing so—that the modern breed of professional planners and administrators will be equal to their opportunities. To dwell on what has been irretrievably lost is of no use except to strengthen a resolve to prevent fresh follies and vandalisms. Some of the Chase's features are of such obvious excellence that it would require a congenital barbarity to neglect them. Its manor houses, its churches, its village groupings of farmhouse and cottage are a constant delight to anyone who visits Tarrant Monkton, Martin, Chettle, Fontmell Magna, Cranborne itself and many more. For the archaeologist the Chase is one of the principal grounds of British prehistory. Hod Hill and Hambledon, Ackling Dyke and Badbury Rings, Bokerley and Worbarrow—the great names ring out in a splendid litany of classic sites that every student longs to visit. And for the naturalist there are still pleasures in abundance even if the blackcock has long since gone from Cranborne Common and the southern heathland between Ringwood and Wimborne. The Dartford warbler keeps its foot-hold along the southern borders of the Chase, and the stone curlew has not quite justified Hudson's pessimism about its survival on the chalk downs, to which it has an obstinate attachment. In May 1767 Sir Joseph Banks, returning from Kingston Lacy to Eastbury saw 'on Blandford Horse Course two remarkable birds seeming to be of the genus Charadrias. Some shepherds informed me that they came here to breed but are exceeding difficult to shoot . . . they were near as large again as grey plover, had a white spot in each wing and whistled exceedingly shrill, not unlike a man.'

A fair description of stone curlew which I could verify 200 years later, marvelling at the brilliant lemon-yellow eye and the low subdued grunts of the hen bird returning to the nest, which I at first mistook for the sounds of a passing hedgehog. To such moments memory adds the splendour of the chalk downland flora—the varieties of orchid; cowslips and rock rose; above all perhaps the predominant blues of harebell, scabious, meadow cranesbill and chicory. This theme of blue seems to be taken up again by the butterflies of the chalk.

Here, in Cranborne Chase, are still the prodigality and the variety that are Nature's gift; and the craftsmanship and artistry that are Man's. It is our privilege to inherit them; our duty to bequeath them.

APPENDIX

BIBLIOGRAPHY

INDEX

APPENDIX

The Bounds of the Chase

THE ACCEPTED DEFINITION of what are termed the outer or greater metes and bounds of the Chase is contained in the *Quo Warranto* of Edward I, issued in or about the year 1280. The circumstances in which this document was produced have been described in chapter two. In his *Chronicle of Cranborne* Wake Smart reproduced it in its original form, as follows:

> De Bolebrigg in Wylton usque ad Herdecote per aquam de Nodre usque ad molendinum de Dyninton et de molendino de Dyninton usque ad molendinum de Tyssebyr et de molendino de Tyssebyr usque Wycham de Wycham per aquam de Noddre usque ubi Semene cadit in Noddre et sic per aquam de Semene usque Semenehened et de Semene-hened usque Kingesethe juxta Schaston, de Kingesethe usque Schaston scilicet usque Sleybrondesgate de Sleybrondesgate usque ecclesiam sancti Rombaldi de Ecclesia Sancti Rombaldi usque la Guldeneoke, del a Guldeneoke usque ad aquam de Sturkell et per aquam de Sturkel usque ad ripariam de Stures et per ripariam de Stures usque ad pontem de Hayford et de ponte de Hayford usque ad pontem de Blaneford et de ponte de Blaneford usque ad pontem de Crauford et de ponte de Crauford usque Alwynesbrigg subtus Wymborn, de Alwynebrigg per aquam de Wymborn usque Waldeford usque Wychampton, de Wychampton usque pontem Petrae, de pontem Petrae usque longam Hayam quae ducit ad le Muledich, de Muledich usque Kynges de Kynges usque viam quae ducit ad Lestesford per medium Estewode, de Lestesforde per aquam de Craneburn usque la Horewyethe et de la Horewyethe usque Albeslake et de Albelake usque la Horeston, de Horeston per chiminum usque ad magnum pontem de Ringeswode, de magno ponte de Ringeswode usque ad pontem de fforde de ponte de fforde usque ad pontem de Dunton, de ponte de Dunton usque Aylwardsbrigg, de Aylwardsbrigg usque ad predictum pontem de Bolebrigg in Wylton.

The document was not making any innovations. It merely confirmed the unanimous verdict of the jury at New Sarum in 1245, which was appointed by Henry III following a complaint by Richard de Clare, who was a ward from 1230 to 1245, that during his minority his inheritance had been neglected. What the jury examined, and endorsed, was a perambulation made during the period when King John, as Earl of Gloucester, was personally interested in the bounds of the Chase. We can say, therefore, with some confidence, that the definition of Cranborne Chase as we know it was established in the late twelfth century—if not earlier.

Most of the perambulation is easy to paraphrase in modern terms. Significantly it began at the ancient capital of Wiltshire, since New Sarum had not yet arisen to overshadow Wilton. From Bulbridge the line ran with the River Nadder to the mills at Dinton and Tisbury and on to the junction of the two rivers Nadder and Sem. The Sem now became the boundary up to its source at Kingsettle. With no suitable river line to follow the boundary skirted round the eastern side of Shaftesbury, past St Rumbold's church, to the little Stirchel stream which helps to form the Manston Brook as a tributary of the Stour. Securely linked with a river system the boundary followed the Stour past the bridges at Shillingstone (Hayward Bridge), Blandford and Tarrant Crawford to the junction at Wimborne of the Stour with its tributary the Allen (or Win burn). Here the boundary left the Stour to follow instead the Allen up to Witchampton and the stone bridge near Knowlton church.

The next stage, linking the rivers Allen and Crane, is somewhat obscure in detail. The perambulation broke away from the Allen between Knowlton church and the Horton Inn, kept to the north of Woodlands and met the Crane in the vicinity of Romford. Following the Crane to Ebblake the boundary then left the river and followed the road to the great bridge at Ringwood. At Ringwood it again had a secure and unmistakable river line—the Avon—to the three bridges at Fordingbridge, Downton and Harnham (Aylward's Bridge) and so to the starting point at Wilton.

In March 1931 Trelawney Dayrell-Reed published (Proc. Dorset Nat. Hist. & Arch. Soc.) a detailed clarification of the obscure sector between the Allen and the Crane. It is a convincing analysis, although he may be in error in placing *above* Romford the junction with the Crane at 'Lestesford'. A perambulation of Horton manor in 1589 suggests that Lestesford may have been below Romford at what is now Does Hatches.

To express the Inner Bounds in modern terms is a far more difficult matter, if only because at no point did they touch a river or stream. Their definition depended on less immutable landmarks. This is how they were recorded in 8 Edward I:

a Chetteslehened usque Grymesdych et de Grymesdych usque ad

Henlegh, et de Henlegh usque la Denne et de la Denne usque Gyssich Sci Andreae usque Brandon et de Brandon usque Stubhampton et per medium villae de Stubhampton usque ad capud de Rythersdeane, de Rythersdeane usque regalem viam quae ducit de Blaneford usque Schaston et a via illa usque Thenersdenne et de Thenersdenne usque ad capud de Westewode per viam quae dicitur Rugwyk quae ducit versus Salesberye et de [via quae ducit ad] Salesbyrye usque bundas Wyltes quae se extendunt inter Asmere et Esgrove et sic usque Staunton et de Staunton usque Mortesgresmore et de Mortesgresmore usque Singhok et de Singhok usque Sondeputte, de Sondeputte usque ad capud de la Lunge Crofte et sic usque Wermere de Wermere usque Bukedon de Bukedon per metas et bundas quae dividunt Dorset et Wyltes usque Cheteleshened.

In terms which would be recognized on a modern map this could be paraphrased as:

From Chettlehead Copse to Grim's Ditch and Sixpenny Handley; from Handley to Dean and Gussage St Andrew; thence through the middle of Stubhampton to the Blandford–Shaftesbury road. Follow that road to Tennerley Ditch, which is the Cross Dyke just past the Fontmell Magna–Ashmore crossroad and continue to the head of West Wood by the road called the Ridgeway which leads towards Salisbury: from this to the Wiltshire boundary which stretches between Ashmore and Ashgrove, and so to a series of obscure landmarks before joining the shire rack at Buckden and following it back to Chettlehead Copse.

Some sections are quite clear. The southern boundary from Handley through Dean, Gussage St Andrew and Stubhampton to the Blandford–Shaftesbury road is unambiguous. The eastern end is less precise because Grim's Ditch has several parts, but we may reasonably assume a boundary running from Chettlehead Copse through Verndtich to somewhere near Bokerley Junction before turning towards Handley. The western end is clear enough along the royal road up to Tennerley Ditch and what is now the minor road past Compton Abbas airfield. This would lead naturally to the ridgeway that passes Win Green and—as the Ox Drove—heads towards Salisbury. In passing it is worth mentioning that the ridgeway, the Roman road which is now the B3081 and the county boundary all meet at the long barrow on Ashmore Down which must have been a familiar landmark to our ancestors.

But what should we make of Staunton, Mortesgresmore, Singhok and the rest? What meaning should we give here to that pervasive word 'Buckden'? This is perhaps the moment to turn to the early map-makers and see what solutions they offered.

I know of no map before 1600 which pays any specific attention to the Chase boundaries. The maps which do so belong to the period in the early 1600s when the Chase was passing from the Crown to the Cecils. Chapter four refers to three such maps, of which a fuller account is now required. The Exchequer Commission of 1616, directed to Sir Francis Popham, Sir John Dauncy, Sir Anthony Hungerford and Thomas Hinton, required the preparation of a map identifying the bounds which had become a matter of dispute. According to West the intention was to have a surveyor employed by each side to set out the conflicting versions in a composite map, but Salisbury's surveyor was withdrawn after his counsel objected to certain directions. The map was therefore completed by the other surveyor alone, and it is virtually certain that it was Thomas Aldwell's map—of which a facsimile was published by General Pitt-Rivers. Another map of this period which has survived was presumably commissioned by Salisbury's opponents. Wake Smart reproduced it in *A Chronicle of Cranborne*: it is said to have been drawn by Richard Hardinge of Blandford in 1618 and faithfully copied in 1677 by Matthew Hardinge. It is a much less detailed map than Aldwell's and shows only the more contracted version of the Inner Bounds. The third map which is relevant is Norden's, which was not prepared for the Exchequer suit but reflects nevertheless a concern about boundaries which had already in 1605 become a bone of contention between Robert Cecil and Pembroke.

What light do Aldwell, Hardinge and Norden collectively throw on the precise locations of what Aldwell renders as Mortonsgore, Sticking Oke, Sandpitt, Longcroft, Wermere and Buckden? Very little that is conclusive, unfortunately. Although the maps are so closely contemporary it is difficult to correlate these minor names of landmarks. There is, however, a general consensus that the inner bound could be interpreted as following the Dorset–Wilts county boundary southwards from the point where the ridgeway met it between Ashmore and Ashgrove—in modern terms the junction of the B3081 and the minor road from Compton Abbas airfield.

This stretch of the county boundary ran past Wiltshire Woods and Tollard Green, turning east at a point close to Bursey Lodge and skirting the southern side of Tollard Park to reach a point on Farnham Common or Farnham Down named as 'Buckden'. Hardinge follows this line and en route indicates Longcroft, Levermere (for Wermere or Larmer) and 'hok' (for Sticking Oke). He does not show anything recognizable as Mortonsgore or Mortesgresmore—which Norden locates in the vicinity of Ashmore and Wiltshire Woods. Buckden is common to all three maps. Rather surprisingly Norden follows the same general course here as Hardinge, implying that Wiltshire was wholly excluded from the Inner Chase—a view not shared by Lord Salisbury in 1616. The request to Norden to make a fresh perambulation before the Exchequer case is therefore understandable, and so perhaps is his disinclination.

To appreciate the contrary argument we must examine Aldwell's map, which is a much more elaborate affair than Hardinge's. Some of the information it gives is especially valuable—notably in the naming of copses and in the outlining of each individual walk. On this matter of the Inner Bounds it shows some of the key words in two different places, in order to embody the two conflicting interpretations. In particular it confirms the positions of Longcroft, Lavermere Gate and Buckden along the county boundary east of Bursey Lodge and adjoining the southern side of Tollard Park. However, none of the other names mentioned above appears on the county boundary. Sandpitt is shown well to the west of the boundary, as it is by Hardinge; and we have to look elsewhere for Mortonsgore, Sticking Oke, etc. They figure only on Aldwell's alternative interpretation.

To pursue this we must return to the point where the ridgeway meets the county boundary—approximately where in modern terms the B3081 is joined by the minor road from Compton Abbas airfield. Aldwell now follows the ridgeway to pass Win Green and take the route along Monks Down and beyond—the Ox Drove as we know it today. And it is in this area, between Win Green and Monks Down, that he places in close succession Stonedene, Mortonsgore, Sticking Oke and Sandpitt. The next landmark in the original perambulation was the head of Longcroft: continuing along the Ox Drove Aldwell located Longcroft north of Bridmore, and this is particularly significant. On Aldwell's map the boundary between Rushmore Walk and Staplefoot Walk starts from the point designated 'head of Longcroft' and runs past Bridmore to Bridmore Green. The copses beside Bridmore Green are named Longcroftes, Little Longcroftes, Young Longcroftes and Old Longcroftes—which does suggest that the 'real' Longcroft is here and not on Farnham Common. Moreover the other copses in the vicinity of Bridmore Green include Parsons and Blindwitch—names which, with 'Longcrastes', occur in Thomas West's deposition of 1594. All these copses are in Wiltshire, of course, and West describes them as part of the East Buckden. Finally it is worth noting that modern Ordnance Survey maps preserve the name 'Longcroft' for copses east of Bridmore Green.

Two final points remain in the original perambulation—the positioning of 'Wermere', and beyond it of 'Buckden' which in either plan is to be found on the county boundary. Aldwell located Wermere, with the alternative name of Lavermere, on the Ox Drove in a blank area between Manwood Copse and Norrington. The modern equivalent would be approximately at Bigley Buildings.

'Buckden' occurs twice between Wermere and Chettlehead Copse. The first occasion is at approximately the point where the minor road from Ebbesborne Wake joins the Ox Drove. As it is not on the county boundary some other explanation is needed to justify 'Buckden' here. It may be connected with the fact that it marks the boundary between Staplefoot Walk and Cobley Walk. The further use of Buckden is in a position equivalent to the modern site of East Chase Farm. Here Aldwell's Greate Ditch, Cowsetten and Cobley Lodge correlate easily with modern names; and the county boundary is at hand to be followed over the short distance to Chettlehead Copse.

All in all the case for tracing the northern boundary of the Inner Chase along the Ox Drove and not round the southern side of Tollard Park seems to me a strong one. There is one remaining consideration which strengthens it still further. In the original perambulation the passage from place to place is expressed by 'usque ad', meaning 'as far as' or 'up to'; and by 'per', meaning 'by way of' or 'along'. It is an important distinction that the first reference to the county boundary is 'usque bundas Wyltes' while the second is 'per metas et bundas quae dividunt Dorset et Wyltes'. The implication is that the Inner Chase follows the ridgeway to the point where it meets the county boundary and then proceeds to the next landmark, Staunton, which is not on the county boundary; whereas in the second instance, at Buckden, the Inner Chase proceeds along the county boundary to its final destination at Chettlehead.

SELECT BIBLIOGRAPHY

PRINCIPAL LOCAL SOURCES

Anecdotes and History of Cranbourn Chase: William Chafin. 1818.

A Chronicle of Cranborne and the Chase of Cranborne: T. W. Wake Smart. 1841.

A History of the Forest or Chace known by the Name of Cranborne Chace: William West. 1816.

A Short Guide to the Larmer Grounds, Rushmore, King John's House and the Museum at Farnham, Dorset: Lt.-Gen. Pitt-Rivers, FRS, FSA. Undated (*c.* 1900).

King John's House: Lt.-Gen. Pitt-Rivers. Published privately 1890.

A Memorandum respecting the keepers: Anonymous MS. Dorset CRO D396/M36 & M38.

Deposition of Thomas West of Handley, 1594: Dorset CRO D396/M6.

Survey of the Lands of William, First Earl of Pembroke. Roxburgh Club, Oxford, 1909.

The Cecil family archives at Hatfield House.

FOREST AND CHASE ADMINISTRATION

The Royal Forests of England: J. Charles Cox. London, 1905.

'Game & the Poacher in Shakespeare's England': Anthony Dent. *History Today* XXV, 11 (1975).

'Game Laws in Wiltshire 1750–1800': P. B. Munsche (*Crime in England 1550–1880*, ed. J. S. Cockburn) London, 1977.

The New Forest: John R. Wise. London, 1883.

HUNTING AND FIELD SPORTS

Thoughts on Hunting: Peter Beckford. 1781.

Half a Century of Sport in Hampshire: the shooting journals of the second Earl of Malmesbury. Ed. by F. G. Aflalo. London and New York, 1905.

Tally Ho!: Henry Symonds. Blandford, 1899.

British Hunts and Huntsmen. London, 1908.

The Meynell of the West: A. Henry-Higginson. London, 1936.

Peter Beckford: A. Henry-Higginson. London, 1937.

The Sports and Pastimes of the People of England: Joseph Strutt. London, 1801, revised by J. C. Cox, London, 1903.

The Noble Art of Venerie or Hunting: George Turberville. 1576; Oxford, 1908.

NATURAL HISTORY

The Roe Deer of Cranborne Chase: Richard Prior. London, 1968.
Living with Deer: Richard Prior. London, 1965.
The Natural History of Wiltshire: John Aubrey, ed. John Britton. London, 1847.
The Naturalist in Central Southern England: Derrick Knowlton. Newton Abbot, 1973.
British Animals extinct within historic times: J. E. Harting. London, 1880/1972.
The Birds of Wiltshire: A. C. Smith. London and Devizes, 1887.

ARCHAEOLOGY

Pitt-Rivers Museum, Farnham: General Handbook. 1929.
The Archaeology of Wessex: L. V. Grinsell. London, 1929.
The Archaeological Journal. Vol. CIV, 1947.
Collins Field Guide to Archaeology in Britain: Eric S. Wood. London, 1963.
Discovering Regional Archaeology—Wessex: Leslie Grinsell and James Dyer. Tring, 1971.
General Pitt-Rivers: M. W. Thompson. Bradford-on-Avon, 1977.
Excavations in Cranborne Chase, 1887–98: General Pitt-Rivers. 4 Vols (privately published).
A Memoir of General Pitt-Rivers: Harold St George Gray. Taunton, 1905 (privately published).
The Ancient Earthworks of Cranborne Chase: Heywood Sumner. 1913.

COMMUNICATIONS: RIVER, ROAD AND RAIL

Ancient Trackways of Wessex: H. W. Timperley and Edith Brill. London, 1965.
The Mail-coach Men of the Late Eighteenth Century: Edmund Vale. London, 1960.
The Old Roads of Dorset: Ronald Good. Bournemouth, 1966.
A Topographical Survey of the Counties of Hants, Wilts, Dorset, Somerset, Devon and Cornwall, commonly called the Western Circuit: William Tunnicliff, Land Surveyor. Salisbury, 1791.
All the Works of John Taylor, the Water Poet. London, 1630/1973.
The Salisbury Avon: Ernest Walls. London, 1929.
The Exeter Road: C. G. Harper. London, 1899.
Lieutenant Colonel Paterson's Book of Roads. London, 1808.

HISTORY

Lucerna: H. P. R. Finberg. London, 1964.
Gibbon's Journal: intro. D. M. Low. London, 1929.
The Story of the Rev. Peter Ince: T. H. L. Jones. London, 1936.
Domesday Geography of S.W. England: H. C. Darby and R. Welldon Finn. Cambridge, 1967.
Thomas Gerard's Survey of Dorsetshire: Rev. Mr Coker. London, 1732.
The History and Antiquities of the County of Dorset: John Hutchins. London, 1861–64 (3rd edition reprinted 1973).
Reliquae Baxterianae (Writings of Richard Baxter), 1696.
A Memorial of the Nonconforming Clergy of Wilts and East Somerset in 1662: Mayo Gunn. London, 1862.
Smuggling Days: K. Merle Chacksfield. Christchurch, 1966.
The Hundred of Chalke: Charles Bowles. Shaftesbury, 1830.
Old Poole Town: Olive Knott. Sherborne, 1975.
The History of Modern Wiltshire: ed. Richard Colt Hoare. London, 1830.
The Hundred of Dunworth and Vale of Noddre: James Everard, Baron Arundell. London, 1829.
A Short History of Breamore: Anthony Light and Ian Dampney. Privately, undated (*c.* 1973).
The House of Pitt: Sir Tresham Lever. London, 1947.
Victoria County History (Dorset): ed. W. Page. London, 1908.
Victoria County History (Wiltshire). London, 1959.
Historical Monuments of the County of Dorset. HMSO. Vols. 3, 4 and 5.
Dorset: J. H. Bettey. Newton Abbot, 1974.
The History of the King's Works: ed. H. M. Colvin. HMSO, 1963.
'An eighteenth century dilettante architect, John Pitt of Encombe': Edmund Marsden, *Country Life* (9 September, 1976).
The Ladies of Alderley: ed. Nancy Mitford. London, 1938.
The Stanleys of Alderley: ed. Nancy Mitford. London, 1939/1968.
Ashmore: E. W. Watson. Salisbury, 1890.
Damerham and Martin: E. H. Lane Poole. Tisbury, 1976.
Family and Fortune: Lawrence Stone. Oxford, 1973.
Short History of Broad Chalke: H. M. Trethowan. Over Wallop, undated.

GENERAL

A Shepherd's Life: W. H. Hudson. London, 1910.
Dorset: A *Shell* guide: Michael Pitt-Rivers. London, 1966.
Country Houses of Dorset: Arthur Oswald. London, 1959.

Travels through England: Dr Richard Pococke, ed. J. J. Cartwright. London, 1888/99.

The Life of Thomas Hardy: F. E. Hardy. London, 1928/30.

Hampshire: Arthur Mee, revised E. T. Long. London, 1967.

Dorset: Arthur Mee, revised E. T. Long. London, 1967.

Wiltshire: Arthur Mee, revised C. L. S. Linnell. London, 1965.

Inside Dorset: Monica Hutchings. Sherborne, 1965.

A Dorset Heritage: Viola Bankes. London, 1953.

A Tour Through England and Wales: Daniel Defoe.

Romney: Humphry Ward and W. Roberts. London and New York, 1904.

Rambles by 'Patricius Walker': William Allingham. London, 1873.

Journal of an Excursion to Eastbury and Bristol in May and June 1767: Sir Joseph Banks. Dorset Nat. Hist. Arch. Proc., XXI, 1899.

A Tour through the South of England during the Summer of 1791: E. D. Clarke. London, 1793.

Memories: Kegan Paul. London, 1899/1971.

Turf Celebrities: William Day. London, 1891.

A Journey into Cornwall: George Lipscomb. Warwick, 1799.

The New British Traveller: George Augustus Walpole. London, 1782.

The Journeys of Celia Fiennes: ed. Christopher Morris. London, 1949.

Observations on a Tour through England and Scotland: C. Dibdin. London, 1801.

The Englishman's Food: J. C. Drummond and Anne Wilbraham. London, 1939/1964.

Literary Recollections: Rev. Richard Warner. 1830.

A Wiltshire Parson and his Friends: Garland Greever. London, 1926.

The Wessex Heathland: Ralph Wightman. London, 1953.

AGRICULTURE AND COMMERCE

Bound to the Soil: Barbara Kerr. London, 1968.

A General View of the Agriculture of the County of Dorset: William Stevenson. London, 1815.

A General View of the Agriculture in the County of Dorset: John Claridge. London, 1793.

The Bath & West: Kenneth Hudson. Bradford-on-Avon, 1976.

Rural Rides: William Cobbett. London, 1830.

The Verwood and District Potteries: David Algar, Anthony Light and Penny Trehane. Ringwood, 1979.

Industrial Archaeology in Southern England: Kenneth Hudson. Dawlish and London, 1965.

INDEX